Teaching Migration in
Literature, Film, and Media

Teaching Migration in Literature, Film, and Media

Edited by

Masha Salazkina and Yumna Siddiqi

The Modern Language Association of America
New York   2025

To order MLA publications, visit www.mla.org/books. For wholesale and international orders, see www.mla.org/bookstore-orders.

The MLA office is located on the island known as Mannahatta (Manhattan) in Lenapehoking, the homeland of the Lenape people. The MLA pays respect to the original stewards of this land and to the diverse and vibrant Native communities that continue to thrive in New York City.

Options for Teaching 66
ISSN 1079-2562

Library of Congress Cataloging-in-Publication Data

Names: Salazkina, Masha editor | Siddiqi, Yumna editor
Title: Teaching migration in literature, film, and media / edited by Masha Salazkina and Yumna Siddiqi.
Description: New York : The Modern Language Association of America, 2025.
Series: Options for teaching, 1079-2562 ; 66 | Includes bibliographical references.
Identifiers: LCCN 2025005094 (print) | LCCN 2025005095 (ebook) | ISBN 9781603296892 (hardcover) | ISBN 9781603296908 (paperback) | ISBN 9781603296915 (EPUB)
Subjects: LCSH: Emigration and immigration—Study and teaching (Higher) | Emigration and immigration—Social aspects | Emigration and immigration in literature | Emigration and immigration in motion pictures | Mass media and immigrants
Classification: LCC JV6013.5 .T43 2025 (print) | LCC JV6013.5 (ebook) | DDC 304.8071—dc23/eng/20250320
LC record available at https://lccn.loc.gov/2025005094
LC ebook record available at https://lccn.loc.gov/2025005095

Contents

Introduction: Teaching Migration   1
  Masha Salazkina and Yumna Siddiqi

Part I: Key Concepts and Frameworks

Border as Method in a Film and Media Studies Context   39
  Malini Guha

Fugitive Aesthetics: Teaching Refugee Cinema Aporetically   48
  Bruce Bennett and Katarzyna Marciniak

Teaching Migration through Mobilities   59
  Gaoheng Zhang

Approaching Displacement: Genealogical Reflections and a
  Teaching Example from a Pennsylvania Rust Belt Classroom   70
  Jutta Gsoels-Lorensen

A Transportable/Transnational Cinema: Wapikoni Mobile   85
  Kester Dyer

Migrant Literature and the United Nations Convention
  on Refugees   102
  William Arighi

Disability in Narratives of Migration   111
  Alexander Dawson

Climate Migration and Deranged Realism in
  Amitav Ghosh's *Gun Island*   120
  Hsuan L. Hsu and Rebecca H. Hogue

Whiteness and Migration Studies   127
  Claudia Sadowski-Smith

Part II: Geopolitical and Pedagogical Contexts

Hip-Hop-Based Education and Italian Studies:
A Culturally Responsive Approach to Teaching
Migration and Contemporary Italy   139
  Lisa Dolasinski

Orban Wallace's *Another News Story*: Media Coverage
of the "Migrant Crisis" in Europe   148
  Eszter Zimanyi

Questioning the Possibility of Return
in Francophone Literatures   156
  Kristen Stern

The Impact of Emigration on Narrativizing the Arab Spring   165
  Elizabeth Rich

Migration and #FamiliesBelongTogether   175
  Jocelyn Frelier and Paige Andersson

Pedagogical Approaches to Contemporary Latin American
Literature: Narco-Narratives and Central American Migrants
in Mexico   184
  B. Judith Martínez-García

Dual Citizenship: Migration and the Imagined Borderlands
Community in Three Chicano-Themed Films   193
  Spencer R. Herrera

Beyond Empathy: Teaching Central American Migration
through Film and Literature   202
  Manuel Chinchilla

Part III: Pedagogical Approaches and Methods

Border Migrants: A Comparative Pedagogical Approach   213
  Weixian Pan

(Un)Reading Jonas Poher Rasmussen's *Flee*   220
  Darshana Sreedhar Mini

Traveling Identities: Migration in Literature and Film
  at a Liberal Arts College   228
  Eva Rueschmann

Migrating Scenes: Teaching an Undergraduate Seminar
  on Migration and Movement in the Hispanic World   236
  Marilén Loyola

Learning through Service:
  Migration in the Spanish-Language Classroom   244
  Megan Thornton Velázquez

We Need More Stories: Disrupting Dominant Narratives
  of Migration through Digital Collaboration   250
  Emily S. Davis and Délice I. Williams

The Migrant Reality Treatment   258
  Juan Llamas-Rodriguez

A Macro-Micro Approach to Migration
  through Digital Exploration   266
  Karen Little

Notes on Contributors   273

Masha Salazkina and Yumna Siddiqi

Introduction: Teaching Migration

Migration, both forced and voluntary, increasingly shapes our contemporary globalized world. Not only are people moving to seek opportunities, unite with family, flee war and persecution, and escape poverty, they are fleeing climate disasters and dramatic changes in the environment. In fact, the symbolic, political, and ideological significance of migration far exceeds the magnitude of migration as a statistical phenomenon. While international migrants number about 300 million, and internal migrants perhaps another 800 million, migration as a phenomenon greatly influences all facets of our society and culture. In the last seventy years, movements—of goods, capital, information, culture—have increased in scope and intensity, shaping the lives of people in increasingly profound ways. At the crux of contemporary discussions of globalization, migration has become key to our geopolitical imaginary and individual identities. In this volume we bring together essays that reflect on developing and teaching courses and offer possible models for expanding curricular and pedagogical practices to address the varied and complex nature of migration through cultural texts.

Attending to migration in our humanities classrooms is crucial as we come to realize the important role that literature, film, and other media play not only in reflecting but also in constituting all aspects of migratory experiences. Popular media, from news to movies, is permeated by narratives that are often directly responsible for creating the public opinion, expectations, and reception of migrants. An array of tracking and portable digital media devices is used by people who are crossing borders and by those who control and manage this flow. Governmental agencies increasingly rely on different forms of media not only as a means of information and training but also as tools for management and logistics. When it comes to migration, the borders between representation, discourse, and practice are blurred. Even those of us who are eager to respond to the need to include migration and migratory experiences among the subjects we teach find ourselves on shifting grounds. As Katarzyna Marciniak and Bruce Bennett note in their introduction to *Teaching Transnational Cinema: Politics and Pedagogy*, the politics and ethics surrounding the "use" of migrants and their experiences in a North American classroom can be quite problematic (5). Contributors to our collection are well aware of this conundrum and offer various ways to combat the tendency to reproduce such power structures. One solution to this problem—as proposed by Tyler Morgenstern, Krista Lynes, and Ian Alan Paul in a recent anthology and taken up by several essays in this volume—is to "interrogat[e] how a wide range of mediating processes and representational practices work to constitute 'migrant crises' as objects of political contention, affective investment, and legal maneuver" (28). Another, related approach is to explore the different modalities of migrants' own discursive, literary, and media production. But for those of us who teach the complex subject of migration in a variety of contexts, having a better sense of the historical and geopolitical frameworks and disciplinary paradigms that give shape to the discussions of migration may be the first and most necessary step.

Historical and Geopolitical Frameworks

Three interlinked and overlapping developments have been particularly influential in shaping geohistorical movements during the twentieth and twenty-first centuries: colonialism and decolonization, the Cold War, and globalization and urbanization. This introduction provides a broad framework for understanding these historical dynamics and the intellectual and political paradigms they offer for the study of migration more generally. We focus on the way these movements and paradigms have affected academic disciplines and areas of study that are most relevant to the teaching of literature, film, and other media in university classrooms today.

European Colonialism and Slavery: Displacement and Forced Migration

If capitalism emerged in the West, the initial accumulation of capital— what Karl Marx called "primitive accumulation"—was spurred not only by the enclosures of common land in Europe but also by the enslavement, forced migration, forced labor, trafficking, indenture, colonial occupation, Indigenous genocide, and settlement by Europeans of racialized people, whose land, labor, and bodies were violently appropriated and turned into commodities, and whose cultures and societies were ravaged. As a long line of intellectuals, including C. L. R. James, Oliver Cromwell Cox, Walter Rodney, Frantz Fanon, Cedric Robinson, Robin Kelley, and Ruth Wilson Gilmore (*Geographies*), have argued, racial capitalism is fundamental to and inextricable from modernity, from its inception at the end of the fifteenth century through the present. That said, the specific histories of slavery, indenture, colonial occupation, and settlement are varied and complex, propelling the migration and displacement of enslaved, Indigenous, colonized, transported, and (relatively) free people.

Equally varied are the histories of resistance to transatlantic slavery, European colonial settlement, and occupation. Such resistance dates back to the beginnings of European dominance, but it was in the late nineteenth and twentieth centuries that liberation struggles gained momentum and were most successful. Between 1945 and 1989, many of the territories occupied by Europeans became independent nations; those territories not only occupied but also settled by Europeans, including North America, Australia, New Zealand, and parts of Central and South America, while independent from Europe, remain settler colonies. The European colonial powers had already "underdeveloped" the territories they had ruled, as the Guyanese historian Walter Rodney famously put it. Many newly liberated nations continued to experience the economic dominance of former colonial powers, a relationship for which Ghana's first prime minister and president, Kwame Nkrumah, coined the term "neo-colonialism." The disadvantaged economic circumstances of postcolonial nations, ongoing and crippling debt payments, and the corruption of elites stymied economic progress in the Global South. The postwar period saw a boom in Western economies, labor shortages, and relatively open-door policies that attracted migrants from the Global South to the Global North and those from the East to the West, spurring what the Jamaican poet Louise Bennett humorously called "colonization in reverse." The most prominent of these early postcolonial migrations were those of Afro-Caribbeans to the United Kingdom beginning in 1948; South Asian migration to the United Kingdom, which peaked in the 1950s; and North African migration to France, which also gained momentum after World War II as both nations recruited workers.

Immigration from Europe to North America occurred in waves, initially of British, Irish, and French immigrants and then of people from elsewhere in Europe, all of which continued the project of settler colonization that started in the beginning of the sixteenth century. The greatest of these waves was between 1880 and 1920, when roughly twenty million Europeans arrived in North America. European working-class immigrants were variably racialized during the nineteenth and early twentieth centuries, increasingly benefiting from "the wages of Whiteness" (Roediger) and both escaping and participating in extreme anti-Black violence. By contrast, the subsequent racialization of migrant workers from Asia and the Caribbean reinforced economic exploitation and violence with systems of indenture, exclusion, and the denial of citizenship.

After 1960, European migration to North America was surpassed in volume by that of people from other parts of the world. This migration has made post-1960 arrivals complicit with Europeans in the ongoing dynamics of settler colonialism in North America and Australia. At the same time, this late-twentieth- and early-twenty-first-century migration has further bifurcated along racial and class lines, with cosmopolitan migrants making up part of a wealthy global elite with greater access to capital, jobs, mobility, and citizenship, while subaltern migrants are trapped in low-wage jobs and subjected to precarity, violence, and, increasingly, incarceration.

World War II, the Cold War, and Migration

While migration is, of course, a historical process that goes back to the beginning of human time and spans the globe, the focus of most of the essays in this volume is on international migration from the Global South to North America and Europe during the twentieth and twenty-first centuries. Because the volume is addressed to teachers in North America and the United Kingdom, such a focus is certainly justifiable—and yet it also obscures the experience of many migrants who move within and between nation-states across the Global South. Even those who make the journey to North America and Europe are often internally displaced within their countries of origin or from other countries first, further complicating the necessary understanding of the geopolitical contours of these processes. And yet migration, especially in the media, continues to be treated as a phenomenon that affects primarily Europe and North America, with its discussions engaging notions of governmentality, sovereignty, and human rights as applicable to those regions rather than the realities faced by the rest of the world. In terms of absolute numbers, migration within the Global South is estimated to be as substantial as migration from the Global South to the Global North, though less significant in terms of the remittances vital to neoliberal logics of development (Awad and Natarajan 48–49; Nawyn).

Such bias extends to—and at least in part stems from—positing World War II as a pivotal moment within the history of global migration. Indeed, roughly forty million Europeans were displaced after World War II and the onset of the Cold War. The way that migration is constructed, legally and institutionally, today is very much a product of this historical moment. A number of the international organizations that deal with migrants today were created during this time, including the United Nations High Commissioner for Refugees founded in 1950, which became the principal institution of the international refugee regime. The International Organization for Migration, or, as it was first known, the Provisional Intergovernmental Committee for the Movement of Migrants from Europe, was formed in 1951 to help resettle approximately one million people displaced by the war. It evolved from a logistics agency into the main migration agency of the United Nations. While many displaced Europeans resettled on the Continent, others migrated to Australia and Canada, furthering the ongoing project of European settler colonialism there.

As Liisa Malkki reminds us, "the refugee" is always a historically and geopolitically specific construct. Though particular to Europe, the post–World War II context was crucial for establishing the terms for contemporary global constructions of refugees as objects of knowledge and subjects of administration. The refugee camp became paradigmatic for this construction:

> The segregation of nationalities; the orderly organization of repatriation or third-country resettlement; medical and hygienic programs and quarantining; "perpetual screening" and the accumulation of

documentation on the inhabitants of the camps; the control of movement and black-marketing; law enforcement and public discipline; and schooling and rehabilitation were some of the operations that the spatial concentration and ordering of people enabled or facilitated. Through these processes, the modern, postwar refugee emerged as a knowable, nameable figure and as an object of social-scientific knowledge. (Malkki 498)

It is important to note that the refugee camp was at this time military in design, and it was only later that the so-called refugee problem was shifted from a military to a humanitarian domain. Refugee law and legal instruments were also developed in the postwar period, including the most widely used legal definition of *refugee*:

[T]he term "refugee" shall apply to any person who[,] . . . owing to well-founded fear of being persecuted for reasons of race, religion, nationality, membership of a particular social group or political opinion, is outside the country of his nationality and is unable or, owing to such fear, is unwilling to avail himself of the protection of that country; or who, not having a nationality and being outside the country of his former habitual residence as a result of such events, is unable or, owing to such fear, is unwilling to return to it. (United Nations)

History and geopolitics determine not only how the refugee is constructed but also the optics of refugee recognition and treatment. Despite their institutional framing in terms of purportedly color-blind universal human rights, inequalities are built into the treatment of refugees, inequalities that depend on both the origin of the refugee and the location of their asylum seeking. Given the dynamics of colonial rapine, neocolonial debt, the effects of structural adjustment plans and neoliberal globalization, the corruption of postcolonial elites, political and religious repression, and catastrophic climate change, refuge seekers tend to come from the countries of the Global South. This leads to the wholesale understanding of refugeeism as a "Third World problem," the historical and geopolitical "First World" roots of which are obscured. And yet contrary to common assumptions, most refugees do not travel to the Global North, seeking shelter in neighboring countries instead. Because immigration to the Global North has become increasingly restrictive overall, as many as seventy-five percent of refugee seekers remain in low- and middle-income countries, forming part of the larger pattern of migration within the Global South ("Refugee Data Finder"). Given increasing discrepancies between the narrow legal definitions of who can be considered a refugee and the wide range of pressures leading to large-scale migration, the generic use of the term *refugee* tends to obfuscate the fact that this category accounts for only about one-tenth of all migrants globally (Awad and Natarajan 52). This is the reason why we, alongside other scholars of critical migration studies, use the broader, more inclusive category of "migrant."

More than World War II as such, it is the Cold War that further propelled displacement and migration, not least because of the two superpowers' proxy wars across the world. The massacre of half a million communists in Indonesia in 1965 and 1966 by the United States–backed Suharto regime, and the resulting migration of ethnic Chinese Indonesians to China, is but one instance of the terror and violence to which "Third World" peoples were subjected as they sought self-determination and embraced leftist politics. This is the event that gave its name—"the Jakarta method"—to various mass killings of leftists orchestrated by United States–backed regimes, many of which resulted in new waves of migration (Bevins). Communist regimes were also responsible for large-scale displacements of people. To give just one example, the departure of the United States from Vietnam in 1975, the expulsion of Chinese Vietnamese from South Vietnam, and Vietnam's invasion of Cambodia in 1979 led to migrations of half a million refugees and the setting up of refugee camps all over Southeast Asia. The historical patterns of large-scale migrations from the Caribbean likewise reflect the impact of Cold War politics in the region. Thus, after the 1959 revolution in Cuba, the Trujillo regime, and the US invasion of the Dominican Republic in 1965, migration from both Cuba and the Dominican Republic to the United States increased dramatically. The so-called dirty wars in South America spanning the period from 1954 to 1990 spurred migrations from Argentina, Paraguay, Brazil, Bolivia, Uruguay, Chile, Ecuador, and Peru. In all these countries, United States–backed dictatorships engaged in the brutal repression of real and imaginary subversives, political opponents, and civilians through death squads nationally and internationally. The 1980s saw similar developments in Central America—in Guatemala, El Salvador, Honduras, and Panama—where the United States provided military training and funding to back dictators and attack popular elected leaders. These internal wars led to the movement of migrants, a movement that continues today as refugees flee from political repression, violence, poverty, and corruption. Similar dynamics of global Cold War politics (before and after the fall of the Berlin Wall) have continuously affected the ongoing migration from and across the Middle East, North Africa, and South Asia.

The Cold War also defined immigration policy in the United States. Until World War II immigration policy in the United States had been framed in relation to domestic concerns. The Immigration Act of 1924, also known as the Johnson-Reed Act, established an implicitly racist quota system based on national origins that favored immigrants from Europe and excluded immigrants from Asia. Between 1945 and 1965, the quota system continued, but through a series of laws and executive actions, special accommodations were made for Europeans displaced after World War II and the drawing of the Iron Curtain. During and after the quota system, refugees from communist countries—namely, the USSR, Hungary, Cuba, and Vietnam—were given avenues to immigrate to the United States. In line with Cold War policy, the Immigration and Nationality Act of 1952, also known as the McCarran-Walter Act, excluded putative subversives and introduced a question regarding communist affiliation to the immigration and travel application form. As recently as October 2020, the United States Citizenship and Immigration Services issued a directive rehearsing the position that any visitor to the United States is familiar with from the visa application form: "In general, unless otherwise exempt, any intending immigrant who is a member or affiliate of the Communist Party or any other totalitarian party (or subdivision or affiliate), domestic or foreign, is inadmissible to the United States" ("USCIS"). Although barriers to immigration from the non-European world decreased with the Immigration and Nationality Act of 1965, and labor and family immigration became the determining factors in access to immigration, Cold War anti-communism is still a guiding principle of the United States Citizenship and Immigration Services.

Globalization and Urbanization

The dual Cold War and postcolonial context is also crucial for understanding globalization, especially in relation to migration. This contemporary period, usually understood as starting at the beginning of the 1980s, is characterized by the greater connectedness and interdependence of polities, economies, societies, cultures, and environments across the globe. Critics and proponents of globalization view this connectedness very differently: while neoliberal journalists such as Thomas Friedman claim euphorically that it has had equalizing effects (summarized in his famous claim that now "the world is flat"), leftist scholars, from Fredric Jameson to Thomas Piketty, underscore its exacerbation of inequality and exploitation.

Regardless of the political lens through which it is viewed, however, migration is understood to be one of the defining features of globalization. Scholars such as Hein de Haas, Stephen Castles, and Mark Miller go so far as to speak of the "globalization of migration," writing that the "large-scale movements of people arise from processes of global integration" (3). In fact, in contrast to the flows of capital, information, and goods, the global migration of people has not increased during this period; what has increased is the unevenness of its distribution patterns. As Mathias Czaika and de Haas note, "Migration has globalized from a destination country perspective but hardly from an origin country perspective, with migrants from an increasingly diverse array of non-European-origin countries concentrating in a shrinking pool of prime destination countries" (283). It is worth noting that a large proportion of this migration from the Global South to the Global North is to the so-called global gateway cities, where migrants make up as much as twenty percent of the population (Bravo).

Migration has also been distributed unevenly in another, albeit connected, sense: it has largely been from rural to urban areas. If one considers the time span of the last five hundred years, the era of (Western capitalist) modernity, then this pattern of migration from rural to urban areas stands out. In 1800 less than ten percent of the world's population lived in rural areas; by 1900 the urban population had risen to sixteen percent; by 1950 it was about one billion out of three billion, or thirty-three percent; in 2018 it was about fifty-five percent (Ritchie and Roser). In his magisterial study *The Country and the City*, Raymond Williams explores the significance in English literature and culture of this demographic shift from the country to the city, which was spurred by England's industrial revolution. We see similar movements from rural to urban areas in nations all over the world that have been shifting from primarily agrarian to extractive and manufacturing industrial economies, though now in the context of finance capitalism and different imperial dispensations. These migrations from rural to urban areas have been treated extensively in literature and film across the world, constituting one of major themes in, for example, Chinese documentary media of the last decades.

While Williams says very little about the country and the city in the rest of the world, or about Britain's imperial history and colonial capitalism, *The Country and the City* frames migrations from the Global South to the Global North (specifically to England) as part of this movement from the rural to the urban (289–306). And yet migration within the

Global South plays an important part in this process as well. A truly global account of migration in its multiple forms demands a rethinking of the concepts and frames that have shaped the field of migration studies away from the binaries that have tended to structure it. As Ibrahim Awad and Usha Natarajan argue, "Much of the dominant discourse on migration turns on binaries: some migrants are voluntary, others are forced; some are international and others are internal; some are legal and others are irregular; and, perhaps the most formative of the binaries, some are migrants whilst others are refugees" (52). All these binaries are problematic to begin with, as many of the essays in this volume show, and their closer examination in the classroom can open up conceptual space to challenge and reconsider many of the assumptions still governing dominant discourses on migration that many students take for granted.

Studying Migration in the Humanities: Intellectual Genealogies

Social scientists have studied migration for decades using empirical methodologies, focusing on statistics, data, and modeling. A glance at the entry for "migration" in the *International Encyclopedia of the Social Sciences* reveals the dominant terms and frameworks for its study: labor flows, cost-benefit analysis, push-and-pull factors, chain migration, and integration, to name but a few ("Migration"). Such analysis, while it varies in its political tendencies, is closely tied to the needs of social, political, and economic policy. At its most state-centered, migration studies has been geared to the territorial rationalities of the nation-state and the management of populations. The emergence of critical migration studies—associated with the work of Sandro Mezzadra and Brett Neilson, Nicholas De Genova, and others—has been distinguished by a profound critique of nation-state rationalities and a questioning of how the objects and terms of analysis, such as the migrant and the border, are constructed and to what ends. With the influence of critical theory, many scholars have moved away from seeking empirical data to focus on the production and uses of knowledge about migration. It is here that the humanities more generally and the fields of literary, film, media, and visual studies in particular can offer significant scholarly intervention while simultaneously providing students with unique analytical tools that enable them to understand and take a critical stance on the world around them. It is therefore not surprising that some of the most exciting interventions in this area in recent decades come from highly interdisciplinary, critical-practice-based models, such as the work of the Forensic Architecture research group (forensic-architecture.org).

In the last thirty-five years, scholars of the humanities have drawn attention to the cultural dimensions of migration. Anthropologists have spearheaded the study of culture in motion, as it crosses national borders. In *Routes: Travel and Translation in the Late Twentieth Century*, James Clifford emphasizes the ways in which cultures are just as crucially creations of the movement of peoples—whether these movements are voluntary, leisurely, under duress, or violent—as they are rooted in particular places. As Clifford suggests, "Practices of displacement might emerge as *constitutive* of cultural meanings rather than as their simple transfer or extension" (2). With the incursion into the field of scholars such as Clifford, there is a new focus on cultural meanings, social values, and ethical relationships in the context of migration and on the artistic and cultural production of people on the move. And with this turn, the study of migration has become increasingly interdisciplinary, with scholars drawing on critical theory to analyze different kinds of texts of migration, be they ethnographic, literary, filmic, digital, visual, or musical.

The historical and geopolitical developments that have spurred migration since 1945 have generated different critical discourses and disciplinary fields. In this volume we refer mostly to the theoretical discussions and cultural contexts that come to the fore when teaching migration in Europe and North America, discussions that are themselves shaped by a combination of historical contexts, disciplinary fields, and specific intellectual and artistic genealogies. In the United States, ethnic studies, Latinx and border studies, Black studies, Indigenous and Native American studies, diaspora studies, postcolonial literature, and world literature are all formations that have arisen out of different understandings and trajectories of migration. Furthermore, it has become apparent that the historical experience of migration and its effects has been constitutive for a number of other academic fields that have shaped educational practices today, including feminist, gender, and sexuality studies; legal studies; and labor studies, as these approaches, in turn, increasingly reshape literary, film, and media-specific scholarship. A brief sketch of how some of these fields, and key artists and thinkers associated with them, have shaped approaches to migration suggests that the (moving) terrain of migration studies is fragmentary, with diverse and at times competing geographies and histories. It is precisely the recognition and exploration of mutual entanglements of these seemingly fragmented histories and geographies as stemming from the global thrust of modern imperialism and capitalism, as Lisa Lowe argues in *The Intimacies of Four Continents*, that remains a crucial task for the study of migration from a humanities perspective.

Diaspora and Global Black Studies

In the United States, African American studies was shaped by a radical tradition of Black intellectuals and activists, such as W. E. B. Du Bois, Marcus Garvey, Paul Robeson, and Malcolm X, who were explicitly Pan-Africanist, anti-imperialist, and in some cases internationalist and anti-capitalist in their analyses and political stances. As the academic discipline of African American studies grew in the United States, it became domesticated within a national frame. In the emergent academic field of global Black studies, by contrast, the significance of migration and diaspora has been key. The term *diaspora*, formulated first in relation to the Jewish Diaspora, has dominated the framing of the enslavement of African people, forced migration, and forced labor. In the last thirty years Africana studies and global Black studies have gained prominence across North America and Europe, with scholars in these fields focusing on Black migration and diaspora across the world. Contemporary scholars of Black culture in North America and Europe increasingly study interwoven cultural movements and migrations across the United States, Europe, and Africa that involve multiple displacements, privileging some of the conceptual frameworks that have come out of global Black studies and formulating new ones, such as the Black Mediterranean.

Stuart Hall's essays on the Afro-Caribbean diaspora and Paul Gilroy's work on diaspora and on the Black Atlantic (*Black Atlantic, There Ain't No Black*) have been crucial to this shift. The writings of Hall, who was extremely influential as a public intellectual in the United Kingdom, were inseparable from his personal experience of diasporic (dis)locations. Hall argues that Caribbean national and diasporic identities are closely connected and intertwined and that in general an open rather than a closed, unified conception of identity recognizes the historical contingencies and transcultural dynamics of diasporas. One of the defining historical conditions of the Caribbean diaspora, he notes, is the violence of "conquest, expropriation, genocide, slavery, the plantation system, and the long tutelage of colonial dependency" (210). So, he suggests, the elements that make up a syncretic Caribbean culture exist within relations of power that are profoundly asymmetrical. Hall argues that the Caribbean diaspora is shaped by vectors of continuity and discontinuity that reach across Africa, Europe, and the Caribbean. Gilroy, who did his PhD at Birmingham University with Hall, popularized the term *diaspora* in Black studies with his book *There Ain't No Black in the Union Jack*, a critique of the implicitly White and national framing of British cultural studies as a field and of the occlusion of immigrant cultures in Britain. In *The Black Atlantic*, Gilroy developed the notion that the Black Atlantic was a cultural formation that emerged from the movement and circulation across the western coast of Africa, the eastern coasts of North and South America, the Caribbean, and Europe. Gilroy has been criticized for emphasizing the fact of connection through movement and for failing to adequately acknowledge the violence that was its defining condition, but it is undeniable that he made migration and the notion of diaspora central to contemporary Black studies.

In the United Kingdom, Black and British Asian studies are closely aligned and overlap because of the history of Black and Asian postcolonial migration to Britain, which increased sharply after World War II, as Britain looked to the Caribbean and South Asia to meet its acute need for labor. Anti-racist activists in the United Kingdom have long rallied with the call "We are here because you were there." Many writers and filmmakers have focused on Black and British migration, in fact multiple migrations, across different historical periods. In their work, they take stock of the long history of Black and Asian presence in the United Kingdom, portraying the experiences of Afro-Caribbeans in World War II, chronicling the challenges and achievements of the Windrush generation,[1] and plumbing the violence of and silence about the partition of India and its lasting memories among British South Asians. They confront racism and document resistance, addressing the shift from a more unified Black and Asian cultural politics to the proliferation of Black and Asian British identities and exploring queer Black and British Asian sexualities. The range and volume of work in these areas is ever-expanding.

Within the North American context, critical race scholars have offered new historical and conceptual frameworks for thinking through the relationship between migration and racialization, taking the Middle Passage as a foundational moment for the racialization of people forcibly brought from Africa to North America (Sharpe 25–102). Centering race in the accounts of migration, critical race scholarship has provided crucial insights into, among other things, the direct relationship between the realities of racial capitalism and the ongoing complicity of its legal and cultural forms with the project of imperialism.

Postcolonial Studies

The publication in 1978 of Edward Said's *Orientalism*, an analysis of the role of Western (that is, European and North American) literature in furthering imperialism, was a landmark event for the emergent field of postcolonial studies. Said argued that by representing those who were designated not White as inferior in varied and shifting ways, Orientalist texts framed colonial domination as a beneficial civilizing mission. The movement of peoples was a central dimension of imperialism, both in colonies of occupation and of settlement. Soldiers, administrators, merchants, adventurers, and workers traveled to the places Europeans traded with, conquered, and ruled while maintaining strong ties with their motherlands and established expatriate communities, cultures, and institutions. The circulation of colonial administrators not only was crucial for colonial administration but also gave imaginative shape to what came to be the post-colonial nation-state, as Benedict Anderson argues (113–40).

In *Culture and Imperialism*, Said further extended his discussion of Orientalism to the ways in which the writing of colonized people responded to their condition. The global reach of the Portuguese, Spanish, Dutch, British, and French empires meant that many millions of colonized subjects—including enslaved peoples, sailors, soldiers, indentured agricultural workers ("coolies"), merchants, and thinkers—circulated and migrated across the world. Students, artists, and intellectuals also undertook "the voyage in" to the metropolitan centers of the European empires, participating in movements and debates there (Said, *Culture* 216, 239–61). Scholars in the field of postcolonial studies have documented the voices of these migrants and studied the histories and the works that came out of these dynamic imperial formations. The post–World War II movements of colonized peoples have created large diasporic and migrant communities and cultures and have inspired literature, films, and scholarship focused on the experience and legacy of migration, not only in Britain but also in France, Spain, Portugal, and the Netherlands.

Despite the successes of tricontinental national liberation movements after World War II, neocolonialism continues in many parts of the world by way of political interference and economic control. Post-1980s globalization has spurred migrations from the Global North to the Global South as a result of colonial and comprador underdevelopment, corruption, civil war, debt, and climate change. Since the end of the Cold War, the United States has waged, promoted, and funded wars in Afghanistan, Iraq,

Syria, Libya, and Yemen. Russia has, after rolling back its occupation of Afghanistan, conducted military operations in Chechnya and now Ukraine. The lingering effects of former imperial dynamics and new quasi-imperial wars have spurred the movement of millions of refugees. Postcolonial scholars, writers, and filmmakers have taken up the challenge of portraying and analyzing these complex movements, turning to history, anthropology, political theory, and other fields and also experimenting with media and form.

Ethnic Studies

While postcolonial migration to Europe largely became the subject of literature, film, and new media after World War II and has only recently been widely studied by scholars and addressed in classrooms, in the North American context there has long been an alternative tradition of thinking about migratory flows and their impact on society and culture. Ethnic studies emerged out of student protests and strikes in the San Francisco Bay Area in 1968 and as a result of the demands of the Third World Liberation Front and the Black Students Union at San Francisco State College (now San Francisco State University) that the curriculum reflect the histories and experiences of racialized and marginalized groups in the United States and that the academy hire more faculty members of color and ensure equal access to education. In 1969, in response to these mobilizations, ethnic studies departments were set up at San Francisco State College and the University of California, Berkeley, and in the last fifty years, hundreds of ethnic studies programs have been set up at universities and colleges in the United States, and ethnic studies courses are widely taught in high schools as well. Ethnic studies has focused particularly on the experiences of African Americans, Asian Americans, Latinx Americans, and Indigenous Americans.

It is worth noting that the call for ethnic studies emerged out of anti–Vietnam War protests, anti-racist organizing by the Black Panther Party, and solidarity with anti-colonial struggles. This context allowed students to reflect on their own antecedents and understand migration to North America as part of the larger process of colonial settlement and imperialism and its logics of exclusion and racialization. In the years that followed, many artists, writers, and scholars asserted and explored their identities as racialized minorities who had been forcibly transported to or had migrated to the United States, arguably engaging more fully in the struggle for recognition than in the politics of solidarity. This is not to say that these are mutually exclusive, but identity-based and solidarity-based cultural formations in the last decades of the twentieth century have tended to diverge in their politics. Today, the different areas of ethnic studies are seeing a turn (or return) to the activist social movement and internationalist thinking of the field's beginnings, and the significance of migration is central to this thinking.

Asian American Studies

Asian migration to North America began with the arrival of indentured workers from China in the mid-1800s to prospect for gold and to build railways on the continent, and this migration is thus intimately tied to settler colonialism and racial capitalism. The legal discrimination against and exclusion of Asians from the United States started with the Chinese Exclusion Act of 1882, which banned the immigration of Chinese workers, and was followed by the passage of the Immigration Act of 1924, which banned immigration from Asia entirely. In Canada, Chinese head taxes were introduced immediately after the completion of the Canadian Pacific Railway, which Chinese migrant workers had helped build in 1885, followed by rising taxes and the passage of the Chinese Exclusion Act of 1923. In these ways, Asian migration was racialized earlier and in more legally explicit ways in North America than in the United Kingdom. Japanese Americans and Japanese Canadians were also subjected to a racialized detention regime with their internment in camps during World War II. This internment set the dubious precedent for the carceral detention and deportation regime for migrants from the Caribbean and Latin America that we have seen in the last thirty or forty years, which particularly affected Haitian migrants.

While the second wave of immigrants from South, Southeast, and East Asia who arrived in North America from the 1970s onward have not been subjected to the same explicitly legal discrimination, such as being been barred from US citizenship, as earlier Asian migrants were until 1943, the students who protested in 1968 were addressing ongoing racism, cultural exclusion, and Eurocentrism when they demanded radical changes to the curriculum. More recent waves of Asian migration to North America have occurred under different conditions than those of earlier generations. With the Immigration and Nationality Act of 1965, the United States showed a preference for family and professional immigration, which has meant, for example, that South Asian professionals who immigrated to the United

States have made South Asians the wealthiest minority in the United States, one strongly invested in neoliberal capitalism. Arguably, the framing of East and South Asian Americans as a so-called model minority has served to absorb and neutralize difference within neoliberal and racial capitalism, naturalizing it and forestalling its criticisms. In response, diasporic and migrant Asian writers, filmmakers, and scholars have been engaged in a wide range of critical and artistic work through the lens of migration, bringing forward anti-capitalist and anti-imperialist critique and queer of color perspectives and combating the dominance of the nation form in fact and imagination.

Latinx and Border Studies

Together with the student protests that led to the founding of ethnic studies in the San Francisco Bay Area, the East Los Angeles walkout of fifteen thousand high school students with a list of demands to the Los Angeles Board of Education—including compulsory bilingual, bicultural education for Mexican American students, more hiring of Mexican American teachers and administrators, firing of teachers who showed prejudice to Mexican and Mexican American students, the introduction of Mexican food to cafeterias, the promotion of community participation in foods—was the backdrop for the founding of the first Latina/o studies program in the United States at California State University, Los Angeles, in the fall of 1968. "We didn't cross the border, the border crossed us" has long been a Chicanx activist rallying cry, referring to the historical fact that the United States annexed Florida, Louisiana, and the northern half of Mexico in the early 1800s, and after the United States' imperial advance on Texas in 1845 led to a war with Mexico, the United States also annexed California, Arizona, New Mexico, Colorado, Nevada, and Utah in 1848. Generations had endured displacement, dispossession, precarity, discrimination, and violence in the US-Mexico borderlands and border states, and it was this history of US settler colonialism as well as their resistance to it and their cultural history that students wanted addressed.

Gloria Anzaldúa begins *Borderlands / La Frontera: The New Mestiza*, a landmark book for Latinx and border studies, by laying out the historical conditions of the Rio Grande Valley, where she grew up and which she describes as a space of multiple movements, a borderland, since the late nineteenth and early twentieth centuries. She emphasizes the cultural admixture and fluidity of this border, celebrating "the new mestiza" of the book's title, a queer woman of mixed culture and consciousness who has made her way in the borderlands, despite the displacements and dep-redations of racial capitalism and the militarization of the borderlands and the US government's calculated attempt to turn it into hostile terrain. Anzaldúa's book is itself a hybrid, borderland text that blends poetry, mem-oir, history, geopolitical analysis, and philosophy and is written in Span-ish and English. It initiated a focus on border identities and has become a celebrated manifesto of queer Chicana feminism.

Like Anzaldúa's work, the work of the artist, writer, and activist Guill-ermo Gómez-Peña that focuses on the border cultures of Mexico and the United States has been fundamental for Latinx and border studies. Gómez-Peña has lampooned the violence and absurdity of border logics and bor-der regimes, incorporating spoken word, pop art, Indigenous rituals, and audio and video installations into his provocative performances alone and with other artists. He aims to dissolve and disrupt not only national, eth-nic, linguistic, and racial borders but also the borders of gender and sexu-ality. Gómez-Peña's work is as politically, culturally, and artistically relevant to thinking of migration and its effects now as it was forty years ago.

With the so-called prevention-through-deterrence policy initiated with the infamous omnibus 1994 crime bill passed by Bill Clinton and the zero-tolerance policy initiated under the administration of Donald Trump, the US-Mexico borderland has been increasingly weaponized. This is furthered through US government tactics such as cutting off water supplies and criminalizing citizen assistance to migrants. Those who face the dangers and brutality of the journey through Latin America to the US border and the horrendous deterrence and detention regimes at the border are often Indigenous people who have been displaced from their homes and lands in Central and South America. The work of activist artists, writers, and filmmakers can help students engage with these horrific realities, which are numbingly routinized by the corporate media.

Indigenous and Native American Studies

Migration may not, at first glance, appear to be an obvious object of study for Indigenous and Native American studies, functioning very differently in this geopolitical and historical context than it does for the other academic disciplines we have touched on in this introduction. As such, the relation-ship between migration and Indigeneity deserves a lengthier discussion. Indeed, scholars of Indigenous and Native American studies have been wary of the ascendance of postcolonial studies as a field not least because there is no "post" to settler colonialism in North America or elsewhere. Nor does the field stand comfortably under the umbrella of ethnic studies, for, as the Choctaw scholar Jodi Byrd argues, such a construction occludes the violent, ongoing dispossession of native lands by White settlers, a process in which, paradoxically, other racialized migrants were and continue to be implicated. This means that Indigenous sovereignty is contravened by the presence of not only White settlers but also enslaved and transported Africans, indentured laborers, and postcolonial migrants (Byrd). To make sense of the ways that Indigenous people have contended with migration in colonial and postcolonial modernity, it is important to debunk the specious notion that because they themselves were migratory, Indigenous people traditionally had no conception of land ownership. Some Indigenous people were and are nomadic, some more settled. Historically, different bands have articulated Indigenous rights to the land in different ways. In the 1960s and 1970s, when Native Americans were mobilizing in North America, for example, the Indigenous tribes of British Columbia forcefully asserted their claim to land in a declaration issued by the Union of British Columbia Indian Chiefs in 1976:

> We, the native people of the tribes of British Columbia, hereby declare and affirm our inalienable right of native title and aboriginal rights to the land, the minerals, the trees, the lakes, the rivers, the streams, the seas, and other resources of our native land. We declare that out native title and aboriginal rights have existed from time immemorial, exists at the present time, and shall exist for all future time. ("Union" 3–4)

Indigenous people did and do have a different relationship to the land than that which developed in Europe in the early modern period and which Europeans imposed on the rest of the world. Indigenous people traditionally view land not as a commodity, something that has a quantifiable value and can be individually owned, bought, and sold, but rather as an integral and unalienable part of their communities and their identities. The Palyku novelist, illustrator, and law professor Ambelin Kwaymullina explains:

> For aboriginal peoples, country is much more than a place. Rock, tree, river, hill, animal, human—all were formed of the same substance by the Ancestors who continue to live in land, water, sky. Country is filled with relations speaking language and following Law, no matter whether the shape of that relation is human, rock, crow, wattle. Country is loved, needed, and cared for, and country loves, needs, and cares for her peoples in turn. Country is family, culture, identity. Country is self. (12)

Traditionally, the land and the natural environment are the ground of spirituality, social relationships, culture, law, and governance. The land requires care, and its health is seen as crucial to the health of all living beings. In North America, Indigenous tribes considered specific territories their homelands; at the same time, the use of the land was shared and negotiated with other tribes at gatherings and through rituals and ceremonies (Riley and Carpenter 78). As Glen Coulthard argues in *Red Skin, White Masks: Rejecting the Colonial Politics of Recognition*, the "primitive accumulation" that Marx discussed in volume 1 of *Capital* involved Europeans' violent appropriation of the territories of Indigenous people, and, as cannot be stressed enough, this process is ongoing, underwritten by the force of nation-state sovereignty.

European settler colonialism involved what Patrick Wolfe calls "the elimination of the native"—that is, the destruction of Indigenous people's culture and ways of life as well as displacement, dispossession, and genocide (387). In "Decolonizing Indigenous Migration," the Indigenous legal scholars Angela Riley and Kristen Carpenter provide an excellent discussion of Indigenous people's experience of migration in North America after the arrival of Europeans. The so-called doctrine of discovery, whereby lands that were not already under the dominion of a European government could be claimed by newly arrived Europeans by conquest or purchase, did not put an end to conflict among European powers; often, Indigenous peoples were embroiled in such conflicts, land was further divided, and Indigenous people continued to be displaced. Later, as the United States expanded with the Louisiana Purchase and embraced the notion of manifest destiny with the conquest and annexation of large parts of Mexico, Indigenous people saw their lands occupied and their territories divided by national boundaries in the North and the South. In the 1830s the United States passed removal acts that resulted in the violent dispatchment of Indigenous people from their homelands and their forced migration to reservations in militarized marches, including the Trail of Tears, the Trail of Death, and the Long Walk. The conditions in these reservations were often harsh. The 1887 General Allotment Act worsened these conditions by allowing the US government to divide up commonly owned reservation land, give allotments to some Indigenous people who were recognized as citizens, and sell off the supposed surplus Indigenous land to White settlers, expelling more Indigenous people (Wolfe 404).

Today, the violent displacement and migration under duress of Indigenous peoples in the West continues most dramatically in Latin America, from where people travel hoping to cross the US-Mexico border. In the 2021 fiscal year, the United States Border Patrol recorded at this border more than 1.6 million expulsions and apprehensions of people seeking refuge from poverty, political violence, criminal violence, and climate catastrophe, conditions caused in large part by the dirty wars backed by the United States. A large number of the migrants from Central America are Indigenous peoples, "who are uniquely and acutely impacted by poverty, lack of enforceable property rights, the destruction of land due to climate change, extractive industry, and governmental interference" (Riley and Carpenter 103). Indigenous people are also being pushed out of Amazonia by the destruction of their habitats and by violence.

To counter past and ongoing settler colonial occupation and violence, Indigenous land defenders and environmentalists across North and South America have mobilized against the policies and actions of right-wing anti-Indigenous politicians and mining and oil conglomerates at the cost of their lives (Le Billon and Lujala). Many also oppose liberal accommodationist multicultural politics. Coulthard rejects what he calls "the politics of recognition" advanced by the Canadian settler nation-state and often accepted by Indigenous communities, a politics that folds Indigenous claims to nationhood within Canadian nation-state sovereignty. He calls instead for a politics that emerges out of "grounded normativity . . . the modalities of Indigenous land-connected practices and longstanding experiential knowledge that inform and structure our ethical engagements with the world and our relationships with human and nonhuman others over time" (13). Such a shift from land-as-territory to land-as-relationship would require a rethinking of the very concept of migration. It would mean thinking of migration outside the framework of state sovereignty, borders, territoriality, and ownership, as movement in the context of deep mutual care for all living things and the land that sustains us. Riley and Carpenter maintain that "decolonizing Indigenous migration first requires conceptualizing and advancing a paradigm in which Indigenous practices and lifeways inform and reform migration in the settler state. This inquiry must begin by acknowledging and respecting Indigenous worldviews, which are rooted in Indigenous Peoples' deep connection to the natural world" (71).

While all these movements emerged from shared political and cultural concerns about the violence and the enduring impact of colonial and neo-imperialist expansions and their effects on the composition of contemporary cultures and experiences of people, they often differ in their understanding of the identity of the object of their study and accompanying theoretical frameworks and terms. The different movements have responded to the political situations and goals of the people on whose behalf they have spoken, therefore giving sometimes overlapping and sometimes conflicting accounts of migration. This multiplicity of perspectives is reflected in the multiplicity of artistic methods that writers and filmmakers have employed in their explorations of migration.

Literature, Film, Media, and Migration

In addition to being a thematic emphasis and a locus of cultural practices, the experience of migration has produced its own expressive forms, both literary and audiovisual. This has been the case historically; the condition of exile has given rise to specific narrative forms and modes of poetic experimentation. Consider, for example, Samuel Selvon's *The Lonely Londoners*, in which the language shifts between and mixes Creole and Standard English and the passages swerve into a stream of consciousness narrative reminiscent of Virginia Woolf. Recent developments in both the flows and the intensity of migration and the degree of its mediation, enabled by new technologies, have created exciting new kinds of texts, texts that are themselves hybrid and mixed and that experiment with literary and cinematic form. For instance, *Flee*, directed by Jonas Poher Rasmussen, brilliantly interweaves animated documentary of a young man's telling of the hidden story of his flight from Afghanistan to Denmark many years before and actual documentary footage of events in Afghanistan at the time of his flight. Writers, artists, and filmmakers explore migration in a range of media, including literature, films, graphic texts, audiovisual works, and television. As the essays in this collection demonstrate, the use of a variety of these forms has enormous potential in the classroom. This is why this collection brings together literature, cinema, and other media, and many of our contributors move across these forms.

Many of the creative and critical projects that center on migration bring into question not only the divisions between different media and genres but also the lines separating aesthetic representation and political action. Going beyond political commentary and reflection, many writers, filmmakers, and artists structure their work as activist interventions. *Refugee Tales*, for example, is a collaborative and ongoing project that involves group walks in the South of England as well as storytelling in solidarity with detained migrants. David Herd and Anna Pincus began the project, collecting and publishing stories told to writers by detainees and those touched by the detention regime in the United Kingdom. The purpose of the project is to end the indefinite detention of migrants in the United Kingdom. In the afterword to volume 1 of what is now a four-volume collection, also titled *Refugee Tales*, Herd discusses the conditions of indefinite detention and how the walks and tales mobilize against this policy and practice in the United Kingdom by staking a space in public discourse and on English soil for the telling of migrants' stories. In the United States, artivist media projects such as the *Transborder Immigrant Tool* address the fact that the US government has deliberately turned the US-Mexico border into a desert death trap by using cell phones to guide migrants through the desert to water stations and, incidentally, fortify them with poetry. Projects such as these show not only that the humanities, broadly speaking, have an important role to play in making sense of migration but also that literature, film, and new media are key to mobilizing the aesthetic and political agency of migrants.

Teaching Migration in North American Classrooms

The challenges and opportunities of teaching migration through literature, film, and media are augmented by the fact that students themselves have experienced different forms of migration, either personally or indirectly through family stories. How to engage pedagogically with different positions and experiences—and, for some, their lack—is crucial. The greatest challenge when broaching the topic of migration is negotiating students' personal experiences while also cultivating an understanding of broader dynamics and varieties of migration that goes far beyond the emphasis on the personal and individual; it involves moving past consciousness raising and the paradigms of voyeuristic spectacles of suffering so prevalent today to critical analysis.

Central to such critical analysis is the interrogation of the representation of migration and migratory experiences, starting from positive and negative stereotypes students are exposed to from high school through college and moving on to readings that offer more complex explorations of causes, effects, and experiences of migration, texts that increasingly form part of the new global literary canon. Whether students are asked to revisit the classics and reassess their representations of earlier moments of migration or to consider more recent literary works featuring migrant experiences, discussions of migration can play an important role in reflecting current political and social debates.

Moreover, a focus on migration provides important opportunities for bridging, integrating, and questioning different forms of knowledge students acquire in other classes as well as through mass media and in the public sphere more generally. While the social sciences have provided many important paradigms for analyzing migration, shifting attention to questions of personal experiences, affects, representation, mediation, ideologies, and cultural contextualization is particularly important at present, and nowhere is it more important than in the classroom. Such direct and student-centered engagement can range from textual analysis to an examination of the many functions of media, including literature, in shaping the flows and experiences of migration and its representation to a discussion of historical changes in the way geopolitical flows are culturally mediated and the effects of such mediation.

Structure and Content of the Volume

The aim of this volume is to foster such critical analysis of migration and the cultural texts that it generates by bringing together essays that introduce key concepts and a range of frameworks, theories, and methodologies; focus on topical issues; and discuss literature, films, and new media about migration. Our focus is on twentieth- and twenty-first-century migration, with a diverse collection of essays that have a range of geopolitical purviews. We have divided the book into three parts. Part 1, "Key Concepts and Frameworks," offers brief overviews of some of the theoretical and methodological paradigms that teachers may find useful either for their own course preparation or as instructional materials for students. Essays in parts 2 and 3, "Geopolitical and Pedagogical Contexts" and "Pedagogical Approaches and Methods," as the part titles suggest, engage more explicitly with teaching practices and classroom experiences.

Key Concepts and Frameworks

In the opening essay, Malini Guha elaborates on the concepts of "the border" and "the borderscape" by engaging, on the one hand, with the intellectual genealogy of works by Étienne Balibar, Suvendrini Perera, and Mezzadra and Neilson and, on the other hand, with illustrative media works by Ai Weiwei, Mati Diop, Gianfranco Rosi, and the Forensic Architecture group. Emphasizing that borders are not static objects or geographic markers but complex and dynamic social organisms, the essay makes the case for moving images' unique capacity to make audible and visible processes of world-making that can resist and challenge entrenched hegemonic views of the border and its political and aesthetic regimes. Because the essay addresses some of the key texts in critical migration studies as well as some of the most frequently used audiovisual examples of migration media in the art world, it provides indispensable tools for educators who would like to engage these critical concepts in their teaching.

Bruce Bennett and Katarzyna Marciniak's essay uses Jacques Derrida's concept of "the aporia" as a theoretical entry point into the teaching of refugee cinema as a way to discuss politics, ideology, and representation from a decolonial perspective. Emphasizing uncertainty and indeterminacy becomes a way of challenging the epistemological authority and legitimacy of the teacher—and the student—in the process of knowledge production. This approach is particularly relevant when the knowledge produced in the classroom concerns migrant subjects who themselves have been denied such authority—or, conversely, forced to perform their identities in such a way as to "authenticate" them in the eyes of state authorities, civil society, and the media. Extending this idea to the analysis of the border itself, Bennett and Marciniak discuss the notion of "fugitive aesthetics" as an instantiation of such an aporetic approach to representation, giving several examples from audiovisual media and extending it to pedagogical practices.

Gaoheng Zhang situates migration in relation to other kinds of human mobility, such as tourism and the movement of international students. A focus on this broader category of mobility allows engagement with larger questions related to the circulation of knowledge and cultural products. Providing an overview of cultural studies approaches to mobility, the essay invites educators and students to consider movement as constitutive of both our everyday experiences and the very cultural foundations of knowledge. It calls for a greater need to engage in humanities-specific inquiries by bringing mobility studies into direct conversation with works on Orientalism, postcolonialism, transculturation, diaspora, and globalizations, foregrounding the important role that mobility and migrations play in their construction of their object of study. In conclusion, the essay describes how a syllabus for a course in Italian and comparative literature on mobilities and migration might be constructed—with an understanding that this model can be used in many disciplinary and interdisciplinary contexts.

Jutta Gsoels-Lorensen examines the crucial notion of displacement, which is ubiquitous in discussions of forced movement and migration, situating it in relation to other similar juridical-political terms such as *refugee* and *immigrant*. Drawing on the history and genealogy of these two terms, the essay argues for the importance of the broadest, most inclusive and multidimensional understanding of displacement, beyond the ossified legal categories that still frequently shape our conceptualization of this process. Taking as its case study a body of literary and activist work, the second part of the essay discusses the ways such an approach can help students engage with the difficult histories and lived realities of displacement through their writing and their creative and community work.

Kester Dyer's essay discusses migration in relation to Indigenous experiences within a settler colonial context, taking as its case study the project of the Montreal-based mobile film studio Wapikoni Mobile. Wapikoni Mobile's conditions of production, exhibition, and cinematic cultural formation serve as a valuable means to illustrate the relationship between Indigenous mobility, colonial legacies, and decoloniality. Focusing on the multivalent role of transportation and mobility in the development of Canadian cinema and their divergent meanings for different communities, the essay outlines the ambivalent and yet powerful history of movement and migration within both the Indigenous and settler colonial Canadian imaginaries. As such, it offers a reflection on the relationship between migration, settler colonialism, and Indigenous histories that would make an important and original addition to courses on Indigeneity and migration.

William Arighi suggests that the 1951 United Nations Convention Relating to the Status of Refugees, also known as the Geneva Convention, can usefully be read as a literary text alongside other contemporary refugee and migrant narratives to contextualize in a powerful way the legal and political struggles that asylum seekers and other migrants experience. While exposing the importance of institutions like the United Nations, as well as their failures to secure basic human rights, this approach allows students to assess the impact of the Geneva Convention on the subsequent global flow of migration and the narrative and rhetorical tropes developed in response to it and to question the role of individual governments and agencies in this process. Students can consider the boundaries and limitations of legal discourses and personal narratives and understand empathy as a critical tool, avoiding the habitual sentimentalization associated with it.

Alexander Dawson's contribution to the volume takes up the concept of disability in relation to migration studies. The essay challenges assumptions, present in mainstream representations, that immigrants are able-bodied, making a strong case for taking a postcolonial intersectional approach to discussions of disability in migration narratives. It lays out the foundation of such an approach and gives examples of literary texts that could be used as important sites for the exploration of these issues in the classroom. The essay is particularly useful for preparing courses at the intersection of migration studies, postcolonial studies, and disability studies.

Hsuan L. Hsu and Rebecca H. Hogue's essay analyzes Amitav Ghosh's novel *Gun Island*, considering migration in the context of the contemporary climate crisis. Hsu and Hogue argue that unlike many widely taught dystopian novels that displace climate migration onto another time and space and obscure the geographies and histories of existing climate migrants, Ghosh's novel places the present-day climate migrant at the center. They propose teaching the novel together with Ghosh's nonfiction work *The Great Derangement: Climate Change and the Unthinkable* as a way to understand contemporary climate migration as a radical disruption of bourgeois temporal, spatial, and ecological regularity. Ghosh, the essay suggests, identifies the migrant as the paradigmatic figure of the Anthropocene and cosmopolitan modernity, both concepts that might be productively explored with students. The authors' critical reading of Ghosh's works suggests how it might be used in a wide range of literature classes—whether organized thematically, regionally, or chronologically—to highlight the exigencies of climate migration.

Claudia Sadowski-Smith's essay grounds discussions of migration in a consideration of race, taking as its focal point the construction of Whiteness. As a crucial prerequisite for participation in supremacist politics, White identity formation is both shaped and threatened by the arrival of new racialized groups. Addressing the intertwined history of the formation of US citizenship, definitions of race, and migration policies in the twentieth century, the essay demonstrates the degree to which Whiteness has, in fact, been a much disputed and highly mutable category. The essay draws attention to the neoliberal changes in the role of a White ethnonational identity that supposedly guarantees those immigrants racialized as White access to citizenship rights, taking as its contemporary example the underexamined racialization of post-socialist (post-Soviet) migration. Drawing on a range of literary sources that largely fall outside the familiar canon of migration literature, the essay takes a global approach to questions of Whiteness as a system of power and set of rights and privileges, an approach crucial for discussions of migration in North American classrooms.

Geopolitical and Pedagogical Contexts

Opening the second part of the collection, Lisa Dolasinski's essay provides a compelling and original context for the study of migration as part of hip-hop-based education, using Italian studies as an example of how hip-hop lyrics, music videos, and social media illuminate the debates and shifts within Italian citizenship laws and migratory experiences from the perspective of young people today. While particularly applicable for courses in Italian studies, this essay offers terrific new ideas for how to approach migration through hip-hop—both conceptually and in its specific pedagogical applications—that will inspire teachers in many areas.

Eszter Zimanyi's contribution takes Orban Wallace's documentary *Another News Story* as a focal point for developing students' critical skills when discussing media representations of migration. Through the analysis of the film's self-conscious emphasis on the practices of looking combined with a consideration of some of the most important recent texts in documentary media scholarship, the essay foregrounds questions about the ethical positions and aesthetic tropes that govern news media. While its emphasis is specific to the discipline of film and media studies, it provides insight and strategies that can be incorporated into courses dealing with broader questions of migration and visuality.

Kristen Stern's contribution to the volume shows how a thematic emphasis on migrants' return to their homeland in francophone literature and film enables conversations about migration grounded in an understanding of narrative conventions, tropes, and genres and their sociopolitical stakes. The essay suggests effective ways of bringing home to students that migratory flows are multidirectional and that there is no "single story" of migration, complicating the limited but all-too-common trope of departure, arrival, and assimilation that students tend to fall back on. Stern proposes as a cornerstone for a course on return migration Aimé Césaire's long poem *Cahier d'un retour au pays natal* (*Notebook of a Return to the Native Land*) and provides examples of different kinds of texts—poetry, fiction and nonfiction prose, fiction and documentary film, and graphic novels that portray the complexity of migration flows. The essay is an invaluable resource for teachers who want to challenge and complicate mainstream portrayals of migration in French and francophone courses as well as in other courses on migration and culture.

Elizabeth Rich's essay places migration—both international and internal—within a larger framework of postcolonial and neocolonial development by focusing on the mediations and narrativizations of the Arab Spring. The essay traces the trajectory of a course dedicated to this topic in a way that shows the interwoven dynamics behind the uprisings in North Africa and the Middle East, focusing on a variety of domains—writing contests, editorial work, literary blogs, literary festivals—where cross-cultural texts are produced and promoted. The essay sketches an approach that could be adapted to other courses, providing suggestions for key readings and viewings that situate the Arab Spring as part of a cluster of issues that shape migration, contemporary culture, and politics—including globalization, interference by Western governments, civil unrest, and economic, environmental, and military involvement.

Jocelyn Frelier and Paige Andersson's essay frames migration in relation to the challenges faced by families and children. It foregrounds the importance of discussing the governmental policies in the United States and France that dictate what constitutes a family unit in the context of migration and what role these policies assign to children and their caretakers. Taking as their case studies cinematic texts such as Diego Quemada-Diez's *La jaula de oro* (*The Golden Dream*), Yamina Benguigui's *Inch'Allah Dimanche* (*Sunday, God Willing*), and Jacques Audiard's *Dheepan*, the authors provide a useful framework to engage students in critical analysis of how families and children bear the consequences of state policies in a way that is attentive to a variety of perspectives.

B. Judith Martínez-García discusses the challenging task of placing migration within the Latin American context specifically in relation to the discussion of drug cartels and narco-narratives. These topics, especially in the case of Central American migration to Mexico, receive highly sensationalized treatment in the media, thus frequently affecting students' prior perception and judgments of these issues. The essay provides discussions of primary literary texts that might be used in the classroom to dismantle widespread stereotypes and provides theoretical sources to convey the systemic nature of drug violence and pedagogical tools for scaffolding its critical analysis.

Spencer R. Herrera's discussion of three Chicano-themed border films—*Born in East LA, Lone Star*, and *The Three Burials of Melquiades*

Estrada—expands Anderson's notion of the nation as an "imagined community" to consider categories of belonging in the specific context of the history of the construction of the US-Mexico borderlands and its contemporary legacies. Taking up cinematic genres and modalities familiar and easily accessible to students, the essay provides ways to engage their understanding of this complex history as a shared text. It thus radically reconfigures students' assumptions about what constitutes border crossing and denaturalizes assumptions about national and cultural belonging.

Manuel Chinchilla's essay approaches empathy as a central category for student engagement with migration narratives. It argues for the need to go beyond empathy by resisting the normalization of the representation of migrants as suffering victims and moving toward a recognition of migrants as empowered subjects with individual and collective agency, despite their vulnerabilities. To make this case, the essay focuses on the reading of several key texts—Marc Silver's experimental documentary *Who Is Dayani Cristal?*, Valeria Luiselli's autobiographical essay *Tell Me How It Ends*, and two poems by Javier Zamora from his book *Unaccompanied*. Chinchilla argues that a comparison of these texts with a focus on how they differently figure migrant's experiences and differently position the implied reader or viewer can enable students to engage in a critical and empathic discussion of migrants' experiences.

Pedagogical Approaches and Methods

In her essay, Weixian Pan explores the use of comparative methodologies in classes on global media centered on questions of mediation of border crossing in two distinct contexts: the US-Mexico border and the mainland China–Hong Kong border. An essay and a film serve as the two main points of reference for students, making for a productive conversation about techno-specificity and affective economy in transborder movements. Pan also describes collaborative assignments based on students' personal experiences with border crossing, which are further reframed in relation to the more systematic and hyper-technologized optics of border surveillance. The essay also offers discussion questions for *The Crossing* as a shared canvas for students to test out these new analytical languages in understanding border crossing in different sociocultural contexts.

Darshana Sreedhar Mini's contribution similarly centers on a film—the animated documentary *Flee*—using a formal survey and focus group discussions among college students studying media and communications. Students are asked to respond to a set of questions pertaining to empathy and migrant experiences and to identify the aesthetic techniques used in the film. In tracing the range of interpretative possibilities to facilitate conversations around empathy and social justice in classrooms, the method Mini proposes examines how migrant media emerges as an overarching framework in the way students understand the tensions, elisions, and fault lines that construct their perceptions of the Global South.

Eva Rueschmann discusses the construction of a course that is tailored specifically to a small liberal arts college environment, an interdisciplinary humanities seminar, Traveling Identities, that brings together a wide range of texts and offers varied formats for assignments. The essay provides a clear structure and a set of key concepts to ground students' exploration of migration and identity, proposing a focus on the gendered nature of migrant journeys, on the recurring trope of memory, and on intergenerational relationships in diasporic communities. Providing a list of additional texts and films that lend themselves to discussions of these themes and tropes, the essay is a valuable resource for instructors in the planning stage of a course on migration.

Marilén Loyola's contribution describes in detail an upper-level Spanish-language course that explores the ruptures and losses that come from migration while highlighting the creativity and resilience of migrants. The course addresses four different trajectories of migration—Africa to Spain, Latin America to Spain, Europe to Latin America, and Latin America to the United States—to study the social and cultural history of the Hispanic world. Bringing together theoretical readings, current events, news articles, and a variety of cultural productions, including theater, films, novels, short stories, and poetry, the course conveys the rich, often painful experiences of Hispanic migration.

Megan Thornton Velázquez also discusses using migration as a topic in a Spanish-language classroom but in the context of experiential learning and community-based service, where migration becomes not only the object of study but also a way for students to enter into a dialogue with Latinx (im)migrants about their experiences. Combining the practice of teaching English as a second language and the real-world use of Spanish, the course Thornton Velázquez describes offers concrete methods for integrating students' understanding of the realities and legacies of migration and their reflections on service learning.

Open access public cultural work is at the center of the course described by Emily S. Davis and Délice I. Williams, a course based on the web project *Moving Fictions: Exploring Migration in Modern Literature*, which was developed as part of several undergraduate English literature classes. The project aims to problematize mainstream narratives that either romanticize or negatively stereotype migrants by bringing together a wide variety of texts, including personal narratives of migrants. The essay discusses in detail the practical and ethical dimensions of structuring and teaching a public humanities course on migration.

Juan Llamas-Rodriguez's contribution elaborates on one assignment that engages with students' media-making skills in a real-world scenario. Students are asked to develop a media production about migrants patterned on a traditional TV show treatment. They are first asked to consider how they aim to represent migrants. Combined with critical theoretical readings on both media and migration, this practice-based activity is designed to force students to contend with the ideological assumptions that underpin common representations of migrant realities and to challenge students to formulate, in a hands-on way, creative alternatives to the mainstream representation of migrants.

In the concluding essay of this final part, Karen Little explores a methodological framework that brings together micro and macro levels of analysis of migration using tools from the digital humanities. This methodology, Little argues, can produce a powerful interplay between large archival data, on the one hand, and individual narratives, on the other. The essay describes in detail how students and researchers can make sense of the intertwined and complex individual histories embedded in archival data with mapping tools and other forms of data visualization. Discussing such projects as Britt Rusert's "New World: The Impact of Digitization on the Study of Slavery" and considering various historical contexts for forced migration, the essay proposes mapping as an effective way to maintain a dual focus on specific experiences and iterations of migration and the larger patterns they form, both of which are indispensable for students' understanding of how the past shapes the present.

Collection of Syllabi

A collection of syllabi centering on migration designed for different levels of undergraduate and graduate courses in film and media studies, world literature, critical theory, English, and Spanish is available online on *Knowl-*

edge Commons (teachingmigration.mla.hcommons.org). Accompanying some of these syllabi are descriptions of assignments. The collection is intended to provide instructors with a wide range of resources as they design individual courses or curricula, formulate topics, consider exercises and approaches, and choose texts and films for reading or viewing.

The first Homo sapiens, scientists now believe, lived in Africa about 300,000 years ago. The history of human migration began about 60,000 years ago, when groups of these modern humans began to travel out of Africa, first to Asia and then, about 40,000 years ago, to Europe. Around 15,000 years ago, these modern humans entered North America and then South America (Bellwood). Human history is the history of moving people, though in the past this movement was less rapid and extensive than it is in the era of globalization. It is only relatively recently that we have come to understand ourselves and act in the world as members of fixed populations; the nation-state as a political formation is only about five hundred years old, despite the tendency of some nations to project their people into a primordial and mythical national past. We might do well to remind ourselves and our students that a migration-centered epistemology might be a much-needed historical corrective to the contemporary assumptions of the normativity of a stasis-centered world.

Note

1. On 22 June 1948, the HMT *Empire Windrush* arrived at Tilbury Docks in Essex, bringing hundreds of passengers from the Caribbean. They were responding to the British government's efforts to recruit workers following labor shortages in Britain. Between 1948 and 1971, roughly 500,000 people migrated from the Caribbean to Britain; they came to be called the Windrush generation.

Works Cited

Anderson, Benedict. *Imagined Communities: Reflections on the Origins and Spread of Nationalism.* Verso, 2006.

Anzaldúa, Gloria. *Borderlands / La Frontera: The New Mestiza.* 2nd ed., Aunt Lute Books, 1987.

Awad, Ibrahim, and Usha Natarajan. "Migration Myths and the Global South." *Cairo Review,* vol. 30, 2018, pp. 46–55.

Bellwood, Peter. *The Five-Million-Year Odyssey: The Human Journey from Ape to Agriculture*. Princeton UP, 2022. *JSTOR*, https://doi.org/10.2307/j.ctv28sc829.

Bennett, Louise. "Colonisation in Reverse." *Caribbean Quarterly*, vol. 54, nos. 1–2, Mar.-June 2008, pp. 52–53. *ProQuest*, www.proquest.com/scholarly-journals/colonisation-reverse/docview/221158204/se-2.

Bevins, Vincent. *The Jakarta Method: Washington's Anticommunist Crusade and the Mass Murder Program That Shaped Our World*. PublicAffairs, 2020.

Bravo, Jorge. "Sustainable Cities, Human Mobility and International Migration: Report of the Secretary-General for the Fifty-First Session of the Commission on Population and Development." 28 Feb. 2018. *United Nations*, www.un.org/development/desa/pd/sites/www.un.org.development.desa.pd/files/unpd_200802_bravo_introduction_of_the_report.pdf.

Byrd, Jodi A. "Weather with You: Settler Colonialism, Antiblackness, and the Grounded Relationalities of Resistance." *Critical Ethnic Studies*, vol. 5, nos. 1–2, 2019, pp. 207–14.

Clifford, James. *Routes: Travel and Translation in the Late Twentieth Century*. Harvard UP, 1997.

Coulthard, Glen Sean. *Red Skin, White Masks: Rejecting the Colonial Politics of Recognition*. U of Minnesota P, 2014.

Cox, Oliver C. *Capitalism and American Leadership*. Philosophical Library, 1962.

Czaika, Mathias, and Hein de Haas. "The Globalization of Migration: Has the World Become More Migratory?" *International Migration Review*, vol. 48, 2014, pp. 283–323.

De Genova, Nicholas. "Spectacles of Migrant 'Illegality': The Scene of Exclusion, the Obscene of Inclusion." *Ethnic and Racial Studies*, vol. 36, no. 7, 2013, pp. 1180–98.

de Haas, Hein, et al. *The Age of Migration: International Population Movements in the Modern World*. 6th ed., Guilford, 2020.

Fanon, Frantz. *The Wretched of the Earth*. Translated by Constance Farrington, Grove Press, 1963.

Flee. Directed by Jonas Poher Rasmussen, Final Cut for Real / Sun Creature / Vivement Lundi! / Mostfilm / Mer Film / Vice Studios / Left Handed Films, 2021.

Friedman, Thomas L. *The World Is Flat: A Brief History of the Twenty-First Century*. Thorndike, 2005.

Geographies of Racial Capitalism with Ruth Wilson Gilmore. Directed by Kenton Card, Antipode Foundation Film, 2020, antipodeonline.org/geographies-of-racial-capitalism/.

Gilroy, Paul. *The Black Atlantic: Modernity and Double Consciousness*. Harvard UP, 2000.

———. *There Ain't No Black in the Union Jack: The Cultural Politics of Race and Nation*. George Allen and Unwin, 1987.

Hall, Stuart. "Thinking the Diaspora: Home-Thoughts from Abroad." *Identity and Diaspora*, by Hall, edited by David Morley, Duke UP, 2019, pp. 206–36. Vol. 2 of *Essential Essays*.

Herd, David. "Walking with Refugee Tales." Afterword. Herd and Pincus, vol. 1, pp. 133–43.

Herd, David, and Anna Pincus, editors. *Refugee Tales.* Comma Press, 2016–21. 4 vols.

James, C. L. R. *The Black Jacobins: Toussaint L'Ouverture and the San Domingo Revolution.* Vintage Books, 1989.

Jameson, Fredric. "Globalization and Political Strategy." *New Left Review,* vol. 4, 2000, pp. 49–68.

Kelley, Robin D. G. Introduction. *Race Capitalism Justice,* special issue of *Boston Review,* edited by Walter Johnson and Kelley, winter 2017, pp. 5–8.

Kwaymullina, Ambelin. "Seeing the Light: Aboriginal Law, Learning and Sustainable Living in Country." *Indigenous Law Bulletin,* vol. 6, no. 11, May-June 2005, pp. 12–15.

Le Billon, Philippe, and Päivi Lujala. "Environmental and Land Defenders: Global Patterns and Determinants of Repression." *Global Environmental Change,* vol. 65, 2020, https://doi.org/10.1016/j.gloenvcha.2020.102163.

Lowe, Lisa. *The Intimacies of Four Continents.* Duke UP, 2015.

Malkki, Liisa H. "Refugees and Exile: From 'Refugee Studies' to the National Order of Things." *Annual Review of Anthropology,* vol. 24, 1995, pp. 495–523.

Marciniak, Katarzyna, and Bruce Bennett. Introduction. *Teaching Transnational Cinema: Politics and Pedagogy,* edited by Marciniak and Bennett, Routledge, 2017, pp. 1–25.

Marx, Karl. "So-Called Primitive Accumulation." *A Critique of Political Economy,* by Marx, translated by Ben Fowkes, Penguin Classics, 1992, pp. 870–940. Vol. 1 of *Capital.*

Mezzadra, Sandro, and Brett Neilson. *Border as Method; or, The Multiplication of Labor.* Duke UP, 2013.

"Migration." *International Encyclopedia of the Social Sciences,* edited by William A. Darity, Jr., 2nd ed., vol. 5, Macmillan Reference USA, 2008, pp. 156–59.

Morgenstern, Tyler, et al. "In and against Crisis." Introduction. *Moving Images: Mediating Migration as Crisis,* edited by Krista Lynes et al., Transcript Verlag, 2020, pp. 27–47.

Nawyn, Stephanie. "Migration in the Global South: Exploring New Theoretical Territory." *International Journal of Sociology,* vol. 46, no. 2, 2016, pp. 81–84.

Nkrumah, Kwame. *Neo-colonialism: The Last Stage of Imperialism.* International Publishers, 1966.

Piketty, Thomas. "We Must Rethink Globalization or Trumpism Will Prevail." *The Guardian,* 16 Nov. 2016, www.theguardian.com/commentisfree/2016/nov/16/globalization-trump-inequality-thomas-piketty.

"Refugee Data Finder." *UNHCR,* 24 Oct. 2023, www.unhcr.org/refugee-statistics/.

Riley, Angela R., and Kristen A. Carpenter. "Decolonizing Indigenous Migration." *California Law Review,* vol. 109, no. 63, 2021, pp. 63–139. *Colorado Law Scholarly Commons,* U of Colorado, Boulder, scholar.law.colorado.edu/faculty-articles/1319.

Ritchie, Hannah, and Max Roser. "Urbanization." Sept. 2018. *Our World in Data*, Feb. 2024, ourworldindata.org/urbanization.

Robinson, Cedric. *Black Marxism*. 2nd ed., U of North Carolina P, 2000.

Rodney, Walter. *How Europe Underdeveloped Africa*. Verso, 2018.

Roediger, David R. *The Wages of Whiteness: Race and the Making of the American Working Class*. Verso, 1991.

Said, Edward W. *Culture and Imperialism*. Vintage Books, 1994.

———. *Orientalism*. Penguin Classics, 2003.

Selvon, Samuel. *The Lonely Londoners*. Penguin Classics, 2006.

Sharpe, Christina. *In the Wake: On Blackness and Being*. Duke UP, 2016.

"Union of British Columbia Indian Chiefs Declaration." 17 May 1976. *Union of British Columbia Indian Chiefs*, www.ubcic.bc.ca/ubcic_publications.

United Nations. Convention Relating to the Status of Refugees. 28 July 1951. *OHCHR*, 1996–2024, www.ohchr.org/en/instruments-mechanisms/instruments/convention-relating-status-refugees.

"USCIS Issues Policy Guidance regarding Inadmissibility Based on Membership in a Totalitarian Party." *USCIS*, 2 Oct. 2020, www.uscis.gov/news/alerts/uscis-issues-policy-guidance-regarding-inadmissibility-based-on-membership-in-a-totalitarian-party.

Williams, Raymond. *The Country and the City*. Spokesman, 2011.

Wolfe, Patrick. "Settler Colonialism and the Elimination of the Native." *Journal of Genocide Research*, vol. 8, no. 4, Dec. 2006, pp. 387–409, https://doi.org/10.1080/14623520601056240.

Part I

Key Concepts and Frameworks

Malini Guha

Border as Method in a Film and Media Studies Context

Ai Weiwei's feature-length documentary *Human Flow* and Mati Diop's short film *Atlantique* (*Atlantics*) model two different approaches to the question of what a border is and, just as significantly, what a border does. Images of barbed wire fences, towering walls, and squalid refugee camps abound in *Human Flow*, which is dedicated to portraying human displacement and migration on a global scale. These images are standard illustrations of "the linear border," which denote stable physical boundaries that are intended to bring a halt to populations on the move (Mezzadra and Neilson 4). The border, in this instance, is akin to a line drawn on a map (vii). These sites are especially conducive to the project of "the border spectacle," which frequently features militarized depictions of border controls as grand displays of power (Casas-Cortes et al. 67). But the film's director, featured prominently throughout, is granted unfettered mobility as he travels from Lebanon to Calais, from camps set up perilously close to active railway tracks to the vast expanse of the sea. *Human Flow*'s primary focus on linear borders is matched by its insistence on cartographic certainty and, more precisely, on the naming of each and every location traversed in the film. Linear borders, which demarcate geographic territories in definitive and often spectacular fashion while promoting a view of themselves as sites of exclusion, are typically how borders have been discussed across a range of disciplinary contexts and in the public domain. However, it is the reoccurring images of the ocean shot from above in *Human Flow*, and especially those that blur the line between sea and sky, that inadvertently trouble understandings of the border as linear, certain, and stable and as a particular kind of spectacle. The very notion of the ocean as border is described by Suvendrini Perera as part of the "malignant perversity of recent regimes of border control in the West," which includes walls that "rise out of the oceans" and the phenomenon of "the immaterial visa" (205). And yet, as Perera observes, the itineraries of "uncertain transit" and, tragically, the unmarked sites of burial "allow for new spaces across the lines drawn in the sea" (205).

Conversely, Diop's short film *Atlantique* exudes cartographic as well as temporal uncertainty and instability. At the film's core are a group of men who gather around a fire and discuss what appears to be a journey across the sea that has already transpired. Their story is initially articulated through a voice recording emanating from a record slowly spinning in low light. This voice describes the ferocity of waves and winds that they faced while sailing on a pirogue. Later, when seated around the fire, they discuss a previous journey where a central character named Serigne recalls passengers who could transform themselves into fish and recounts the root cause of his departure, which is "the dust in his pockets" (00:07:17). The spatial coordinates of this narrative are never visualized but gradually emerge through dialogue—the men are Senegalese, and Spain, via Mauritania, is their final destination. The only image that corresponds directly to their narration of the journey is one of the ocean taken from a great distance, from which one can barely make out a pirogue struggling to keep afloat. Diop's refusal to show suffering or death ensures that the border spectacle is resisted. As *Atlantique* continues, we learn that Serigne has died on this journey and has somehow materialized for this conversation with his friends. The film remains deliberately hazy about whether Serigne died on his first journey or on a second journey that may have been triggered as part of a deportation from Spain. And yet, it is the ocean that Serigne situates in opposition to both Europe and Africa that are discussed as sites of inclusion and exclusion. As he observes, the ocean is borderless. Lines of text appear near the end of the film, which explains that the feverish condition of a patient makes him long to "flow into the ocean" (00:12:59) as he sees trees and flowers on the other side. This is an excerpt from a conversation between the surgeon Jean-Baptiste Sevigny and the engineer-geographer Alexandre Corréard, who both survived a shipwreck of the French ship *Méduse* in 1816, which charted a path from Senegal through Mauritania to Saint-Louis (Pattison). *Atlantique* disrupts the notion of definitive borders of various kinds, extending from the ocean to time itself. These instances of temporal, physical, and cartographic instability create space for a broader questioning of what a border is in the first place, since borders in the film are as frequently transcended as they are imposed. To return to Perera's assertion regarding new spaces that are borne from transit through the seas, *Atlantique* engages more directly with the question of time by forging relations across different facets of past and present that resonate with the borderless image of the sea. While *Human Flow* moves across a series of seemingly stable border regimes that reference different though often interrelated histories of conflict, displacement, and exclusion, *Atlantique* provokes a meditation on the question of what counts as a border and how such boundaries are always already porous and susceptible to breach.

These two examples demonstrate the difference between viewing the border as a geographic entity and approaching the border as a method, an idea developed by Sandro Mezzadra and Brett Neilson. It is the latter concept, taking hold across numerous disciplinary contexts, that can be productively incorporated into film and media studies and, particularly, in the study of migration in cinema and media. As Maribel Casas-Cortes and colleagues assert, migration is the phenomenon that forces borders into varying states of transformation, while the inherent instability of border regimes is constantly managed by the state and other state-led actors (69). In effect, they assert that "migration is a coconstituent of the border as a site of conflict and as a political space" (69). Despite the kind of dynamism, friction, and turbulence that such a description of the relationship between borders and migration elicits, as Mezzadra and Neilson claim, the border is most often associated with walls and defined solely as a site of exclusion (viii, 7). They trace the origins of the linear border, as a representational form, to the cartographic traditions of the most recent European-led age of empire (4). The image of the border as a line that delineates clearly defined geographic territories is a fiction of modern mapping that eschews the messiness and, more often than not, the violence that accompanies the constant making and unmaking of borders.

Mezzadra and Neilson's notion of the border as method returns a sense of dynamism and instability to scholarly discourse by shifting the question away from what a border is to what a border does and the forms of knowledge that can emerge from thinking with borders rather than simply about them. Border as method is grounded in the notion that the border is a material form as much as it is an epistemology, a method of both comprehending and configuring worlds. Mezzadra and Neilson stage a number of interventions within dominant understandings of borders when presenting their notion of border as method. As they argue, the border was never simply a dividing line, but circumstances of contemporary globalization are marked by what they refer to as "the proliferation of the border" (2), which extends beyond physical boundaries to encompass all the mechanisms that manage and seek to control migrant populations "where they are" (Casas-Cortes et al. 73). One prominent case study cited by Mezzadra and Neilson concerns the "splintering" of borders in the Palestinian context (8), which include walls, checkpoints, roadblocks, military zones, and so on, an observation indebted to many thinkers, including the Israeli British architect Eyal Weizman and the work of the interdisciplinary group led by him, Forensic Architecture. The changing nature of border regimes is attributed to the declining significance of national borders as the dominant mechanism of regulating mobility, particularly in relationship to questions of labor (Mezzadra and Neilson 2). The proliferation of the border is indelibly linked to what Mezzadra and Neilson term the "multiplication of labor," which denotes the acceleration of heterogeneous labor processes on a global scale, whereby populations are transformed into "the commodity of labor power" by the workings of borders (21, 20). The often fraught and antagonistic methods by which the multiplication of labor occurs across border regimes "facilitate processes of production, dispossession and exploitation" (23).

But even more to the point, borders are not merely geographic in their form or their orientation (Mezzadra and Neilson 28). As Mezzadra and Neilson observe, a border is "a complex social institution," and as such, a more expansive notion of borders is needed to comprehensively address their functioning (3). This mode of expansion situates cognitive borders alongside geographic ones (59). Additionally, the authors question an understanding of both the proliferation and the heterogeneous nature of borders as sites of exclusion. Instead, as they put it, "one of our central theses is that borders, far from serving merely to block or obstruct global passages of people, money or objects, have become central devices for their articulation" (ix). And lastly, borders do not represent worlds but, rather, participate in their very formation. Mezzadra and Neilson seek to revisit the "ontological moment concealed in modern mapping" in order to take stock of the world-configuring function of the border and to situate this moment as a starting point for imagining the possibility of other worlds (36). They revive the concept of *fabrica mundi* as part of this endeavor, a concept that can be traced back to the sixteenth century. A term with a complex origin story, *fabrica mundi* denotes, Mezzadra and Neilson argue, "a cartographer's awareness of the fact that representing the world on a map also means *producing* it" while simultaneously disavowing this act of creation (31–32). Thus, it is an expression that directly addresses the friction that lies at the heart of the world-making function of the border. As the authors note, a shift to border as method speaks to an investment in apprehending the struggles of the present, which they claim is more politically urgent than solely advocating for a borderless world (14).

While the genealogical underpinnings of border as method are wide-ranging, it is worth considering how Mezzadra and Neilson draw on the work of Étienne Balibar and Perera in particular while also revising it. Mezzadra and Neilson's engagement with the work of these scholars is key to grasping the most significant attributes of border as method. Certainly, and as is acknowledged by Mezzadra and Neilson, Balibar lays the foundation for border as method when he notes in his canonical text *Politics and the Other Scene* that borders do not have a transferrable and stable "essence" that is "valid in all places and at all times, for all physical scales and time periods, and which would be included in the same way in all individual and collective experience" (75). This lack of essence, or what Balibar refers to later as the "polysemic" nature of borders (81), situates them as heterogeneous at the level of experience, a claim that Mezzadra and Neilson stretch further in their delineation of the inherently heterogeneous nature of borders. Balibar also gestures toward what Mezzadra and Neilson describe as the proliferation of borders when he declares that there is "nothing less material than a border" (81), a claim grounded in a series of earlier assertions concerning the internalization of borders, which ensures that they are both "everywhere and nowhere" (78). But perhaps most significantly, Mezzadra and Neilson situate border as method as a way of engaging the paradox of defining the border. In a conundrum that echoes that associated with the concept of *fabrica mundi*, Balibar writes, "The theorist who attempts to define what a border is is in danger of going around in circles, as the very representation of the border is the precondition for any definition" (76). In moving away from the problem of definition to that of method, Mezzadra and Neilson shift their emphasis to the question of how the border, as an object of knowledge, is constituted as such. As they write, "It is by rescuing and reactivating the constituent moment of the border that we make productive the vicious circle that Balibar identifies" (17).

The dynamism of border as method is also partly indebted to Mezzadra and Neilson's extension and reworking of Perera's concept of the borderscape. The "borderscape" is a term that Perera coins through her assessment of the complexities of border making and unmaking in the now notorious Pacific Solution, which she combines with Michel de Certeau's notion of "spatializing practices" (qtd. in Perera 203). The Pacific Solution denotes the use of "onshore detention centers, deterritorialized zones, and the offshore arrangements" to detain as well as contain asylum seekers in Australia (Perera 203). The borderscape is "mobile and multidimensional," very much in opposition to the tradition of modern mapping that renders borders linear and static (206). Her central claim is that the geographies made by borderscapes frequently escape the conventions of modern mapping (208). In contrast, she observes that the earliest medieval maps preserved itineraries that illustrated a wide range of "border practices" (208). Her concept of the borderscape revives the itinerary as form, which "weave interrelations, engender border practices, reanimate contested sovereignties, and give rise to new geographies, spatial identities, and territorial claims and counterclaims" (224). Mezzadra and Neilson reconfigure the borderscape into their notion of border struggles. While they retain Perera's delineation of the constantly shifting nature of the border as both spatial and temporal phenomenon, they believe that the concept of border struggles makes room for considerations of political subjectivities as they are articulated and disarticulated by "everyday border practices" (Mezzadra and Neilson 13). One example the authors draw on involves female migrant care and domestic laborers. These figures often reside in the "shadow of" borders long after they have reached their destinations for numerous reasons, including what Mezzadra and Neilson refer to as an "ethnicization" that fractures this segment of the labor market, the lack of legal documents for some, and the forms of abuse that many of these workers face at the hands of their employers (108). As they write, border struggles of the "everyday" variety that are frequently eclipsed by more visible overtures such as public protests "open a new continent of political possibilities" that are not limited to the two most recognized poles of border conflicts, namely those pertaining to quests to obtain citizenship, on the one hand, and radical political organization, on the other (14).

The question of conceptual translation is embedded into Mezzadra and Neilson's view of border as method. They draw from Antonio Gramsci's notion of the "structural friction" that should exist between concepts and concrete situations, which they argue is mobilized by border as method (Mezzadra and Neilson 9). Claiming that the notion of border as method is applicable to a cinema and media studies context involves a certain conceptual translation as well as an acknowledgment not only of structural friction but also of the structural affinities between the method and moving images. To begin, there is no question that the linear border has occupied a place of prominence in cinema and media; across a range of work, maps are employed as a way of orienting viewers to specific times and places. The challenge is to find border images and sounds that do not correspond to the most recognizable attributes of a border, such as a line on a map or a physical boundary. In taking up this challenge, border as method becomes especially productive in a film and media studies context, as a way of moving past the most recognizable images and sounds of border regimes and into the domain of proliferating and heterogeneous borders.

In one of numerous articulations of the aims of border as method, Mezzadra and Neilson write, "Rather than organizing a stable map of the world, the processes of proliferation and transformation of borders we analyze in this book aim at managing the creative destruction and constant recombining of spaces and times that lie at the heart of contemporary capitalist globalization" (6). Montage is among the first words to come to mind when engaging in a conceptual translation of borders as a way of "managing the creative *destruction* and constant *recombining* of spaces and times" (my emphasis). We can situate montage as one way that films, among other moving-image works, configure borders through medium-specific means. A pertinent example is Gianfranco Rosi's documentary *Fire at Sea*, a film that alternates between the depiction of the everyday activities of a young boy named Samuele, who lives in Lampedusa, in the heart of Italy's so-called migration crisis, and groups of migrants who are forced to move through Lampedusa's border regime. After being "rescued" at sea, they are subjected to the spectacle of the border as they are disinfected en masse and made to don bright yellow aluminum blankets to guard against the cold (00:29:44–00:33:45). The most striking aspect of the film is that Samuele and most of his fellow islanders do not come into physical contact with these migrants. Montage is used to demonstrate the complex dynamics of inclusion and exclusion at work in the film; while the migrants are able to enter Lampedusa, they remain completely separated from life on the island. And yet, Rosi also shows us how the life of the islanders is not entirely unaffected by what is happening. Samuele develops a lazy eye, and his struggles with vision acquire a metaphorical quality in the film. He and his friends also play games where they pretend to be at war. The presence of borders in this film extends far beyond the familiar aspects of the border regime to encompass the cinematic equivalent of "everyday border practices" as well as matters of form and style. In Rosi's hands, montage becomes an act of "bordering" (Mezzadra and Neilson 48).

Montage is also one method by which the film configures a world, and of course, it is not a stretch to argue that film and media constitute modern-day incarnations of *fabrica mundi*. However, films like *Fire at Sea* develop "itineraries," to draw on Perera's language (208), to show us how borders give rise to "elusive and mobile geographies" that facilitate our thinking beyond entrenched views of geographic and cognitive borders (Mezzadra and Neilson 8). We can go so far as to claim that moving-image works have the potential to "rescue" the ontological moment where, as specifically defined by Mezzadra and Neilson (17), the very act of representing borders has a world-configuring function. Moving images have the potential to make this process of world-making visible and audible. As a teaching tool, border as method can push students not only to conceptualize the border more expansively but also to turn their attention to the border-configuring function that style and form accumulate in this context. This is not a call to abandon a focus on the presence of linear borders in film and media but rather to consider the most obvious depictions of the border alongside those that are no less present but perhaps more difficult to see and hear. On more than one occasion, Balibar advances the need for a "phenomenology of the border," which is an interdisciplinary undertaking that ensures that discussions of migration and borders are not restricted to their legal aspects (*Politics* 83; "At the Borders" 315). Film and media can produce a phenomenological experience of the border and, in turn, can also orient critical thinking toward a recognition of the experiential realities of border regimes. The reciprocal nature of this work is vital to pedagogical endeavors and particularly for those researching in an interdisciplinary vein. And finally, many of the authors cited in this essay, including but not limited to Mezzadra, Neilson, and Balibar, work from within a Marxist-oriented scholar-activist paradigm, which involves both studying and participating in a wide range of border struggles. As Mezzadra and Neilson explain, "[W]e can say that method for us is as much about acting on the world as it is knowing it," or, more precisely, "it is about the relation of action to knowledge" (17). Elsewhere in the text they draw our attention to the ways in which a political praxis can productively inform a theoretical one where, for example, they had to confront the disparities that arose between the desire of the activist to dismantle border regimes and the tremendous risks incurred by migrant populations trying to cross these borders (10). This aspect of their work and aspects of the work of other authors referenced in this essay offer yet another path for film and media studies students, particularly for those who want to participate in the building of better worlds while also researching the ones we presently inhabit.

Works Cited

Atlantique. Directed by Mati Diop, Anna Sanders Films / Le Fresnoy Studio National des Arts Contemporains, 2009.

Balibar, Étienne. "At the Borders of Citizenship: A Democracy in Translation?" *European Journal of Social Theory*, vol. 13, no. 3, 2010, pp. 315–22.

———. *Politics and the Other Scene.* Translated by Christine Jones et al., Verso, 2002.

Casas-Cortes, Maribel, et al. "New Keywords: Migration and Borders." *Cultural Studies*, vol. 29, no. 1, 2015, pp. 55–87.

Fire at Sea. Directed by Gianfranco Rosi, 01 Distribution, 2016.

Human Flow. Directed by Ai Weiwei, AC Films / Participant Media, 2017.

Mezzadra, Sandro, and Brett Neilson. *Border as Method; or, The Multiplication of Labor.* Duke UP, 2013.

Pattison, Michael. "Anywhere but Here: Close-Up on Mati Diop's 'Atlantiques' and 'Snow Canon.'" *MUBI*, 21 Mar. 2018, mubi.com/en/notebook/posts/anywhere-but-here-close-up-on-mati-diop-s-atlantiques-and-snow-canon.

Perera, Suvendrini. "A Pacific Zone? (In)Security, Sovereignty, and Stories of the Pacific Borderscape." *Borderscapes: Hidden Geographies and Politics at Territory's Edge*, edited by Prem Kumar Rajaram and Carl Grundy-Warr, U of Minnesota P, 2007, pp. 201–27.

Bruce Bennett and Katarzyna Marciniak

Fugitive Aesthetics:
Teaching Refugee Cinema Aporetically

What does it mean to introduce Jacques Derrida's concept of aporia to our classrooms? Why grapple with such a complex idea vis-à-vis refugee cinema? How useful might it be pedagogically? Working on transnational cinema and, most recently, on refugee cinema specifically—on films concerned with forced migration and the politics of violent uprootings and dispossession—we keep returning to the concept of aporia as a particularly potent theoretical move that helps us engage with decolonizing questions of politics, ideology, and representation.

The word *aporia* expresses doubt, an impasse. Its ancient Greek origin, *aporos*, means "impassable" ("Aporia"). In philosophy, an aporia refers to a difficulty in establishing a stable truth, since an aporia signifies the presence of evidence both for something and, simultaneously, against that something. In our understanding, being aporetic thus points to nonbinarism, toward a wavering border. The cinematic figure of the refugee always invokes this wavering—these are the bodies that flee, that move, that cross borders and various barriers, often in perilous circumstances. However, this impetus to move is often paradoxically juxtaposed with images of stasis, enclosure, and waiting, with being stuck in makeshift tents. Ai Weiwei's documentary *Human Flow*, for example, offers multiple images of such paradoxes: we see human movement on a global scale, people walking and carrying their children and their possessions, and we also see people immobilized. One image that particularly stands out is that of a woman's back; sitting at a table, she has her arms extended, and she draws her hands to her face, signaling that she is not ready to face the camera. She utters an anxious sound (1:04:34). This brief moment feels deeply moving and upsetting at the same time. Her gesture and the sound she makes might be read as a refusal to engage, a refusal to be represented. The spectators understand that all of this is simply too much for her, returning us to a well-known statement by Teresa de Lauretis that "violence is engendered in representation" (33). Thus, the concept of aporia becomes particularly relevant to the figuration of refugeeism, exemplified by experiences positioned between hospitality and hostility, mobility and stillness, visibility and invisibility, and a willingness to be represented and a refusal to be represented: in other words, the wavering border.

Derrida acknowledged his fascination with aporias: "the old, worn-out Greek term *aporia*, this tired word of philosophy and logic, has imposed itself upon me" (12). Aporias obscure clarity and certainty; they frustrate. Rather than overcome or resolve aporias, Derrida posits their critical potential: "I was then trying to move not against or out of the impasse but, in another way, *according to* another thinking of the aporia, one perhaps more enduring" (13). Thinking *"according to . . .* the aporia," according to ambivalence and indeterminacy, is certainly hard to implement pedagogically because, overwhelmingly, students in Western spaces are interpellated as what Trinh T. Minh-ha calls "an all-knowing subject," one that "owns" its knowledge (932).[1] And as teachers, we, too, are interpellated into positions of knowledge, and, by extension, invested with the authority to teach others.

Teaching aporetically thus becomes a subtle provocation, one that we believe is necessary while approaching knowledge in general. However, this way of thinking is especially instructive when teaching refugee cinema, with its representations of dispossession, privation, and trauma. It allows us to dwell on the insidiousness of borders, their ambivalence, and the violence of the asylum process itself. That is, refugees, often unlike other migrants, are institutionally forced to perform their refugee identities in order to prove that they are indeed genuine refugees. In John Haptas and Kristine Samuelson's *Life Overtakes Me*, for example, a film featuring refugee children in Sweden in a coma-like condition known as resignation syndrome, the liminal state of the children prompts politicians to ask whether this is a genuine condition or whether they were poisoned by their parents, a reiteration of the perpetual skepticism with which all refugee claims are treated. Are they genuine and thus deserving of hospitality, or are they bogus, intent on securing fraudulent access to the welfare systems, housing, and employment rights of the country's citizens by pretending to be asylum seekers? In a related context, discussing queer migrations in European cinema and "homophobic mispractice of credibility and assessment" (Williams 6), James Williams posits the notion of "the burden of queer proof" (6)—the necessity to prove one's queerness and thus one's legitimacy as a refugee vis-à-vis Western expectations of "queerness." We see the weight of such "proof," for instance, in *Fremde Haut* (*Unveiled*), directed by Angelina Maccarone, when the protagonist, Fariba, an Iranian queer refugee, paralyzed by the necessity to disclose herself to German authorities, assumes a dead man's identity to enter Germany. She becomes an aporetic figure: a lesbian masquerading as a straight man, exposed to all kinds of xenoracist insults as a foreigner. In a different context, the short film *Choke*, by the Palestinian American director Rolla Selbak, takes as its focus the way that a queer Muslim rising mixed martial arts star struggles with celebrity culture's demand for self-exposure.

Grappling with such aporetic thinking, Derrida is helpful in his claims that an aporia is not something to be resolved: "what is at stake in the first place is therefore *not the crossing of a given border*" (18; our emphasis). In other words, he is inviting us to ponder the uncomfortable, violent implications of proliferating borders and thus their "duties":

> The *duty* to respond to the call of European memory, to recall what has been promised under the name Europe, to re-identify Europe. . . . The *same duty* also dictates welcoming foreigners in order not only to integrate them but to recognize and accept their alterity. . . . The *same duty* dictates respecting differences, idioms, minorities, singularities, but also . . . opposition to racism, nationalism, and xenophobia. (18–19)

Thus, aporias and their ambiguities command respect for difference, for reidentification, and for reenvisioning what is possible. They command the duty to think outside the privileged boundaries of the sanctioned "I" and its prejudices.

Furthermore, the concept of aporia is equally important when approaching the very definitional ambiguity of the refugee, a term that encompasses a wide range of positionalities: a refugee, an internally displaced person, a stateless person, and an asylum seeker. Such definitional ambiguity is also historically rooted: for example, Charles Simic, a US-based poet from post–World War II Yugoslavia, writes, "'[D]isplaced persons' is the name they had for us back in 1945" (119). In turn, in her well-known text "We Refugees," Hannah Arendt claims, "[W]e don't like to be called 'refugees.' We ourselves call each other 'newcomers' or 'immigrants'" (69). Moreover, a central debate in refugee and forced migration studies turns on the question of how wide the category of "the refugee" can be expanded before it becomes critically and politically useless. For example, in the context of queer migration, Eithne Luibhéid writes:

> I use the term *migrant* (rather than make distinctions among legal immigrants, undocumented immigrants, refugees, asylum-seekers, or short-term visitors) when referring to anyone who has crossed an international border. In my view, such distinctions are less reflections of empirically verifiable differences among queer migrants, who often shift from one category to another, than techniques of nation-state power that remain centrally implicated in neocolonial hierarchies and that classify migrants in order to delimit the rights that they will have or be denied, and the forms of surveillance, discipline, normalization, and exploitation to which they will be subjected. (186)

While Luibhéid selects the category of "the migrant" as most useful, Achille Mbembe, commenting on "penitentiary geography" and angrily pondering the nomenclature we are discussing, writes, "Refugee camps? Camps for displaced people? Transit zones? Detention centers? Emergency accommodation centers? Jungles? . . . Let us sum up all of the above in a single phrase, the only one which paints a truthful picture of what is going on: camps for foreigners" (*Necropolitics* 102).

This point takes us to our earlier preoccupation with foreignness and aporias. We believe that refugeeism and thus, by extension, foreignness, invite us to think according to this other logic: "*according to* . . . the aporia.*" We do not aim to collapse refugeeism and foreignness into one category, but, since refugees inevitably enter the treacherous material and conceptual territory of foreignness, we want to argue that refugeeism, like foreignness, is critically aporetic.[2] Unlike Luibhéid, who privileges the concept of the migrant, we emphasize the figure of the refugee—a legal category for the forcibly uprooted—despite all its contingencies, because we are discussing refugee cinema specifically. The United Nations High Commissioner for Refugees understands refugees as "persons fleeing armed conflict or persecution" ("UNHCR Viewpoint"), and this designation allows the refugee access to various forms of assistance and to protection or asylum under the principles of international law. By contrast, migrants are defined as people who choose to move to improve their lives and face no impediments should they return home. In practice, the distinction between these two categories is not so clear-cut, with governments in some cases reluctant to recognize refugees, and so questions of definition—or "refugee status determination"—can acquire an urgent political and humanitarian significance. Thus, the refugee is a figure who brings into focus questions of meaning, identity, individual agency, and history that are often a central concern of film studies.

Rather than resolve this definitional ambiguity, in our classrooms we examine cinema's role in tracing the changing understandings of the category of the refugee. Here we have recourse once again to *Human Flow*, in which Hanan Ashrawi, a Palestinian politician, explains, "Being a refugee is much more than a political status. It is the most pervasive kind of cruelty that can be exercised against a human being. . . . You are forcibly robbing this human being of all aspects that would make human life not just tolerable but meaningful in many ways" (40:18–40:58).

Such definitional ambiguity is expressed in many films, but David Fedele and Kumut Imesh's *Revenir* (*To Return*) represents paradoxes of refugee identity with a particular intensity. The film, a reverse refugee journey, recounts the attempt by Kumut Imesh, who now lives in France, to retrace the route he followed after being forced to leave the Ivory Coast ten years earlier as a student activist. The intention, he explains, was "to show the reality of migrants on the road, when they are forced to leave their country. To shoot this reality by someone who has lived it. From the perspective of a migrant himself" (00:04:15–00:04:29). However, his French refugee passport does not give him a right to travel, and so, frustrated by the slow process of visa applications, he sets off to travel as an undocumented migrant, keeping a video record of his journey from Ghana toward Libya.

Whereas at the beginning of the film, Imesh understood the journey as a simulation of refugeeism undertaken by a filmmaker or investigative journalist in order to document the reality of this experience, as the journey progresses, from the perspective of others, that distinction is indiscernible or irrelevant. At the end of the film, forced to return to France (in an ironic inversion of the more common refugee trajectory), Imesh reflects that the French refugee passport confers on him an interstitial, aporetic identity: "With this document, I realize that I am now considered neither African nor European. I am somehow stuck in the middle. It doesn't give me the right to travel as a European, and I had also lost my freedom to travel as an African in my own continent" (01:13:12–01:13:30). Imesh learns that his designation as a refugee confers on him a spectral, differential identity that is neither one thing nor the other—that eludes the grasp—and the film concludes with an intertitle explaining that Imesh hopes "to soon be able to leave this identity of 'refugee' behind him" (01:15:12), thereby escaping its stigma and his ensnarement in what Imogen Tyler describes as "stigma-craft" (1791), "the mechanisms through which stigma is produced, the processes through which it becomes attached to bodies" (1791–92). Tracing the historical roots of the "stigma machine of racism," she argues that "racism is a primary technology of statecraft in contemporary Europe," and *Revenir* is a poignant document of this idea (1786).

A Fugitive Aesthetics

In an overview of the dominant theoretical perspectives on the study of international migration, Douglas S. Massey and colleagues argue that this field of research comprises "only a fragmented set of theories that have developed largely in isolation from one another, sometimes but not always segmented by disciplinary boundaries" (35). However, they suggest, the complexity of shifting patterns of migration and flight demands an inter-disciplinary, multifaceted approach "that incorporates a variety of perspectives, levels and assumptions" (35). For example, within the theory of "cumulative causation," which is concerned with the interplay of socio-economic context and migration decisions, "[t]he last and perhaps most difficult factor to measure in testing for cumulative causation is culture, which requires information about beliefs, values, and normative practices" (58). Teaching refugee cinema can make a valuable contribution to an understanding of the cultural circumstances of forced displacement and migration, and to emphasize the concept of the aporia is to confront the complexity of this object of study.

One helpful way of acknowledging the pedagogical importance of thinking aporetically is to consider how the unstable identity of the refugee figure might extend to the category of the refugee film itself. That is to say, rather than treat the refugee film as a stable genre with a codified set of narrative and stylistic conventions, we are more interested in asking whether some refugee films can be seen as exemplifying a fugitive[3] aesthetics, a way of seeing and experiencing the world that extends across media boundaries. Refugee cinema encompasses an extremely broad range of material that includes campaigning films produced by NGOs and charities, such as Vanessa Redgrave's *Sea Sorrow*; documentary reportage, such as Yasmin Fedda's *Queens of Syria* and Rokhsareh Ghaemmaghami's *Sonita*; independent cinema (ranging from comedy to horror to drama), such as Aki Kaurismäki's *The Other Side of Hope*, Remi Weekes's *His House*, Philippe Lioret's *Welcome*, and Kaouther Ben Hania's *The Man Who Sold His Skin*; gallery installations, such as Candice Breitz's *Love Story* and Alejandro González Iñárritu's *Carne y arena* (*Flesh and Sand*); and self-produced video material by current and former refugees, such as Hassan Fazili's *Midnight Traveler*, Behrouz Boochani's *Chauka, Please Tell Us the Time*, and Amel Alzakout's *Purple Sea*.

This material, which circulates through varied platforms, distribution systems, and media, encompasses quite diverse ideas about the social function of cinema as well as different assumptions about imagined audiences. This vast archive poses a question about classification, inviting us to consider where the boundaries around this field of cinema might be drawn, and in doing so, invites us to reflect on one of the principal themes of refugee cinema, the violence of borders. While such a taxonomy is provisionally helpful in enabling us to gain some critical purchase on this broad cinematic field, it is crucial to acknowledge the risk of reproducing the inflexible bordered thinking that underpins the institutional processes that are designed to classify asylum seekers as genuine and deserving or inauthentic and unwelcome. *Life Overtakes Me* and *Unveiled* are particularly evocative in this context. Both films lay bare the further trauma faced by asylum seekers who are trying to gain recognition as genuine refugees by the legal systems of European countries.

To discuss refugee films in relation to a fugitive aesthetics, rather than as a genre, allows us to identify continuities, connections, and perspectives that might be less visible within a more restricted frame. We use the term *fugitive aesthetics* to describe the variety of ways in which refugee films express different aspects of refugees' experiences. We put the concept to work in the analysis of themes and formal features of a range of examples, from classic Hollywood films such as Lewis Milestone's *Arch of Triumph*, which explores the experiences of European refugees in pre–World War II Paris, to avant-garde cinema such as Jean-Luc Godard and Anne-Marie Miéville's *Ici et Ailleurs* (*Here and Elsewhere*), which deploys footage of Palestinian refugee camps in a complex reflection on the efficacy of political cinema. Characteristic themes of refugee films include masquerade and performance, the instability of identity, and misrecognition, mistranslation, misunderstanding, racism, and, in some cases, xenophilia. These thematic concerns are expressed through such formal qualities as fractured narratives that are characterized by gaps, interruptions, and delays; stylistic heterogeneity; and a mise-en-scène that foregrounds certain landscapes, spaces, and means of transport. In exploring the subjective experience of flight or escape, many refugee films lead the spectator through a wide range of affects that encompass anxiety, desperation, humor, and hope.

The Hungarian film *Jupiter's Moon*, directed by Kornél Mundruczó, is a compelling example of a fugitive aesthetics. It tells the story of Aryan, a Syrian refugee who is shot by a border officer when trying to cross from Serbia to Hungary and discovers that he can levitate. He is given shelter by a medic who works at a chaotic refugee camp, and the indebted doctor recruits Aryan to make money from his credulous clients, charging them extra for a demonstration of Aryan's miraculous healing powers. *Jupiter's Moon* is a magic realist fable that juxtaposes implausible fantasy sequences with passages from a tense thriller (as the border guard who shot Aryan at the beginning tries to hunt him down). The film makes no attempt to resolve or explain the impossible scenario (as dream, hallucination, or allegory) or to situate the narrative precisely (since the noirish imagery, the shots of military helicopters flying low over the city, and the title's reference to Europa, one of Jupiter's largest moons, appear to set the film in a heightened or alternative reality—another Europe). The film makes extensive use of handheld camera, long takes, and sequence shots, and the bobbing, panning camera moves almost continually, reinforcing the sense of disorientation and instability experienced by the refugee protagonist. This dynamic mobility is especially pronounced in the sequences where Aryan levitates, spinning silently and gracefully through the air while the camera dances sympathetically around him.

In the context of a refugee narrative, the motif of levitation is especially evocative; it captures a sense of dislocation. Aryan is not firmly located in Budapest but is suspended in an indeterminate purgatorial interzone between different places, between life and death. This motif realizes the strength of the desire for escape that drives people to risk their lives to cross borders, but in rendering Aryan as an angelic figure (bearing bulletwound stigmata), the film insists on an obligation to care for refugees and to recognize that they may be a gift rather than a drain or a threat. Indeed, toward the end of the film, the doctor, Stern, confesses to Aryan, "I'm so ashamed. I wanted to keep you for myself. Childish. You know, I realized that when you left—that you have brought us a message, haven't you? People just forgot to look up" (01:39:46–01:40:46).

However, rather than conclude with a blandly optimistic celebration of European hospitality and cosmopolitanism, the film ends far more ambiguously. During a destructive police raid on the hotel where he was hiding, Aryan is cornered on an upper floor by the policeman who shot him at the beginning. Trapped, Aryan throws himself through a plate-glass window high above the ground, but rather than fall to his death, he hangs suspended in the air. Watched by astonished onlookers below, he floats into the sky above the city, tumbling slowly as helicopters hover around him. In a discussion of Jacques Audiard's *Dheepan*, Özlem Köksal and Ipek A. Çelik Rappas call for "allegorical filmic moments, for the visibility of refugees and migrants as fictional characters with desires and identities other than those fixated on wounds and injuries, a visibility that allows refugees room outside a frame of violence and crisis" (267). The metacinematic ending of *Jupiter's Moon* achieves this emphatically, with an apotheosis that hovers uncertainly between fantasy and reality. The climax could be interpreted as a suicide, but the film refrains from concluding with that morbid, desperate spectacle. In staging Aryan's leap as a breathtaking public performance, it moves Aryan from the marginal spaces inhabited by cinematic migrants to the very center of the narrative as an ambiguous emblem of both hope and accusation.

The Aporetic Classroom

Teaching refugee cinema, with all its contingencies and indeterminacies, returns us to the concept of the "pedagogy of anxiety" that must necessarily accompany the introduction into the classroom of these films about trauma (Marciniak, "Pedagogy"). As pedagogues, we are tasked with making borders unclear, with relinquishing the bordered thinking and sense of secure knowledge that is typically assumed to be the end point of teaching. While such pedagogical ambition is a challenge, it is necessary, because at the heart of our teaching is the obligation to uncover our implication in the uncomfortable histories and unstable geographies we study. One moment in *Jupiter's Moon* speaks directly to this idea: when Aryan asks Stern whether he knows of a safe place, Stern replies, "There is no safe place from injuries of history" (01:40:55–01:40:59). Teaching refugee cinema aporetically requires us to recognize that the classroom, too, is a place in which we must confront the injuries of history.

Notes

1. We discuss this issue at length in our introduction to *Teaching Transnational Cinema: Politics and Pedagogy*: see Marciniak and Bennett, "Teaching Transnational Cinema."

2. We are drawing here on our earlier discussion of aporia in our introduction to a special issue of *Transnational Cinemas*: see Marciniak and Bennett, "Aporias." These ideas are also examined in Marciniak, "Aporias."

3. "Fugitivity" is a concept with particular significance to Black studies in relation to histories of slavery and postcolonialism, but in its concern with strategies of resistance and refusal, it is a valuable term with which to think about refugee and migrant experiences. See, for instance, Mbembe, "In Conversation." See also Papadopoulos and Tsianos on "escape routes" and "the autonomy of migration" and Emejulu on "fugitive feminist" politics.

Works Cited

"Aporia, *N.*" *Merriam-Webster*, 2024, unabridged.merriam-webster.com/collegiate/aporia.

Arch of Triumph. Directed by Lewis Milestone, Enterprise Productions, 1948.

Arendt, Hannah. "We Refugees." *The Menorah Journal*, vol. 31, no. 1, 1943, pp. 69–77.

Choke. Directed by Rolla Selbak, Gemini Twin Productions / Black Poppy Productions / Master Vic Productions, 2018.

de Lauretis, Teresa. *Technologies of Gender: Essays on Theory, Film, and Fiction*. Indiana UP, 1987.

Derrida, Jacques. *Aporias*. Translated by Thomas Dutoit, Stanford UP, 1993.

Emejulu, Akwugo. *Fugitive Feminism*. Silver Press, 2022.

Fremde Haut. Directed by Angelina Maccarone, Fischer Film / MMM Film Zimmermann, 2005.

Human Flow. Directed by Ai Weiwei, AC Films / Participant Media, 2017.

Ici et Ailleurs. Directed by Jean-Luc Godard and Anne-Marie Miéville, Société des Etablissements L. Gaumont, 1976.

Jupiter's Moon. Directed by Kornél Mundruczó, Proton Cinema / The Match Factory / KNM / ZDF/Arte / Pyramide Films, 2017.

Köksal, Özlem, and Ipek A. Çelik Rappas. "A Hand That Holds a Machete: Race and the Representation of the Displaced in Jacques Audiard's *Dheepan*." *Third Text*, vol. 33, no. 2, 2019, pp. 256–67.

Life Overtakes Me. Directed by John Haptas and Kristine Samuelson, Stylo Films, 2019.

Luibhéid, Eithne. "Queer/Migration." *GLQ*, vol. 14, nos. 2–3, 2008, pp. 169–90.

Marciniak, Katarzyna. "Aporias of Foreignness: Transnational Encounters through Cinema." *Subjectivity and the Political: Contemporary Perspectives*, edited by Gavin Rae and Emma Ingala, Routledge, 2017, pp. 91–109.

———. "Pedagogy of Anxiety." *Signs: Journal of Women in Culture and Society*, vol. 35, no. 4, 2010, pp. 869–92.

Marciniak, Katarzyna, and Bruce Bennett. "Aporias of Foreignness: Transnational Encounters in Cinema." *Transnational Cinemas*, vol. 9, no. 1, 2018, pp. 1–12.

———. "Teaching Transnational Cinema: Politics and Pedagogy." *Teaching Transnational Cinema: Politics and Pedagogy*, edited by Marciniak and Bennett, Routledge, 2016, pp. 1–35.

Massey, Douglas S., et al. "Theories of International Migration: A Review and Appraisal." *The Migration Reader: Exploring Politics and Policies*, edited by Anthony M. Messina and Gallya Lahav, Lynne Rienner, 2006, pp. 34–62.

Mbembe, Achille. "In Conversation: Achille Mbembe and David Theo Goldberg on 'Critique of Black Reason.'" Interview by David Theo Goldberg. *Theory, Culture and Society*, 7 Mar. 2018, www.theoryculturesociety.org/blog/interviews-achille-mbembe-david-theo-goldberg-critique-black-reason.

———. *Necropolitics*. Translated by Steven Corcoran, Duke UP, 2019.

Papadopoulos, Dimitris, and Vassilis Tsianos. "After Citizenship: Autonomy of Migration, Organizational Ontology and Mobile Commons." *Citizenship Studies*, vol. 17, no. 2, 2013, pp. 178–96.

Revenir. Directed by David Fedele and Kumut Imesh, 2018.

Simic, Charles. "Refugees." *Letters of Transit: Reflections on Exile, Identity, Language, and Loss*, edited by André Aciman, New Press, 1999, pp. 119–35.

Trinh T. Minh-ha. "Not You / Like You: Postcolonial Women and the Interlocking Questions of Identity and Difference." *The Longman Anthology of Women's Literature*, edited by Mary K. DeShazer, Longman, 2001, pp. 928–33.

Tyler, Imogen. "The Hieroglyphics of the Border: Racial Stigma in Neoliberal Europe." *Ethnic and Racial Studies*, vol. 41, 2017, pp. 1783–1801.

"UNHCR Viewpoint: 'Refugee' or 'Migrant'—Which Is Right?" *UNHCR*, 11 July 2016, www.unhcr.org/news/latest/2016/7/55df0e556/unhcr-viewpoint-refugee-migrant-right.html.

Williams, James S. "Queering the Migrant: Being beyond Borders." *Queering the Migrant in Contemporary European Cinema*, edited by Williams, Routledge, 2021, pp. 3–29.

Gaoheng Zhang

Teaching Migration through Mobilities

In this essay I propose an approach to teaching migration-related literary, cinematic, and media texts within a broader, interdisciplinary context of other forms of human mobility. I characterize the study of mobilities as an intellectual enterprise focused on examining two main critical issues. The first issue relates to the tension between mobility and immobility as manifested by, for example, the encampment of refugees. The second issue concerns the intersection of multiple mobilities, such as the connections between labor migration and leisure tourism or between the movement of international students and the flow of their transnational media consumption between home and destination countries. The mobilities method helps both to sharpen the specificity of migration as a mobility and to place migration in dialogue with the larger story of multiple and intersecting human movements. Moreover, a focus on mobilities allows students to critically engage with larger questions related to the circulation and blockage of knowledge and cultural products, which migration brings about in combination with other mobilities. I am particularly invested in analyzing cultural mobility, which can be defined as mobilities relayed within or about cultural texts, events, and phenomena.

In this essay I examine two questions about migration and mobilities in relation to their application in course designs that involve culture, literature, cinema, and the media. First, how can we appreciate the significance of mobility in interpretive and cultural studies of migration, and in particular, from the perspectives of the mobility-immobility tension and intersecting mobilities? Second, why do we need to mobilize previous cultural studies that have already enriched migration analysis within a larger mobility framework? I contend that a focus on mobilities helps strengthen cultural analysis within migration studies. Further, this scholarly practice provides instructors with a richer and more diversified array of primary texts, as well as critical theories and methods, for teaching migration as it is represented in different types of media.

In a 2018 report for the International Organization for Migration, the geographer Ronald Skeldon states that "[m]obility is an inherent characteristic of all populations unless specific policies or other factors are in place that limit or control that mobility" (4). The critic champions the inclusion of tourism in migration analysis because this industry, often viewed as a short-term mobility, can affect or complicate migration in important ways. For example, tourist visa holders may overstay the limit of their visas and become irregular migrants. Mass tourism may cause local residents to move away from their habitual dwellings. Contemporary educational and work arrangements allow people (e.g., international students and digital nomads) to reside in a place where they do not possess citizenship for a substantial amount of time. Such mobile subjects effectively become migrants without being officially recognized as such.

While Skeldon's analysis from within migration studies develops without overtly considering the "mobilities paradigm" (Sheller and Urry), the sociologist Anne-Marie Fortier writes from this critical perspective in a contribution to *The Routledge Handbook of Mobilities*. Fortier's central message about migration and mobility studies dances around the previously mentioned mobility-immobility tension: whereas migration studies tends to analyze situations of immobility, an existential force in mobility studies is pervasive mobility. Regardless of how we assess Fortier's formulation of this contrast, the critic's remarks on imaginations and affects are useful for this essay because they refer to culture and migration within a mobility frame. Fortier asks, "How is migration imagined? And what is at stake, and for whom, in the deployment of the migration imaginary within the landscape of mobilities?" (69). Fortier considers feelings, desires, affects, and the body through a Marxist psychoanalytic lens, with reference to representations of migration in art, culture, and policy as well as migrants' own representations of migration. For Fortier, migration can function at the interface of the empirical and imagined worlds, shaping "understandings of identity and difference, of borders and boundaries, of our relationship to others 'here' and 'elsewhere'" (69).

The sociologist Anna Xymena Wieczorek goes beyond Skeldon and Fortier in shedding light on the value of understanding narratives of migration through the broader lens of mobility. In *Migration and (Im)Mobility*, Wieczorek begins by disagreeing with Fortier and other academics on their theoretical orientation toward a dichotomy between migration (which carries with it a sense of problem and settlement in one place) and mobility (which exalts the highly mobile lifestyle of expatriates, skilled professionals, leisure tourists, and study abroad students). Instead, Wieczorek reveals that after their initial migration, migrants often talk about migration and mobility together as part of a complex matrix. Migration scholarship actually captures such narratives, but most of the current migration theories are ill-equipped to address such empirical and narrative situations. Thus, the critic advances a "mobilities perspective" (67) on meaning-making narratives written by migrants themselves, proposing three patterns according to varying degrees of post-migration mobility. In so doing, Wieczorek intends to "uncover the plurality and broad spectrum of geographical movements that individuals experience as significant biographical constellations of (im)mobility" (19).

What is the current state of the mobilities scholarship that serves as a backdrop for more culturally sensitive social scientific studies such as Fortier and Wieczorek's, which foster an analysis of mobility within migration studies? Since the two most influential articles on the mobilities paradigm appeared in 2006 (Sheller and Urry; Hannam et al.), prolific scholarship on mobility has appeared in the fields of sociology, geography, anthropology, and cultural studies. This has occurred because issues of mobilities and immobilities touch upon our social and cultural lives in extensive and profound ways, from the students who travel abroad to study at North American universities to the Middle Eastern and African refugees who are detained in camps in Europe. These examples include both cosmopolitan nomad elites (Braidotti) and marginalized groups (e.g., Indigenous people [Clifford]). To be sure, (im)mobility as a style of analysis (Adey et al., Introduction 2) has benefited from mature studies of migration, diaspora, transnationalism, colonialism, and networks. But an analysis of mobility more consciously foregrounds the centrality of movement and stasis in the spatiotemporal coordinates of global issues such as citizenship, belonging, and pluralism. In this way, studies on mobilities encourage us to debate the changing technologies and meanings of transportation and communication. This scholarship also helps unpack power relations within the contexts of nation-states, supranational organizations (e.g., the United Nations and the European Union), and transnational strategies (e.g., China's Belt and Road Initiative), which directly affect the mobilities of human beings and the objects and ideas that they bring, create, and circulate. Indeed, according to Tim Cresswell's simple and elegant definition, mobility is the combined effect of movement, meaning, and power (2–3, 21).

In particular, Cresswell underscores the role that cultural representations play in conveying social meanings and power relations of physical and metaphorical movements that are practiced, experienced, and embodied. Such an understanding of mobilities as both socially and culturally produced and articulated is key to the argument that the concept of mobility is as strongly embedded in the arts and humanities as it is in the social sciences (Merriman and Pearce; Faulconbridge and Hui). Like Peter Merriman and Lynne Pearce and James Faulconbridge and Allison Hui, I believe this is where interpretive studies of migration texts within a mobility framework can begin to both take stock of previous scholarship and forge a new direction in teaching. A great many cultural analyses of diverse mobility forms and events are well-known to humanistic scholars and can be fruitfully used in interpretive migration courses. Culturally contextualized analyses of Orientalism, colonialism, imperialism, and Eurocentrism (Said, *Orientalism*, *Culture*; Fanon; Hardt and Negri; Shohat and Stam); borderlands and in-between spaces (Anzaldúa; Bhabha; Soja); routes and traveling cultures (Clifford); spatial stories (de Certeau); transculturation and contact zones (Ortiz; Pratt; Gilroy); diaspora and migration (Hall, "Cultural Identity," "Local"; Chow); and globalization and localism (Robertson; Appadurai; Bauman; Greenblatt) are all examples of the human sciences' involvement in thinking and theorizing about mobilities. The contributions of this heterogeneous collection of critical theories cannot be reduced to a single aspect of mobilities. But these studies are oriented toward a basic concern with (im)mobility. They also provide a wide range of empirical and narrative case studies involving multiple intersecting mobilities.

Indeed, many of the analyses mentioned above emphasize how social actors understand and experience migrations and mobilities through culture work, such as their narratives of their own migration journeys. This insight is useful for advancing humanistic interpretive scholarship within migration studies. Interpretive cultural analysis has a peculiar status within migration studies: it is neither fully disavowed nor entirely incorporated. Consider one widely used English-language introduction to migration studies, *Migration Theory: Talking across Disciplines* (Brettell and Hollifield). As the editors Caroline B. Brettell and James F. Hollifield demonstrate, many theoretical and methodological frames coexist in individual social scientific and history disciplines, resulting in similar critical concerns about migration. For Brettell and Hollifield, it is fruitful to build bridges among the disciplines surveyed. It is symptomatic of the current lack of bridges between the social sciences and the humanities that a successful anthology on migration theory includes no in-depth examination of any contributions that humanistic disciplines and cultural studies have made to theorizing migration and mobilities. Working within a field like migration studies, which is still largely dominated by social sciences, history, and policymaking, we would do well to highlight the values of cultural and interpretive migration analysis by mobilizing the abovementioned mature humanistic scholarship on mobility forms other than migration. This is another crucial reason why we ought to place migration analysis within a broader mobility framework.

To summarize, the intersection of migration, mobility, and culture in interpretive scholarship has been ongoing in various disciplines for decades. But not until recently did academics begin to stylize this area of inquiry with increasing awareness of the necessity for agenda setting. The place of cultural analysis and criticism within migration studies is yet to be cemented, and adopting a mobility-focused framework within migration analysis can help advance this enterprise. How do these conclusions help build and shape undergraduate and graduate curricula relating to migration within humanities departments? In what follows I describe two courses that I have taught, a graduate seminar in Italian studies and an undergraduate seminar in comparative studies.

The first part of the graduate seminar focuses on theories and methodologies concerning culture and mobility that can be adapted to interpret migration, while the second part of the course considers mobility case studies, both past cases and more current cases about refugees and migrants. In the first part, I introduce the topic by asking students to read works by Mimi Sheller and John Urry, Merriman and Pearce, and Stephen Greenblatt, which showcase both sociological and humanistic studies of mobility. The next two sessions are focused on social scientific works, including classic and contemporary theorists (Heidegger; Simmel; Cresswell; Urry). As previously mentioned, Cresswell's critical stance leans toward cultural analysis of mobility, and his writings provide a natural transition to the next four sessions, which focus on some of the above-mentioned humanistic scholarship on mobility. For the first session, titled "Orientalism and Eurocentrism," students read work by Edward Said (*Culture and Imperialism, Orientalism*) and by Ella Shohat and Robert Stam. For the second session, "Transculturation," I assign work by Fernando Ortiz, Mary Louise Pratt, and James Clifford. For the third session, "Diaspora and Migration," students read works by Robin Cohen, Stuart Hall ("Cultural Identity"), and Rey Chow. For the fourth session, "Glocalization," readings include works by Hall ("Local"), Roland Robertson, and Homi Bhabha. Rather than pair these theories with specific texts, I aim to first familiarize students with basic theories and methods that are available to them in analyzing primary texts through a mobilities lens. At this stage, it is expected that students may either feel intimidated by the variety and sophistication of critical insights studied or remain unconvinced about the value of considering these theories under the rubric of cultural mobility studies. I believe these reactions provide the necessary mindset to effectively transition to the second and more substantive part of the course.

In the second part of the course, we examine several case studies about historical and contemporary mobilities pertaining to Italy but with a global resonance. Here I use a largely chronological order and familiar categories of mobile subjects in order to lend a sense of comfort to students after several weeks of intense study of theories. For the first session, titled "Medieval Merchants," readings include works by Marco Polo and Ibn Battuta. The following session, "Explorers of the 'New World,'" focuses on works by Christopher Columbus and Michel de Montaigne. For the next session, "Grand Tourists," students are assigned works by Montesquieu and Madame de Staël. In a session titled "Colonizers," we discuss Gabriele Salvatores's film *Mediterraneo* and Moustapha Akkad's film *The Lion of the Deserts*. In the next session, "Political Pilgrims," we consider Michelangelo Antonioni's film *Chung Kuo Cina* and Julia Kristeva's *About Chinese Women*. In a subsequent session, titled "Migrants," we discuss literature on Chinese migrants in Italy (Nesi) and France (Cheng). Finally, a session called "Refugees" focuses on Gianfranco Rosi's film *Fire at Sea*. I take care to select primary texts that provide opportunities for comparative studies of languages, cultural perspectives, historical periods, and mobile forms.

When students arrive at the sessions on migrants and refugees, they are usually able to make connections with previous examples of colonialism, tourism, and travel for commerce and evangelization. For example, when discussing a novel about the Chinese migrant-managed fast-fashion sector in Prato, Italy—namely, Edoardo Nesi's *Story of My People*—I encourage students to interpret the conceptual parallels regarding prejudice and racism that emerge when one considers contemporary Italian entrepreneurs' assessment of Chinese migrant workers, Italian colonizers' relationship with their Greek subjects, and northern European grand tourists' attitudes toward (southern) Italians. Thus, a contemporary migration is interpreted within an intricate cultural mobility network that also includes colonialism and tourism from the past, which provided potent strategies aimed at othering certain groups of individuals. Such an analysis of the intersection of culture, mobility, and migration provides an opportunity for graduate students to develop their cultural sensitivity and analytical sophistication.

The undergraduate seminar in comparative studies examines cultural exchanges between China and Italy, the longest-standing East-West cultural communications in written record.[1] In order for students to better understand the importance of a largely understudied topic—Chinese migration to Italy—adopting a mobility framework in teaching is essential. Using this framework, I divide the course into four learning units focused on different mobilities, culminating in a final unit about migration. In the first unit, "Marco Polo and His Contemporary Legacy," we read texts by Polo and Italo Calvino and watch Bernardo Bertolucci's film *The Last Emperor*. The second unit, "The Cultural Revolution," includes readings from Alberto Moravia and Tiziano Terzani as well as Antonioni's film *Chung Kuo Cina*. In "Italian Cinema and China," we watch Vittorio De Sica's *Bicycle Thieves*, Wang Xiaoshuai's *Beijing Bicycle*, Mario Caiano's *My Name Is Shanghai Joe*, and Charles Brabin's *The Mask of Fu Manchu*. The final unit, "Chinese Migration to Italy," includes texts by Roberto Saviano and Nesi, Matteo Garrone's film *Gomorrah* and Sergio Basso's film *Giallo a Milano: Made in Chinatown*, and news accounts of Chinese migrants (Donadio; Max). Throughout the course I privilege primary texts that originate from physical movements across borders but often speak to more symbolic movements. For example, the second unit juxtaposes various Italian intellectuals' views of the Cultural Revolution in China (1966–76), which paves the way for students to debate at the end of the unit whether the texts exhibit manifest and latent Orientalisms (Said, *Orientalism* 201–25) and Orientalist melancholia (Chow 1–15), a tendency for Westerners with knowledge of Chinese high culture to fault contemporary Chinese for failing to live up to the grandeur of their civilization. These insights help students comprehend the circulation of similar ideas that were based on a polarity between communism and democracy and updated to interpret contemporary Italy's Chinese migrants.

The third unit of the course addresses the mobility of cultural ideas and technologies. I ask students to compare two films, De Sica's classic *Bicycle Thieves* and Wang's *Beijing Bicycle*, in order to help students analyze which Italian neorealist ethics and aesthetics are at stake for contemporary Chinese filmmakers who are socially engaged—and why. I contextualize the rise of neorealist cinema in the post–World War II milieu in relation to the destruction occasioned by the war, and I highlight the cinematic movement's ideological opposition to conformist middle-class cinema under the fascist regime. This explanation helps students understand how Wang, too, consciously responded to both sociopolitical circumstances and innovations in the film industry at the beginning of the new millennium in China. Wang's film critiques the treatment of rural migrants in the country's major cities, which were undergoing dramatic urbanization and economic transformation. The director was also part of a film movement in China known as the Sixth Generation Chinese cinema, which was moving away from the state-sponsored film industry and heroic narratives and toward close examinations of humble people in everyday life. Wang may be inspired by Italian neorealist cinema aesthetics and ethics, but his point of arrival is firmly planted in the Chinese reality that he treats. This example helps students analyze the positive stereotyping of Chinese migrants in Italian culture, which often exalts the successful melding of Chinese and Italian cultural components.

The two course designs that I have adopted are meant to promote students' understanding of issues pertaining to a culturally oriented, mobility-centric approach to migration studies. This teaching method also helps move migration studies away from a nation-state-centered approach toward a transnational and transcultural framing. In adapting existing cultural interpretations of other mobile forms, this style of teaching addresses issues that seem obvious but are often not fully spelled out when analyzing migration-related texts. For example, cultural representations of migrants often do not discuss migration as the exclusive form of mobility. I hope that this essay has served as a springboard for further discussions about research-based teaching on migration, culture, and mobility.

Note

1. For an examination of modern cultural mobilities between China and Italy, see Pedone and Zhang. For a discussion of contemporary Chinese migration to Italy from media and cultural perspectives, see Zhang.

Works Cited

Adey, Peter, et al. Introduction. Adey et al., *Routledge Handbook*, pp. 1–20.
———, editors. *The Routledge Handbook of Mobilities*. Routledge, 2014.
Anzaldúa, Gloria. *Borderlands: The New Mestiza*. Aunt Lute Books, 1987.
Appadurai, Arjun. *Modernity at Large: Cultural Dimensions of Globalization*. U of Minnesota P, 1996.
Battuta, Ibn. *The Travels of Ibn Battuta in the Near East, Asia and Africa, 1325–1354*. Translated and edited by Samuel Lee, Dover Publications, 2004.
Bauman, Zygmunt. *Globalization*. Columbia UP, 1998.
Beijing Bicycle. Directed by Wang Xiaoshuai, Pyramide Productions, 2001.
Bhabha, Homi. *The Location of Culture*. Routledge, 1994.
Bicycle Thieves. Directed by Vittorio De Sica, Produzioni De Sica, 1948.
Braidotti, Rosi. *Nomadic Subjects*. Columbia UP, 1994.
Brettell, Caroline B., and James F. Hollifield, editors. *Migration Theory: Talking across Disciplines*. Routledge, 2008.
Calvino, Italo. *Invisible Cities*. Translated by William Weaver, Harcourt Brace Jovanovich, 1974.
Cheng, François. *The River Below*. Translated by Julia Shirek Smith, Welcome Rain Publishers, 2000.
Chow, Rey. *Writing Diaspora: Tactics of Intervention in Contemporary Cultural Studies*. Indiana UP, 1993.
Chung Kuo Cina. Directed by Michelangelo Antonioni, RAI Radiotelevisione Italiana, 1972.
Clifford, James. *Routes*. Harvard UP, 1997.
Cohen, Robin. *Global Diasporas: An Introduction*. 2nd ed., Routledge, 2008.
Columbus, Christopher. *The Four Voyages of Christopher Columbus*. Edited and translated by J. M. Cohen, Penguin Books, 1969.
Cresswell, Tim. *On the Move: Mobility in the Modern Western World*. Routledge, 2006.
de Certeau, Michel. *The Practice of Everyday Life*. U of California P, 1984.
Donadio, Rachel. "Chinese Remake the 'Made in Italy' Fashion Label." *The New York Times*, 12 Sept. 2010, www.nytimes.com/2010/09/13/world/europe/13prato.html.
Fanon, Frantz. *The Wretched of the Earth*. Grove Press, 1963.
Faulconbridge, James, and Allison Hui. "Traces of a Mobile Field: Ten Years of Mobilities Research." *Mobilities*, vol. 11, no. 1, 2016, pp. 1–14.
Fire at Sea. Directed by Gianfranco Rosi, Stemal Entertainment, 2016.

Fortier, Anne-Marie. "Migration Studies." Adey et al., *Routledge Handbook*, pp. 64–75.

Giallo a Milano: Made in Chinatown. Directed by Sergio Basso, La Sarraz Pictures. 2008.

Gilroy, Paul. *The Black Atlantic: Modernity and Double Consciousness*. Verso, 1993.

Gomorrah. Directed by Matteo Garrone, Fandango, 2008.

Greenblatt, Stephen, editor. *Cultural Mobility*. Cambridge UP, 2010.

Hall, Stuart. "Cultural Identity and Diaspora." *Identity: Community, Culture, Difference*, edited by Jonathan Rutherford, Lawrence and Wishart, 1990, pp. 222–37.

———. "The Local and the Global: Globalization and Ethnicity." *Culture, Globalization, and the World-System*, edited by Anthony D. King, U of Minnesota P, 1997, pp. 19–39.

Hannam, Kevin, et al. "Editorial: Mobilities, Immobilities and Moorings." *Mobilities*, vol. 1, no. 1, 2006, pp. 1–22.

Hardt, Michael, and Antonio Negri. *Empire*. Harvard UP, 2000.

Heidegger, Martin. "Building, Dwelling, Thinking." *Basic Writings: From* Being and Time *(1927) to* The Task of Thinking *(1964)*, edited by David Farrell Krell, Harper and Row, 1977, pp. 347–63.

Kristeva, Julia. *About Chinese Women*. M. Boyars, 1977.

The Last Emperor. Directed by Bernardo Bertolucci, Yanco Films / TAO Film / Recorded Picture Company, 1987.

The Lion of the Deserts. Directed by Moustapha Akkad, Falcon International Productions, 1981.

Madame de Staël. *Corinne; or, Italy*. Oxford UP, 1998.

The Mask of Fu Manchu. Directed by Charles Brabin, MGM, 1932.

Max, D. T. "The Chinese Workers Who Assemble Designer Bags in Tuscany." *The New Yorker*, 9 Apr. 2018, www.newyorker.com/magazine/2018/04/16/the-chinese-workers-who-assemble-designer-bags-in-tuscany.

Mediterraneo. Directed by Gabriele Salvatores, A. M. A. Film, 1991.

Merriman, Peter, and Lynne Pearce. "Mobility and the Humanities." *Mobilities*, vol. 12, no. 4, 2017, pp. 493–508.

Montaigne, Michel de. "Of Cannibals." *The Essays of Montaigne*, translated by Charles Cotton, edited by William Carew Hazlitt, 1877. *Project Gutenberg*, 16 Mar. 2023, www.gutenberg.org/files/3600/3600-h/3600-h.

Montesquieu. *The Spirit of the Laws*. Hafner, 1949.

Moravia, Alberto. *The Red Book and the Great Wall: An Impression of Mao's China*. Farrar, Straus and Giroux, 1968.

My Name Is Shanghai Joe. Directed by Mario Caiano, C. B. A. Produttori e Distributori Associati, 1973.

Nesi, Edoardo. *Story of My People*. Other Press, 2012.

Ortiz, Fernando. *Cuban Counterpoint: Tobacco and Sugar*. Duke UP, 1995.

Pedone, Valentina, and Gaoheng Zhang, editors. *Cultural Mobilities between China and Italy*. Palgrave Macmillan, 2023.

Polo, Marco. *Travels of Marco Polo*. J. M. Dent, 1939.

Pratt, Mary Louise. *Imperial Eyes: Travel Writing and Transculturation*. Routledge, 2008.

Robertson, Roland. *Globalization: Social Theory and Global Culture*. Sage, 1992.

Said, Edward. *Culture and Imperialism*. Knopf, 1993.

———. *Orientalism*. Vintage Books, 1978.

Saviano, Roberto. *Gomorrah*. Farrar, Straus and Giroux, 2007.

Sheller, Mimi, and John Urry. "The New Mobilities Paradigm." *Environment and Planning A: Economy and Space*, vol. 38, no. 2, 2006, pp. 207–26.

Shohat, Ella, and Robert Stam. *Unthinking Eurocentrism*. Routledge, 1994.

Simmel, Georg. *Simmel on Culture: Selected Writings*, edited by David Frisby and Mike Featherstone, Sage, 1997.

Skeldon, Ronald. "International Migration, Internal Migration, Mobility and Urbanization: Towards More Integrated Approaches." International Organization for Migration, 2018.

Soja, Edward W. *Postmodern Geographies: The Reassertion of Space in Critical Social Theory*. Verso, 1989.

Terzani, Tiziano. *Behind the Forbidden Door: Travels in Unknown China*. Allen and Unwin, 1986.

Urry, John. *Mobilities*. Polity Press, 2007.

Wieczorek, Anna Xymena. *Migration and (Im)Mobility: Biographical Experiences of Polish Migrants in Germany and Canada*. Transcript, 2018.

Zhang, Gaoheng. *Migration and the Media: Debating Chinese Migration to Italy, 1992–2012*. U of Toronto P, 2019.

Jutta Gsoels-Lorensen

Approaching Displacement: Genealogical Reflections and a Teaching Example from a Pennsylvania Rust Belt Classroom

Displacement is part of a lexicon increasingly utilized in scholarship, the media, cultural expression, and policymaking to frame experiences of forced mobility across a range of contexts, encompassing conflict and war, environmental degradation and climate change, poverty and livelihood insecurity, and other forms of devastation and dispossession, including development projects and gentrification. In this context, it is noteworthy that the office of the United Nations High Commissioner for Refugees also predilects this terminology for its fundamental "Figures at a Glance," firstly establishing that "117.3 million people worldwide were forcibly displaced at the end of 2023" and only secondarily distinguishing between refugees, internally displaced people, asylum seekers, and others. This shift to the language of *displacement* is incisive in that it recognizes deprivations of "livability" (Espiritu et al. 54) that remain outside the purview of existing human rights instruments and the mandates of the global humanitarian apparatus. Novel conceptual formations such as the "climate refugee" and the "climate or environmentally displaced person" (Hassine 11, 14), among others, reckon with this fact; yet contrary to the refugee subject, the aforementioned are, as of now, without any legal import.

The title of Viet Thanh Nguyen's *The Displaced: Refugee Writers on Refugee Lives*, a collection of nonfiction essays testifying to experiences of global forced migration from 1945 until the present, offers a related provocation. Referencing both "refugee[s]" and "the displaced" in conjunction with writing and living, it can be read as commenting on the conceptual fault lines just mentioned; and while the connective colon, not visible on the cover page but implied in the title construction, suggests explication, Nguyen's titular montage productively unweaves its resonant terms, setting their meanings in motion while touching off the narrative-theoretical shuttling[1] that all essays collected in the volume, implicitly or explicitly, perform. The title reaches not only into the legal resonances of *the refugee* but also into the word's other, more expansive and undisciplined, dynamics, punctuating mandatory stories with countercurrent reclamations tied to historical, political, social, economic, cultural, ecological, and affective conditions as refracted through gender, race, class, age, ability, and sexual orientation. Less explication than insistence, therefore, Nguyen's assemblage unmoors the lexicon of displacement from an entrenched epistemics of causality and crisis, including a staunch presentism of disaster shaped by myopia vis-à-vis long-standing historical violences, and asserts experiences and imaginaries of sanctuary defying definition by a single event or a spatial state. The mark of the colon also implies possibilities and practices of emplacement, facilitating instantiations of self and common, inhabitation and solidarity, challenge and protest (Espiritu et al. 60–75, 124–33). In all, Nguyen's montaged title pauses over a genealogy of terms that have historically framed, and continue to frame, the lives of persons forced to move; together with the essays gathered in his volume, it can serve as an important springboard into class discussions about the stakes of conceptual formations.

Displacement and its derivatives are not novel concepts in the response to forced migration. The year 1945 bears special significance in this regard, because the devastations of the Second World War resulted in the uncertain fate of millions who either could not, or did not wish to, return to their erstwhile place of residence. The historian Peter Gatrell estimates their number at approximately sixty million persons in Europe and 175 million total across the globe, the latter a figure equal to about 7.6% of the world's population at the time (3). In anticipation, as David Nasaw's and Gerard Daniel Cohen's work lays out, the Allied forces had started planning for a global humanitarian effort as early as 1943, founding the United Nations Relief and Rehabilitation Administration as an international agency with a mandate to provide and oversee assistance to refugees in the immediate postwar situation (Nasaw 129–33; Cohen 58–61). It was during these early negotiations that the United States advanced the term *the displaced* to categorize people uprooted by war and genocide. Its better-known initialism, *DP*, especially in relation to so-called DP camps, which temporarily housed persons who found themselves with no place to return after 1945, is now indelibly linked to the Allied postwar occupation of Europe (Cohen 4). In class, we approach this history through Art Spiegelman's *Maus II: A Survivor's Tale*, subtitled *And Here My Troubles Began*, in whose final pages Spiegelman's father, Vladek, recollects a "longer," discontinuous "liberation" from the grip of Nazi Germany (104), including extended sojourns in DP camps while waiting for coveted papers to be able to move on (124–25, 129–30). In this context, it is also important to discuss that the DP camps of Central Europe not only reflected but also informed the ideological battles of the postwar moment, helping contour a "Cold War West," with its distinct set of values steeped in individualism and personal freedom (Cohen 28; see also Nasaw 129–43 and Espiritu et al. 87–88). While this is not directly addressed in Vladek Spiegelman's testimony, the restrictive US immigration "quotas" he alludes to, and the multiyear wait they necessitated (124), are fully entwined with these ideological objectives (Nasaw 409–11). The final sections of *Maus II* thus allow students to engage with incisive yet undertaught postwar displacement histories. Importantly, they also set up a discussion of the Eurocentrism of the DP regime and the glaring asymmetries of the global protection commitment, because while shuttering DP camps at the earliest possible time by provision of resettlement options or other permanent arrangements was an avowed goal for the Central European context (1–13), durable solutions for Palestinian refugees after the Arab-Israeli War of 1948, including advancement of refugee rights and repatriation, remain outstanding to this day (Akram 237–38). Yousif M. Qasmiyeh's collection of poems, *Writing the Camp*, responds to this protraction from within the Baddawi refugee camp in Lebanon, articulating multigenerational displacement not as historical predicament but as claim to questions of authorship and archive: "Who writes the camp and what is it that ought to be written in a time where the plurality of lives has traversed the place itself to become its own time" (66–67). This discussion, then, historicizes a consequential Cold War invention: that of the juridico-political entity of the refugee, which rendered the European DP subject obsolete by absorbing it, including its epistemic foundations, entirely.

The 1990s saw the reappearance of the language of displacement, however, with the United Nations High Commissioner for Refugees expanding the scope of its work, at least operationally, from refugees having crossed an international border to so-called internally displaced persons.[2] This shift asserted that "events taking place *inside* a country were a legitimate matter of international concern" (Russell and Tennant 303; my emphasis) and hence brought more persons forced to migrate under the global protection umbrella. Despite this expansion, no specific mandate or concerned UN agency has since been created (Espiritu et al. 37–39; Russell and Tennant 302–12). The standard-setting criteria outlined by the 1998 *Guiding Principles on Internal Displacement* nonetheless mark an important revision, as they broaden the definition of who should be entitled to international protection substantially:

> internally displaced persons are persons or groups of persons who have been forced or obliged to flee or to leave their homes or places of habitual residence, in particular as a result of or in order to avoid the effects of armed conflict, situations of generalized violence, violations of human rights or natural or human-made disasters, and who have not crossed an internationally recognized State border. (1)

While this definition pertains only to internally displaced persons, it implicitly revisits the persecutory framework of the 1951 definition of *refugee* (*Convention* 14) while recasting prevalent spatiotemporal imaginaries underpinning forced mobility, emplotments from departure to arrival, exile to settlement, the lost home to the found one. Many contributors to Nguyen's *The Displaced* write against such coercions of the lived human experience, creating powerful statements regarding the bursts and continuities of displacement; the alinearity of traumatically entwined conditions of mobility and immobility; and the repeated acts of courageous, concerted arriving they necessitate. Lev Golinkin's essay is a case in point. Golinkin writes that "[a]n art museum is a great place to be a refugee" (67). This claim, an enigmatic distillation of a displaced father and son's occupation of art history's publics, does not delineate an escapist fantasy from but rather a space for being a refugee, contouring a notion of sanctuary that refuses firm sorting between passing through and living settled, displacement and arrival. Its force lies in undercutting the conventional yoking of migrancy to the border by weaving transit, asserted belonging, and self-authorship into an act of place-making in a city inconclusively meshed into the family's routes. In the museum, as Golinkin writes, "loitering" is "appreciating" (67), movement *and* occupation, transit *and* emplacement, in synchronicity. By engaging with the pieces in *The Displaced*, then, students can revisit some of the most entrenched tropes related to migrancy and displacement in order to undertake the work of retheorization and response while attending to another's texts and worlds.

All this reverberates through the title of Nguyen's volume, which employs a carefully crafted lexicon of "refugee[s]" and "the displaced," "writers" and "lives," terms that refuse to settle, offering an account while agitating preset semiotic edges. And while there are no colons littered across Nguyen's own introduction to the volume, many of his sentences start and restart,[3] thus materializing the maneuver his title construction announces: not to explain and order but to layer and link, crafting incisive creative-theoretical writing acts reliant on the potentializing difference of iteration. "I remember my displacement," Nguyen says at one point, "so that I can feel for those now displaced. I remember the injustice of displacement so that I can imagine my writing as attempting to perform some justice for those compelled to move" (Introduction 18). The language of displacement can become static and reinculcate perceptions of linear journeys from origin to destination, mistaking *home*—lost and found—for its most important conceptual hinge. Nguyen's double sentence unknows these epistemics, suggesting instead that displacement is always already heterogenous, plural, and multiply linked. This iterative structure is one of the many places in *The Displaced* where students can discern that what is at stake at this global juncture is not a mere refurbishment of postwar regimes of international protection but a reckoning with the global injustices that lie at the root, and exacerbate, contemporary forced migrations on all sides of the border. The lexicon of displacement, unmoored from the event of crisis and administrative accounting, can be harnessed for this important work.

All this was on our minds when my colleague Lee Peterson, a poet and fellow educator, and I decided to teach a course on twenty-first-century forced migration in the fall of 2018, a venture, we agreed, that needed to be devotedly attuned to people, place, and politics. To be sure, college classrooms are unpredictable assemblages of students with a wide array of experiences and points of view, but in seeking to engage this topic in the deindustrialized, depopulating area where our college is located,[4] in a region that has been for decades now a place of departure rather than arrival, we could assume that for many, if not all, of our students, migrancy, in the sense of permanently moving across borders, would not be a lived experience. We also conjectured that almost none of them would have formally studied human mobility and that media and political discourses would be present in our discussions, whether directly or indirectly. To find an entry point into the work of the class, hence, we conducted a simple exercise at the beginning of the semester in trying to predict, collectively, the verbal and especially visual content of an unopened fundraising letter from the United Nations High Commissioner for Refugees such as routinely arrives in people's mailboxes in central Pennsylvania. Upon unsealing it, we found several examples of the visual regime of victimhood foreseen with striking competence. A set of early questions thus presented itself: Where did the group's strangely precise knowing come from? What was its work? What place or places—lived, imagined, projected—did the epistolary epistemics not only render but also elide? And what mappings of distance and proximity undergirded the letter's structure of appeal? From this exercise, we created a semester-long study of displacement understood as heterogeneously plural while intricately conjoined with place-making as assertion and claim.

In hopes of shaping an open, fluid course environment that would keep key thematic questions unsettled, Lee and I devised a collaborative class ecology, including a scholarly upper-level seminar (three credits), a creative writing workshop (one credit), and three excursions to, for us, easily reachable destinations (Washington, DC; Pittsburgh, PA; and downtown Altoona, PA, to meet with the city's mayor). To connect the courses, we maintained an ongoing conversation but did not plan any individual sessions together, relying rather on spontaneous convergences. Accordingly, students themselves assumed the task of ferrying readings, concepts, practices, and even mood and tone back and forth between the two classes. This proved, as per their feedback, somewhat disorienting at the outset, but it prompted all of us to repeatedly situate, and resituate, ourselves in relation to the dual course streams, thus allowing, even at the level of the pedagogical experience, for the idea of place as a passive, preexisting location for human action to come under review. Writing played a special role in this, making the shuttle between the two classes possible. It became a fundamental course habit, whether as a venture at the critical-creative juncture or through a series of writing acts, parenthetical poetic interventions, in various locations and contexts.

In the first phase, Lee and I engaged several twentieth-century texts and foundational human rights documents in preparation for our opening "mobile writing lab" in Washington, DC. On this trip, our first stop was a workshop led by the asylum and immigration lawyer Lindsey Wilkes in the courtyard of her office building, the first of repeated instances where our interlocutor hosted us in a place of their determination. Lindsey walked us through important legal definitions and related jurisprudence, teaching us about both expanding and contracting interpretations of noncitizen law. Hence, the concept of the "border" emerged as an apparatus reaching far into the United States, shaping migrants' lives beyond the point of crossing and, in different ways, for years to come. To make this point most forcefully, Lindsey led us in the study of an already concluded asylum case that, through no fault of her client, came under revision years later and was, fortunately, redecided positively for a second time.[5] Her observations upended conventional conceptions of "arrival," "safety," and the putative protection of adjusted legal status, all modalities of place in one sense or another. Furthermore, Lindsey drew a direct line from the premises undergirding her daily legal work to the voting booth, citing hundreds of changed legal provisions in the sphere of noncitizen law during the first administration of Donald J. Trump alone.[6]

Our second destination that day was the United States Holocaust Memorial Museum, which we approached with the task of witnessing and with the institution's continuous commitment to genocide prevention in mind. Writing accompanied our group through these transitions, providing opportunities for situated chronicling and reflection, with students consistently jotting down notes and observations, gathering materials, cataloging details, and registering responses in preparation for more sustained compositional work at home. Finding and occupying space to write also prompted us to engage with the museum building itself as a site shared with many, and in difference, on a crowded Saturday afternoon. Where to write, and under what assumption of permission, thus became an important consideration, linking our practice to questions previously engaged in class discussions.

The second phase of the course was devoted to reading and discussing twenty-first-century writers of displacement from a range of global contexts, including some of the current and former authors of Pittsburgh's City of Asylum, the site of our second class trip. City of Asylum is an organization that provides residencies to artists, mostly writers but also musicians, who are persecuted on account of their work and thus had to escape violence or conflict in their home countries ("City of Asylum Exiled Writer and Artist Residency Program"). The intention of this visit was to explore some of the residents' work in conjunction with "creative placemaking," as manifested in City of Asylum's signature "house publications," whose facades express artistic endeavors in response to displacement and migration ("City of Asylum House Publications"). The most recent addition, "Comma House," is based on a design by the Bengali writer and activist Tuhin Das, who was forced to leave his native Bangladesh in 2016 after coming under threat from religious fundamentalist groups ("Comma House"; "Tuhin Das"). Das met us in Alphabet City, City of Asylum's event space, for a workshop, including presentations on his activism; his decision to depart from his country and what he has left behind; and, finally, a reading and discussion of some of his recent poems, many composed in Pittsburgh. While we were engaged in listening and studying, however, a white supremacist entered the Tree of Life Synagogue in the Squirrel Hill neighborhood of Pittsburgh, a few miles away, murdering eleven congregants and injuring many others (Robertson et al.). Our trip thus took an abrupt turn: we had reached City of Asylum through the calm routines of a typical Saturday morning; yet, by the time we emerged from our workshop with Das, we found ourselves in a city in partial lockdown after a heinous act of antisemitic violence. That day, 27 October 2018, imprinted itself on the class in many ways, some spoken, many more unspoken. For several students, the established journaling and writing routines seemed to prove valuable, however, as they were able to seize on course texts and the writing endeavor to create space for grappling with the aftermath of the assailant's unfathomable terror.

The final part of the class took a turn toward the domestic—specifically, the assumedly familiar place of our immediate surroundings in central Pennsylvania. We began this section with an interview project, with students actively looking for experiences and stories of displacement in their spheres of daily existence. Once the interviews got underway, quite a few students learned that, despite creating dialogues in contexts they considered home and with interlocutors of some familiarity, they knew neither place nor person as reliably as they had assumed. In an interview conducted by Tessa Strength, formerly Albert,[7] an earlier biographical story was completely revised, with her dialogue partner disclosing that he was a refugee from persecution, not a migrant from Puerto Rico, as she had originally thought. As Tessa reflected, "This was the point I knew that my interview was going in a place I wasn't intending it to go. I quickly discarded some of my questions, as they were not relevant anymore. . . . He wanted to tell his story of how he escaped from Cuba and journeyed to America." The dramatic turn in the interview came as a surprise, not only to Tessa but also to her interviewee's daughter, who was present as a translator, close family member, and friend. It necessitated an adjournment, with the interview completed on a second attempt a few days later. Tessa's interlocutor also took an active interest in the class, in its readings and discussions, and eventually asked Tessa to convey a message to the course participants. Through his proxy in front of us, he thus actively intervened in the claimed site of the settled, exerting a measure of control over his life story and how to frame it.[8]

With this interview task, the class began probing the possibility of translating theoretical insights between starkly different contexts and to engage, cautiously and critically, with the language of displacement in relation to other US settings and circumstances, including the aftermath of the 2007–08 financial crisis. Revisiting the concept of "place" one more time, we turned our attention to global labor, deindustrialization, and decline, especially as they related to our location in the Pennsylvania Rust Belt; Guy Standing's notion of "precarious lives" served as an important theoretical provocation in this endeavor (1–29). We briefly explored the history of labor and deindustrialization in Pittsburgh; sought a conversation with the mayor of Altoona, Pennsylvania, home to our college; and investigated familial labor genealogies with an eye to socioeconomic patterns of inequality as well as the impact of gender, race, and class. The basic course vocabulary thus came under review again, disturbing maps of distance and proximity in favor of a sense of place that is historically dynamic and heterogeneously linked. In a later, thematically similar course, Janet Neigh of Penn State Erie, The Behrend College, and I broadened the scope of our inquiry to include Erie, Pennsylvania, a city likewise located in the Rust Belt but with a decades-long history of serving as an official refugee resettlement area ("USCRI Erie"). To engage this perspective on the local environment, we watched a short documentary entitled *Rust Belt New Americans,* which is based on a photo series by Maitham Basha Agha, a refugee from Iraq who resettled in Erie; we also invited persons affiliated with the Erie office of the United States Committee for Refugees and Immigrants to speak on subjects of their choice. This allowed our classes to study deindustrialization and human (im)mobility comparatively across three cities—Pittsburgh, Altoona, and Erie—all located within the central-western corner of the Pennsylvania Rust Belt yet striking for their variant self-interpretations in relation to a globally mediated here. Most importantly, it brought our classes face-to-face with reflections of place, displacement, and place-making as articulated by refugee speakers in shared Pennsylvania contexts.

The class of fall 2018 culminated in a public reading and presentation, during which each student had five minutes to articulate their—scholarly, creative, experiential—entry points into the matter of forced migration and displacement. All forum contributions were developed in Lee's workshop and creatively processed the course readings and travel that inspired many of the details. Speaking publicly, some for the first time, students responded to the difficult histories and lived realities of twenty-first-century displacements, holding out a creative, ethical insistence that refused not only to bow to entrenched interpretations but also to acquiesce to a seemingly hopeless status quo.[9] The appendix to this essay includes two poems by Madra Furman, titled "Protected Ground" and "Watching the World," as well as a poem by Joseph Miller, "Bildungsroman," all three read that day. In addition, it comprises "(a hundred days)," by Madisyn Lynn Simington, and "(un)Worthy," by Anna Schmitt, both developed in response to pieces in Nguyen's *The Displaced* for a digital gallery of student work in a later version of the class, taught jointly at Penn State Altoona and Penn State Behrend.

Notes

1. The Critical Refugee Studies Collective makes a related point about the simultaneous "creative and critical potentiality" of refugees' self-representation and world-making (Espiritu et al. 11–29, but especially 9, 102–07, 143).

2. To be precise, the United Nations High Commissioner for Refugees had been working with internally displaced persons as early as the 1970s; displacement situations due to climate change and development necessitated a rapid expansion, however (Russell and Tennant 303).

3. During the final phase of preparing this text for publication, I became aware of Vinh Nguyen's *Lived Refuge: Gratitude, Resentment, Resilience*, published in 2023, which theorizes the refugee experience in terms of "experiment," as repeated "try[ing]" and "start[ing] again" (16, 25–26, 34–35).

4. Altoona's population declined from around 82,000 residents in the 1930s ("History of Altoona") to approximately 43,000 residents by July 2022 ("Quick Facts").

5. To allow the group to engage in conversation about specific examples, all client case materials were redacted for anonymity and used with express consent.

6. Lindsey made this point in the fall of 2018 but rendered it more forcefully in a subsequent, online workshop in the fall of 2020.

7. Tessa Strength, née Albert, graduated with a BA in English from Penn State University, Altoona College, where she also worked as a peer tutor in the Writing Commons.

8. Because I could not secure the required permissions, his statement, which constituted a key moment in the course, cannot be reproduced here.

9. An excerpt of Lee's introduction to the forum can be found on her personal website (leepeterson.net/#/news-and-events/).

Appendix

Protected Ground

by Madra Furman

> *Those seeking asylum must show they have suffered past persecution or have a*
> *well-founded fear of persecution on account of a protected ground if they are*
> *returned to their home country. Protected grounds for asylum include race,*
> *religion, nationality, membership in a particular social group, or political*
> *opinion.*
>
> — *Center for Immigrants' Rights Clinic, Penn State Law,*
> *"Family Separation Policy: What You Need to Know" (2018)*

Lights that could incinerate
   a spider
with its first step into the beam.

Chairs that hold static and
   no comfort.

A chalkboard with Spanish
   translated
to English questions,
   questions,
    questions.

A translator.
A child.
Asked to show proof of their tragedy,
   and if not,
be sent back.

Watching the World

by Madra Furman

Watching the world
I open my mouth
   and the scent of daughters
      burning,
   of sons drowning,
pour down my neck.

I try spitting them out,
but inside me,
these lives
linger.

Madra Furman is a graduate of Penn State University, Altoona College, and is currently working as a counselor in a behavioral health care agency focused on youth. Her poem "Protected Ground" was composed in response to Valeria Luiselli's *Tell Me How It Ends* and the workshop on refugee law with Lindsey Wilkes. "Watching the World" was inspired by Warsan Shire's "Ugly."

Bildungsroman
by Joseph Miller

> *(n.) having as its main theme the formative years of one person.*

Before I departed, I'd never even seen a dead body.
Now that I'm home, it's tough to count those I've seen.

They are here WHEN I wake.
And even worse, they are present when I sleep.

At least in waking, they remain motionless.
In my dreams, they writhe constantly.
The cadavers twist around like worms in sludge.
Then suddenly, there is fire. They cinder like coals.

I became a supreme egotist.
Perpetuated by death and loss,
the only person I could pity was myself.

Joseph Miller, a graduate of Penn State University, Altoona College, and a veteran of the US Army, works in Penn State's College of Health and Human Development and Alumni Relations office as a donor relations specialist. His poem is a meditation on the sense of internal displacement and trauma that resulted from his experience as a soldier.

(a hundred days)
by Madisyn Lynn Simington

you wonder how
you will live that
other life
the one where you stayed

to beg as to become
time,
you have had no always
no real reason on the list

every day is a lesson in doubts
that never protected you
remember the first time
you imagine another forever

you wonder how
you will live that
other life
the one where you stayed
with agony

Madisyn Lynn Simington (she/they) is a graduate of Penn State University, Altoona College, and is currently working on an MFA at Penn State University Park. Simington's work explores grief, trauma, and memory through interdisciplinary work such as visual media, writing, and performance. "(a hundred days)" is a found poem created from page 119 of Porochista Khakpour's "Thirteen Ways of Being an Immigrant."

(un)Worthy

by Anna Schmitt

As the devil confirms
[you're not enough]
Their silence escapes
control until
The space they occupy
messy stories
Face their identity
[you're not enough]
Apologize until
remorse for life
Angry as the devil
stories of shame
[you're not enough]

Anna Schmitt (they/them), a graduate of Penn State Erie, The Behrend College, intends to pursue graduate work in English. They currently work in higher education. "(un)Worthy" is a found poem created from page 150 of Dina Nayeri's "The Ungrateful Refugee."

Works Cited

Akram, Susan. "UNRWA and Palestinian Refugees." Fiddian-Qasmiyeh et al., pp. 227–40.

"City of Asylum Exiled Writer and Artist Residency Program." *City of Asylum*, 2024, cityofasylum.org/residencies/.

"City of Asylum House Publications." *City of Asylum*, 2024, cityofasylum.org/creative-placemaking/house-publications/.

Cohen, Gerard Daniel. *In War's Wake: Europe's Displaced Persons in the Postwar Order.* Oxford UP, 2011.

"Comma House." *City of Asylum*, 2024, cityofasylum.org/public-art/comma-house/.

Convention Relating to the Status of Refugees. United Nations, 28 July 1951, treaties.un.org/doc/Treaties/1954/04/19540422%2000-23%20AM/Ch_V_2p.pdf.

Espiritu, Yến Lê, et al. *Departures: An Introduction to Critical Refugee Studies.* U of California P, 2022.

Fiddian-Qasmiyeh, Elena, et al., editors. *The Oxford Handbook of Refugee and Forced Migration Studies.* Oxford UP, 2014.

"Figures at a Glance." *UNHCR*, 2001–24, www.unhcr.org/us/about-unhcr/who-we-are/figures-glance.

Gatrell, Peter. *The Making of the Modern Refugee.* Oxford UP, 2015.

Golinkin, Lev. "Guests of the Holy Roman Empress Maria Theresa." Nguyen, *Displaced*, pp. 67–72.

Guiding Principles on Internal Displacement. United Nations Commission on Human Rights, 11 Feb. 1998, undocs.org/Home/Mobile?FinalSymbol=E%2FCN.4%2F1998%2F53%2FAdd.2&Language=E&DeviceType=Desktop&LangRequested=False.

Hassine, Khaled. *Handling Climate Displacement.* Cambridge UP, 2019.

"History of Altoona." *City of Altoona, Pennsylvania*, 2024, www.altoonapa.gov/history-of-altoona.

Khakpour, Porochista. "Thirteen Ways of Being an Immigrant." Nguyen, *Displaced*, pp. 113–20.

Luiselli, Valeria. *Tell Me How It Ends: An Essay in Forty Questions.* Coffee House Press, 2017.

Nasaw, David. *The Last Million: Europe's Displaced Persons from World War to Cold War.* Penguin Books, 2020.

Nayeri, Dina. "The Ungrateful Refugee." Nguyen, *Displaced*, pp. 137–50.

Nguyen, Viet Thanh, editor. *The Displaced: Refugee Writers on Refugee Lives.* Abrams Press, 2018.

———. Introduction. Nguyen, *Displaced*, pp. 11–22.

Nguyen, Vinh. *Lived Refuge: Gratitude, Resentment, Resilience.* U of California P, 2023.

Qasmiyeh, Yousif M. "The Camp Is Time." *Writing the Camp*, by Qasmiyeh, Broken Sleep Books, 2021, pp. 66–67.

"Quick Facts: Altoona City, Pennsylvania." *United States Census Bureau*, www
.census.gov/quickfacts/altoonacitypennsylvania. Accessed 1 Nov. 2023.

Robertson, Campbell, et al. "Eleven Killed in Synagogue Massacre; Suspect
Charged with Twenty-Nine Counts." *The New York Times*, 27 Oct. 2018,
www.nytimes.com/2018/10/27/us/active-shooter-pittsburgh-synagogue
-shooting.html.

Russell, Simon, and Vicky Tennant. "Humanitarian Reform: From Coordina-
tion to Clusters." Fiddian-Qasmiyeh et al., pp. 302–16.

Rust Belt New Americans. Directed by Jessica Yochim, MenajErie Studio, 2018.
Vimeo, 15 June 2018, vimeo.com/278166907/8ae298b99a.

Shire, Warsan. "Ugly." *Teaching My Mother How to Give Birth*, by Shire, Kindle
ed., Flipped Eye Publishing, 2011.

Spiegelman, Art. *Maus II: A Survivor's Tale: And Here My Troubles Began*. Pan-
theon, 1991.

Standing, Guy. *The Precariat: The New Dangerous Class*. Bloomsbury Academic,
2016.

"Tuhin Das." *City of Asylum*, 2024, cityofasylum.org/portfolio/tuhin-das/.

"USCRI Erie." *U.S. Committee for Refugees and Immigrants*, 2024, refugees
.org/uscri-erie/.

Kester Dyer

A Transportable/Transnational Cinema: Wapikoni Mobile

The word *transportation*, in the context of Indigenous cinema and media, may conjure images of mainstream culture's penetrating and polluting effects, of extractive industries that move in and out of Indigenous territory, seizing natural resources and leaving behind environmental, cultural, and social desolation. The flip side of the Faustian dilemma described by the visual anthropologist Faye Ginsburg, however, suggests that the outward flow of media and cultural perspectives from Indigenous creatives toward the broader public generates dialectical counterincursions. To be sure, the appropriation of mainstream media tools and forms by Indigenous filmmakers has fueled phenomena such as the current Indigenous New Wave, a vibrant cultural movement that has catalyzed opportunities for understanding and pedagogically engaging with Indigenous preoccupations and aspirations. Since this film movement has proven especially dynamic in terms of genre cinema,[1] Wendy Gay Pearson's emphasis on the relevance for Indigenous filmmakers of appropriating and challenging the road movie's forms and conventions is particularly pertinent and edifying. Perhaps not coincidentally, and at the level of institutions rather than of genre, Wapikoni Mobile, the Montreal-based participatory filmmaking initiative aimed at emerging Indigenous artists, is also premised on mobility, the road, and transportation.[2] In this respect, Wapikoni lends itself to an extension of Pearson's argument that the Indigenous road movie may be subversive and can overturn Eurocentric stereotypes of Indigenous peoples as a "vanishing race" in the face of so-called European progress. Thus, Wapikoni's conditions of production, exhibition, and cinematic culture formation serve as a valuable tool to illustrate complementary points about the relationship between Indigenous mobility and decoloniality.

Wapikoni Mobile gets its name from a young woman, Wapikoni Awashish, who was tragically killed in a road accident in 2002. Only twenty years old, Wapikoni had been an energetic leader among the youth of the Wemotaci Atikamekw community and a collaborator of the Québec documentary filmmaker Manon Barbeau. Deeply troubled by Wapikoni's death and by the high levels of youth suicide in this community, Barbeau began to imagine a mobile film production studio as a means of empowering Indigenous youth (Barbeau, "Du Wapikoni mobile" 22). Barbeau cofounded Wapikoni Mobile in 2004 together with the Council of the Atikamekw First Nation and the First Nations of Québec and Labrador Youth Network, with the assistance of the National Film Board of Canada. This project has converted four recreational vehicles into mobile studios that make monthlong stops in various communities, enabling emerging artists and community members to conceive, produce, edit, and exhibit their own films. To date, the project counts more than 6,000 participants[3] from 36 nations and 45 communities around the world who have created over 2,300 audiovisual works and garnered over 240 prizes and honorable mentions. In addition, Wapikoni films are distributed widely in international festivals, and most remain accessible online (Wapikoni Mobile, *Rapport annuel* [2022–23] 1).

As an idea that frames and underpins the Wapikoni project, transportation evokes a sense of carrying large loads, of material and cultural exchange, and of the movement of people by the apparatus. It may also suggest an attachment to a particular location combined with the ability to move within and out of that space of activity. It also brings to mind historical and ongoing traumas associated with movement—for example, the forced removal and relocation of Indigenous peoples, the transportation of children away from their communities to residential schools, and genocidal roadways such as the infamous corridor known as the Highway of Tears, where Indigenous women and girls who find themselves compelled to travel from their communities toward urban centers go missing and are murdered in shocking numbers. Within this context, Wapikoni engages with transportation from multiple perspectives, inducing shifts in representation, perception, and communication that fundamentally redefine intercultural relationships. Even in the current era of transnational cinemas where, as Philip Rosen argues, nation-states and borders yet remain concrete experiences (13), Wapikoni significantly challenges the nation-state paradigm through practical and thematic approaches to transportation. In this respect, the geopolitical context of Québec is notable. Its ambiguous history as a conquered settler nation not only provides it with a historical experience of colonial mechanisms that potentially augments its sensibility to the workings of such oppressive systems but also predisposes it to an appropriation of colonized status and the disavowal of its own role as a colonizer. As such, the origins and situatedness of Wapikoni activities primarily within the territory known today as Québec also elucidate the significance of mobility both in practice and as a malleable cultural symbol. In addition, the Québec film tradition also manifests strong aesthetic links to genealogical markers of mobility, notably to the portable character of the 1960s *cinéma direct*, or direct cinema, movement and the National Film Board's Challenge for Change (Société nouvelle) programs of the late 1960s through the 1980s. But it also evinces links to earlier priest-filmmakers who traveled throughout Québec during the 1930s, 1940s, and 1950s, using their semiamateur films as pedagogical and ideological tools. In this essay, I consider how Wapikoni, by intervening in this sociopolitical, historical, and aesthetic context, influences impressions of national space, borders, and land and creates synergy with contemporary political and cultural movements toward radical reconceptualizations of nationhood in ways that are pedagogically instructive.

From its inception, Wapikoni Mobile proposed an alternative understanding of transportation. Wapikoni Awashish's story is frequently cited as inspirational, and her image is displayed in the organization's mobile studios. The name Wapikoni means "flower" in the Atikamekw language and acts as a powerful symbol that contrasts with the haulage of natural resources by multinational corporations. In fact, Wapikoni was killed when her car drove head-on into a truck carrying lumber that was illegally parked on the road to her community. Wapikoni Mobile therefore explicitly positions itself in contradistinction to the historical and ongoing deployment of transportation as an exploitative endeavor. Instead, its engagement with movement and transportation bears the intent of social change through artistic practice, cultural exchange, and political commitment. Following the implications of Wapikoni's organizing principles, I seek to understand

and highlight how this initiative provokes a reevaluation of national space by diverting Québec's symbolic investment in a national narrative that foregrounds transportation. I interrogate the singularities of this subversion, considering the specificity of Québec, a settler colonial society marked simultaneously by its own subjugation and its strong self-perception as a colonized nation. I argue here that Wapikoni, through its conception, activities, and the thematic concerns of its output, reappropriates the evocative power of transportation from national hegemonies by initiating a sequence of temporal and spatial interpenetrations. To this end, I consider the political and cinematic history of Québec and Canada alongside a selection of Wapikoni films in order to critically examine settler relationships with Indigenous peoples and to illustrate how Wapikoni brings together both the physical and emotional dimensions of transportation in ways that capture the popular imagination and challenge its assumptions.

National Narrative Flows

In his book *Bitter Feast*, the Québec historian Denys Delâge describes how complex communication networks shaped the history of the northeastern American continent prior to the arrival of Europeans and how the Wendat people of Georgian Bay managed a vast system across this region that connected numerous Indigenous communities by means of waterways and trade routes. From the Great Lakes, Delâge writes, "it was possible to travel by water over the whole continent—from the Arctic to the Gulf of Mexico, from the Atlantic to the Rockies" (54). For Delâge, unequal relations of exchange and market capitalism superimposed onto existing structures destroyed the balance of social and interethnic relationships in the seventeenth century (173), an economic penetration inextricably linked with the missionary enterprise, where "the Hurons were faced not only with a commercial monopoly, but with a religious monopoly as well" (166). As Europeans gained control over transportation, Indigenous movement became increasingly constrained, culminating in repressive reserve and education systems put in place by Canada's Indian Act of 1876.

In parallel, cinema in Canada consolidated emerging national myths shaped by transportation. Christopher Gittings, for example, describes the railway as "the master narrative of Canadian nation, *par excellence*" (236). Indeed, the Canadian Pacific Railway's early use of film to promote land settlement in western Canada (Morris 29–39) was later followed by

National Film Board documentaries such as Stanley Hawes's 1944 *Trans-Canada Express*, which proclaims the railway's inauguration of a geographically complete nation. In contrast, Colin Low's 1952 Oscar-nominated short *The Romance of Transportation in Canada*, in Thomas Waugh's words, "implants a rather campy spirit in its animated riff on the epic subject matter of portage canoes, corduroy roads, steamships, continental railways, and bush pilots" (18). Low's remarkably prescient film thus reveals cinema's potential for undermining the celebration of Euro-Canadian dominance over all stretches of the landscape.

In Québec, transportation is mythologized in particular by means of the liminal figure of the *coureur des bois*, situated symbolically between French Canadian and Indigenous worlds (Marshall 240) and at times portrayed in National Film Board shorts like the 1978 vignette *Voyageurs*, and Bernard Gosselin's earlier *Les Voyageurs* (*The Voyageurs*) as a romanticized adventurer whose desire for wealth and westward exploration led to the birth of the Canadian nation and traced the paths of its modern roads and heritage. Indeed, the *coureur* runs through Québec history, storytelling, cinema, and literature, notably in *La chasse-galerie*, Québec's most iconic oral tale, where *coureur*-type characters defy religious dogma and travel by magic canoe, thus memorably combining Indigenous tradition with physical, emotional, and supernatural transportation. The *coureur* lives on in such literary classics as Louis Hémond's *Maria Chapdelaine* and Félix-Antoine Savard's *Menaud, maître draveur* (*Menaud, Master Log Driver*), where the literature scholar Aurélien Boivin notes an eternal dilemma, the need to occupy and possess the land to ensure the survival of the French Canadian race, counterbalanced by the desire for liberty personified by the *coureur des bois* (8). Gillian Helfield's analysis of folk influences on Québec cinema corroborates this dichotomy between two basic archetypes: the *coureur des bois* and the *agriculteur*, or farmer (15). In this regard, the pioneering travel and tourism propaganda of the Québec priest-filmmaker Maurice Proulx, endorsed nationally by the postwar regime of Maurice Duplessis, romanticizes exploration even as it favors an *agriculteur* vision. And although, historically, Catholic missionaries had frowned on the *coureur*'s hybridity, in films like *Les routes du Québec* (*The Roads of Québec*), Proulx neutralizes the *coureur*'s liberating and pluralistic potential to celebrate a notion of travel that validates Euro-Canadian territorial possession.

In Helfield's analysis, the emergence of *cinéma direct* during Québec's Quiet Revolution, despite its "overriding emphasis on the processes of movement and change" (13), nevertheless continued to reaffirm pastoral values (22). Following this, Challenge for Change's francophone counterpart, Société nouvelle, which grew out of the Groupe de recherches sociales (Social Research Group), an initiative that existed from 1966 to 1969 and was formed by Office national du film filmmakers and producers who privileged consultative and participatory methods (Bégin 17; Marchessault 356), not only continued to emphasize portability; as Marion Froger contends, it also displayed a fascination for migrating populations after the failure of agricultural colonization and played out the "l'échappée libertaire" ("libertarian escape") of pioneers continued by the *coureurs des bois* (29; my trans.). At the same time, the creation of the National Film Board's "Indian crews," which challenged dominant narratives, foreshadowed elements of Wapikoni, including pan-Indigenous collaboration and community screenings (Starblanket 39). Indeed, Wapikoni has been described as an inheritor of Challenge for Change and Société nouvelle (Serpereau 57), but as this brief overview suggests, a more far-reaching lineage retraces the enduring sequence of transportation and its iterations through cinematic, literary, historical, and other narrative moments.

Diverting Mainstream Narratives

Embedding itself within the mainstream Québécois and Canadian narratives that link transportation to nationhood, Wapikoni literally merges transportation with audiovisual communication, then redirects the hegemonic current of Euro-Canadian storytelling. Rechanneling the penetration of electronic media into historically immobilized communities, Wapikoni transports technology and skills to communities in order to facilitate the outward flow of ideas, art, opinions, and world senses.[4] One significant way it works to achieve this in Québec and Canada is by appropriating and inverting Indigenous peoples' historical and mythical relationship with the *coureur des bois*, whose mediation of Indigenous knowledge ambiguously facilitated colonial expansion.[5] Indeed, one of Wapikoni's most notable early successes, Canouk Newashish's *Coureurs de nuit* (*Night Runners*), warps the *coureur* myth to fit modern reserve realities, thereby forcing the Québécois spectator to absorb a sardonic critique of the stereotypical Indigenized French adventurer and storyteller. Thus, this short film undermines popular settler conceptions of the *coureur*, effectively echoing the Kanien'kehá:ka scholar Taiaiake Alfred, who insists that "contemporary indigenous peoples' nationhood" should intrude into the colonial state's mythology and thereby deny this state's ability to "maintain its own legitimacy" (83).

Québécois *coureur* stories perform an exoticizing function akin to what the Māori scholar Linda Tuhiwai Smith has denounced as "travellers' tales," misshaping Western understandings of non-Western peoples (81). Wapikoni, however, reworks this model and instead features Indigenous participants as storyteller-travelers who provide counternarratives to pervasive clichés. Even so, Wapikoni does not simply superimpose itself onto Western cultural structures but invokes antecedent Indigenous practices of transportation and exchange (Delâge 93–94), which validate its basis in transportability and movement. Indeed, Delâge, by stressing that it was not trade itself but rather the unequal nature of exchanges that overturned the social equilibrium in place before European arrival (89), mirrors Ella Shohat and Robert Stam's perspective on Eurocentrism in the media, which affirms that "[d]espite the imbrication of 'First' and 'Third' Worlds, the global distribution of power still tends to make the First World countries cultural 'transmitters' and to reduce most Third World countries to the status of 'receivers'" (30). Moreover, "[t]he problem lies not in the exchange but in the unequal terms on which the exchange takes place" (31). Accordingly, in the contemporary era, Wapikoni attempts to redress economic, communicational, and political imbalance by affixing itself to European networks of transportation imagined as the successors of those routes previously traced by Indigenous ancestors.

Wapikoni tackles transportation flows in three main ways: the transgenerational current within communities, communication from Indigenous to non-Indigenous peoples, and finally, pan-Indigenous connections through participant collaborations, public meetings, and other worldwide exchanges (Wapikoni Mobile, *Rapport annuel* [2005] 6). In the first instance, Wapikoni confronts a caesura in the temporal trajectory of communities by emphasizing a reconnection across imposed generational barriers.[6] Thus, Wapikoni responds to the severed continuum between elders and youth enacted by church-run Indigenous residential schools. Instead, the structure of Wapikoni stopovers targets the restoration of intracommunity interaction through participatory filmmaking, which culminates in end-of-visit screenings that create a space for group encounters and dialogue. Thematically, intergenerational communication and healing are often expressed as journeys in Wapikoni films, many of which allude to nomadism or other traditional activities foregrounding mobility. For example, *Coeurs nomades* (*Nomad Hearts*), directed by Joyce Grégoire, deals with homelessness in the director's community in a poignant testimony that features her own father's struggle with homelessness. The plural title of the film clearly implies a communal trauma that extends beyond the film's protagonist and holds accountable the breakdown of social structures. Likewise, Charlotte Poucachiche's *Le voyage* (*The Journey*) posits healing as a lifelong journey, associating traditional Anishinaabe principles with an image of a canoe to suggest both their continuity and movement. *Ka Kushpian* (*My Journey*), directed by Tshiuetin Vollant, frames the ancestral nature of a monthlong canoe trip to Schefferville within a contemporary maturation ritual that asserts a nomadic presence on a vast traditional Innu territory and reconnects with past generations, thus bursting the boundaries of an eight-square-kilometer reserve.

Such appeals to the past challenge dominant geographic assumptions in the present. Debby Flamand's *Meskano* (*The Path*) links healing with movement but focuses on future generations. Flamand and her daughter tackle the latter's depression together by undertaking a 120-kilometer snowshoe journey that connects the Atikamekw communities of Manawan and Wemotaci with a group organized by Stanley Vollant, Québec's first Indigenous surgeon. Thus, Flamand's film valorizes traditional practices as well as contemporary achievements, emphasizing the link between generations as a means to fight internal difficulties, while expressing territorial presence to non-Indigenous society. Other films, such as *Anmani mak Kum* (*Anmani and Kum*) and Evelyne Papatie and Vince Papatie's *Kokom Déménage* (*Kokom on the Move*), stress the persistence and fragility of nomadic activities and rituals performed by elders. Likewise, Mélanie Kistabish's *Le lac Abitibi* (*Abitibi Lake*) retraces a history of forced sedentarization, which led to the concomitant loss of nomadic practices and of Anishinaabeg land. Kistabish's inquiry isolates the key moments of reserve and residential school legislation as determining ruptures, while her use of archival footage of sedentarized school children waiving Québec flags clearly implicates Québec and shatters its perception as a colonized society.

Merging intracommunity communication with external conduits, Wapikoni therefore aims to "rebâtir des ponts entre les gens, les générations et les cultures" ("rebuild bridges between people, generations and cultures"; Dumont; my trans.). Indeed, Barbeau's own initial hopes in this respect are telling: "S'ils renouent avec leurs racines et leur histoire tout en s'ouvrant au monde, ils créeront un lien avec nous qui nous apportera quelque chose d'extrêmement précieux" ("If they reconnect with their roots and their history while opening up to the world, they will create a link with us that will bring us something extremely precious"; qtd. in Dumont; my trans.). Similarly, multiple aspects of transportation are present in the work of the longtime Wapikoni filmmaker Kevin Papatie, who asserts that "se transporter à travers le cinéma, c'est transporter tes idées, ta culture, vers une autre culture. Là, on parle de chemin. C'est de créer des chemins, des ponts interculturels à travers le cinéma qui amèneraient une compréhension à ce qu'on est" ("to transport oneself through cinema means transporting one's ideas, one's culture, toward another culture. So, we are talking about a path then. It means creating paths, intercultural bridges through cinema, which would then bring about an understanding of who we are"; my trans.). In keeping with this, some films deploy travel or its inhibition as didactic devices. For instance, *Wigwas*, directed by Karl Chevrier, articulates the traditional fabrication of a bark canoe as a metaphor for alternative directions for Indigenous and non-Indigenous people alike, affirming the hope that the film itself will help the viewer on their own journey. Chevrier thus equates travel with the filmmaking process, not only as mediation between cultures but also literally as a vehicle that carries us forward toward the resolution of cultural and political differences. From a more overtly political perspective, *Atikuat nimeteut* (*The Caribou Trail*), directed by Pishu Pierre Pilot, links the trail followed by caribou to a train journey and to the camera itself in order to outline the notion of voyage as a narrative of resistance opposing the government's forced immobilization of caribou herds. Conversely, Réal Junior Leblanc's *Blocus 138—Innu Resistance* documents a roadblock protesting Québec's 2011 Plan Nord project to further exploit natural resources on Innu territory, and Eden Malina Awashish's *Rien sur les mocassins* (*Nothing about Moccasins*) similarly depicts the refusal of a journey by denying settler access to knowledge about Indigenous tools of mobility while also addressing the need to bridge intergenerational divides.

Global Indigenous Interconnections

Interconnections between Wapikoni filmmakers across nations contest the isolating structures of the reserve system implemented by the Indian Act of 1876. Participants take part in such initiatives as film collaborators or through meetings at festivals, forums, and other events. These connections encourage the reconceptualization of territory not only as occupied by an Indigenous presence but also as traveled across by mobile Indigenous actors and interwoven with networks. This augments political and cultural clout and influences how national communities continue to be imagined (Marceau 566). In Québec, artists from different nations work together to assert Indigenous presence in ways that undermine mainstream notions of national space. Wapikoni has systematically sought to generate such alliances. Opportunities include collaborations with academic institutions where filmmakers are often partnered with members of other communities to create short films. *Indian Taxi*, for instance, codirected by Kevin Papatie and Abraham Côté—Anishinaabe filmmakers who come from francophone and anglophone communities, respectively—emerges as an ironic view of transportation somewhat reminiscent of Low's *The Romance of Transportation in Canada*.

Although Wapikoni remains most present in Québec, its first stopover in Ontario took place in Wikwemikong in October 2013, and its influence now extends beyond provincial borders across different regions of Canada. In parallel, films like *Vers Vancouver* (*Toward Vancouver*), directed by Bradley Brazeau and Evelyne Papatie, cinematically expresses Wapikoni's desire to uncover suppressed commonalities across provincial borders and mirrors the spirit of Wapikoni itself in its desire to produce counternarratives through the appropriation of roadways. Four Anishnabeg youth undertake a month-long cycle trip, leaving from Val-d'Or then bifurcating north to visit Indigenous communities on their way to Vancouver. Participants recount stopovers where, despite divergent linguistic assimilation into French or English, they can communicate across a continent populated by Algonkian peoples with cognate languages. The exclamation "On est vraiment partout au Canada. C'est juste qu'on est pas inscrit dans la carte" ("We are actually everywhere in Canada. It's just that we aren't written on the map"; *Vers Vancouver* 00:03:17; my trans.) responds to films such as *Trans-Canada Express*, which bind the completeness of Canada to the rail connection but either obscure or co-opt Indigenous presence and identity.

Political dimensions apparent in intercommunity projects find concerted expression in Wapikoni's focus on global Indigenous interconnections. Over the last nineteen years, Wapikoni has developed a considerable range of international connections and continues to cultivate such relationships. As Barbeau repeated during her tenure as Wapikoni's artistic director, "We're trying to create a network of resources for First Nations all over the world so that youth feel less alone, less invisible" (qtd. in Beeston). Activities that seek to promote global Indigenous interconnections feature attendance by filmmakers at international festivals, overseas training opportunities, discussion forums, diplomatic ties between communities, and reciprocal relationships with analogous audiovisual organizations in Bolivia, Columbia, Peru, Chile, Panama, Turkey, Norway, France, and Finland. Opportunities for new encounters also work synergistically with links between communities in Québec. For example, *Finding the Light*, directed by Emilio Wawatie, Shaynah Decontie Thusky, and Raymond Caplin, brings together two Anishinaabe and one Mi'kmaq youth from Québec to shoot a film about their experience at an international Indigenous festival and filmmaking workshop in Inari, Finland. Upon contact with Sámi and other Indigenous groups, the young filmmakers discover a shared history of colonization. Later that year, Wawatie accompanies fellow Wapikoni filmmaker and cofounder of Idle No More Québec, Mélissa Mollen-Dupuis, to New York and eloquently speaks on behalf of Wapikoni at the Thirteenth Session of the United Nations Permanent Forum on Indigenous Issues. Thus, Wapikoni associates itself with the 2007 United Nations Declaration on the Rights of Indigenous Peoples, which, according to James Anaya, questions the validity of the nation-state as the paramount form of human association that all collectivities should necessarily strive toward (9).[7]

Other films also reveal the mobilizing effect of international exchanges. Kevin Papatie's visit to the Chiapas region of Mexico immediately preceded his manifesto-film *Nous sommes* (*We Are*), while Evelyne Papatie's trip to Mato Grosso, Brazil, encouraged her to address her own people audiovisually in a short postcard film titled *Des forêts de Kitcisakik aux forêts de Xingu* (*From the Forest of Kitcisakik to the Forests of Xingú*). In this film, Papatie draws attention to shared concerns and emphasizes her calls for the simultaneous renewal of Indigenous resistance in her own community through the use of parallel editing in the final segment of her film. Finally, *De passage* (*Passing Through*), directed by Sacha Dubé and Billy Roy Mowatt, produced during an exchange to Marseille, inverts the gaze of the sympathetic Western filmmaker intending to highlight Indigenous problems. Instead, this Atikamekw-Anishinaabe filmmaking duo casts a sympathetic eye on the marginalization of the Marseillais in relation to Paris and thereby invites solidarity with non-Indigenous groups.

Subverting Understandings of Mobility

As Pearson highlights, the road doesn't always have to be linear and Eurocentric. It can also imply dead ends, detours, and crossroads (140). According to this scholar, Indigenous filmmakers appropriate the road movie genre for decolonization and stress the concept of "home" as well as family, kinship, and land. Indigenous road movies often lead back to home or family in an indirect, nonlinear way (153–54). Pearson provides as one example the breakthrough Indigenous road movie, *Smoke Signals*, directed by Chris Eyre and produced in the United States, which displays a narrative that is circular rather than linear. Two of its characters, Velma and Lucy, present an obvious reference to the archetypal Thelma and Louise, but their "rez" car only works in reverse. Citing Kerstin Knopf, Pearson highlights that this mocks the masculinism of the road movie genre and suggests paradoxically moving forward by going back to reclaim history through oral storytelling (148). Similarly, individual Wapikoni films and the premise for this initiative as a whole offer the possibility of subverting entrenched understandings of the road, mobility, migration, and transportation in Québec while raising awareness about crucially important historical, social, and political issues beyond this context. For example, James McDougall's *The Routes* literalizes the cyclicality of the road and of journeys by describing a habitual bicycle route taken by the protagonist, which, in an iterative manner, leads him to continuously reencounter locations that propel his personal journey to reconnect with culture and traditions as well as community members affected by the disappearance of Maisy Marie Odjick and Shannon Alexander, two teenage girls from the community of Kitigan Zibi who went missing in 2008. Thus, drawing attention to a striking example of missing and murdered Indigenous women and girls in Québec, *The Routes* simultaneously evokes the significance of this crisis elsewhere in Canada as well as violence embedded in Eurocentric perceptions of Indigenous women more broadly.

Although in many ways specific to Québec's own history of settler colonialism, Wapikoni films and its organizational structure, understood through the notion of transportation, can facilitate the communication of how migration and mobility relate to Indigeneity in multiple ways, often transgressing imposed Eurocentrist-colonialist delimitations such as the reserve system or nation-state borders. The extent of Wapikoni's long-term impact—through its transportation of a broad range of Indigenous voices, in multiple directions, both temporally and spatially, and within a structure that celebrates movement and simultaneously questions its manifestations— still remains unclear. However, the aggregation of crosscurrents described in this essay suggests that the transnational and transportable nature of Wapikoni brings into focus Indigenous presence while drawing attention to Québec's transportation myth epitomized by the *coureur* and its incompatibility with the dominant notion of territorial integrity. By tapping into and channeling this symbolism in a geopolitically specific manner, it proposes ethically motivated and didactic opportunities to rethink nationhood and explore other forms of intercultural association as genuinely collaborative enterprises.

Alfred's Indigenous manifesto, *Peace, Power, Righteousness*, stresses several interrelated points as crucial to building a successful Indigenous challenge to Western hegemony. The most central of these points concerns leadership. In this respect, Wapikoni, though open to all participants, actively encourages the formation of a nucleus of young leaders in each community and aims toward the transferal of skills and responsibilities (Sédillot 71). Importantly, in 2018, Barbeau ceded her role as artistic director of Wapikoni to the Innu leader and rights activist Odile Joannette, a transition Barbeau claims to have hoped for since the early stages of the project (Niosi).[8] Alfred also highlights the need for both community cohesion and transnational solidarity. These criteria are addressed through Wapikoni's focus on intracommunity communication and intercommunity network building across provincial and national borders. In addition, links between Wapikoni and other organizations tend to take shape organically. Once such opportunities arise as coherent and useful, strategic methods follow to develop them (Barbeau, Interview). Finally, Alfred's call for the regeneration of Indigenous political foundations adapted from Haudenosaunee condolence ceremonies accentuates the need to recognize loss. Given Québec's tangible historical experience of oppression under British domination, its long-standing self-perception as a victim of colonialism, as well as subsequent moves to disavow its ongoing responsibilities as a settler colonial state, Alfred's focus on loss suggests a potential area of mutual understanding that lies in the recognition of colonial injuries and their perpetuation. Indeed, for Alfred, "most white people in positions of authority" must "be prodded simply to recognize their dominance over indigenous people" (102). Wapikoni addresses this provocation by means of its prolific output, but beyond this, it also prepares the ground for a significant horizontal shift in communication. It provides a vehicle for repairing damaged links between generations and activates a critical mass of emerging, engaged artists, who, through their coincident incursions into Québec and Canadian film, culture, and politics, announce a concerted reevaluation of Indigenous and non-Indigenous relationships. Although this example is limited to one point of epistemological overlap, its dialogical potential and Wapikoni's apparent consistency with aims corresponding to some

Indigenous intellectual principles intimate the broad pedagogical possibilities that Wapikoni may increasingly form as a distinct response to mainstream audiovisual production, wider sociopolitical challenges, and the global hegemony of the nation-state.

Notes

This essay, adapted from a section of my doctoral dissertation, draws on research that received the Film Studies Association of Canada Gerald Pratley Award in 2014. I have since continued to develop and revise this material for the classroom. This work has also led to Circle Visions, a partnership between Concordia University, Carleton University, and Wapikoni Mobile. I would like to thank all those who contributed to my ongoing reflections on Wapikoni: the Film and Media Studies Association of Canada, members of my doctoral committee, Liz Miller, Circle Visions and Carleton University Summer Institute workshop participants and collaborators, and Wapikoni staff members as well as Manon Barbeau, Kevin Papatie, Raymond Caplin, Tshiuetin Vollant, Jani Bellefleur-Kaltush, Élisa Moar, Délia Gunn, and Lina Jane Gunn, who generously granted interviews.

1. As the prominent Ojibway film critic and producer Jesse Wente stressed in his keynote lecture at the 2017 Film Studies Association of Canada conference, after emerging through films of resistance and self-affirmation over the last few decades, global Indigenous cinema has now entered a phase of development wherein its best works subvert and challenge genre conventions.

2. Although this essay explores Wapikoni in the Québec context, other comparable participatory film production projects exist elsewhere in the world. In Brazil, for instance, Video in the Villages has existed since the late 1980s (Aufderheide; "Apresentação"). In western Africa, the Cinomade project was created in the late 1990s and works to raise awareness and generate debate about HIV and AIDS through cinema (Bouchard; "Cinomade").

3. The number of participants was confirmed to me in an email exchange with Wapikoni staff members.

4. In this essay I opt for the term "world senses" rather than the more common, oculocentric "world views."

5. Wapikoni does not explicitly identify itself as engaging with the *coureur* archetype. However, during the interview I conducted with Barbeau, she explained that the conception of the recreational vehicle as Wapikoni's mobile filmmaking studio, and the fascination with this vehicle as the central metaphor for the project, probably stemmed from and conjures several different non- or anti-institutional influences, including, notably, punk counterculture, the carnivalesque, and nomadism (Interview). As such, the link between the recreational vehicle's effect on the popular imaginary and the *coureur* seems pertinent given the *coureur*'s evocation of liminality, unorthodoxy, nonconformism, and mobility as defining traits.

6. Sédillot notes that several participants express the hope that technology will encourage "better dialogue between generations" (74).

7. Wapikoni also became an official partner of UNESCO in 2017 (Wapikoni Mobile, *Rapport annuel* [2017]).

8. Odile Joannette has since left Wapikoni and was replaced in 2021 by Véronique Rankin (Anishinaabe), Wapikoni's third director and the second Indigenous person to hold this position.

Works Cited

Alfred, Taiaiake. *Peace, Power, Righteousness: An Indigenous Manifesto.* 2nd ed., Oxford UP, 2009.

Anaya, James. "Indigenous Law and Its Contribution to Global Pluralism." *Indigenous Law Journal*, vol. 6, no. 1, 2007, pp. 3–12.

Anmani mak Kum. Wapikoni Mobile, 2012.

"Apresentação." *Video nas Aldeias*, www.videonasaldeias.org.br/2009/vna.php. Accessed 26 Apr. 2024.

Atikuat nimeteut. Directed by Pishu Pierre Pilot, Wapikoni Mobile, 2013.

Aufderheide, Pat. "'You See the World of the Other and You Look at Your Own': The Evolution of the Video in the Villages Project." *Journal of Film and Video*, vol. 60, no. 2, 2008, pp. 26–34.

Barbeau, Manon. "Du Wapikoni mobile et du Vidéo Paradiso vers la maison des cultures nomades: 'Aller vers.'" *Séquences: La revue de cinéma*, vol. 243, 2006, pp. 22–23.

———. Interview. Conducted by Kester Dyer, 5 May 2014.

Beeston, Laura. "Montreal Diary: Wapikoni Mobile Offers a Creative Outlet." *The Gazette*, 25 Oct. 2012, montrealgazette.com/news/montreal/montreal-diary-wapikoni-mobile-offers-a-creative-outlet.

Bégin, Jean-Yves. "Le groupe de recherches sociales de l'O.N.F." *Séquences*, no. 59, 1969, pp. 14–22.

Blocus 138—Innu Resistance. Directed by Réal Junior Leblanc, Wapikoni Mobile, 2012.

Boivin, Aurélien. "Présentation." *Menaud, maître-draveur*, by Félix-Antoine Savard, Bibliothèque québécoise, 1992, pp. 7–20.

Bouchard, Vincent. "Cinomade and the Fight against HIV/AIDS Pandemic in Burkina Faso." *CALL: Irish Journal for Culture, Arts, Literature and Language*, vol. 2, no. 1, 2017, https://doi.org/10.21427/D7R985.

"Cinomade." *Africiné*, 2020, www.africine.org/structure/cinomade/1411.

Coeurs nomades. Directed by Joyce Grégoire, Wapikoni Mobile, 2013.

Coureurs de nuit. Directed by Canouk Newashish, Wapikoni Mobile, 2005.

Delâge, Denys. *Bitter Feast: Americans and Europeans in Northeastern North America, 1600–1664.* Translated by Jane Brierley, U of British Columbia P, 1993.

De passage. Directed by Sacha Dubé and Billy Roy Mowatt, Wapikoni Mobile, 2011.

Des forêts de Kitcisakik aux forêts de Xingu. Directed by Evelyne Papatie, Wapikoni Mobile, 2008.

Dumont, Jean-Guillaume. "Manon Barbeau et l'ONF—Rompre l'isolement par la création." *Le Devoir*, 12 June 2004, www.ledevoir.com/societe/56734/manon-barbeau-et-l-onf-rompre-l-isolement-par-la-creation.

Finding the Light. Directed by Emilio Wawatie et al., Wapikoni Mobile, 2013.

Froger, Marion. *Le cinéma à l'épreuve de la communauté: Le cinéma francophone de l'Office National du Film, 1960–1985*. PU de Montréal, 2009.

Ginsburg, Faye. "Indigenous Media: Faustian Contract or Global Village?" *Cultural Anthropology*, vol. 6, no. 1, Feb. 1991, pp. 92–112.

Gittings, Christopher E. *Canadian National Cinema: Ideology, Difference and Representation*. Routledge, 2002.

Helfield, Gillian. "'I' Y Ava't un' Fois' (Once Upon a Time): Films as Folktales in Québécois Cinéma Direct." *Folklore/Cinema: Popular Film as Vernacular Culture*, edited by Sharon R. Sherman and Mikel J. Koven, Utah State UP, 2007, pp. 10–30.

Indian Taxi. Directed by Kevin Papatie and Abraham Côté, Wapikoni Mobile, 2011.

Ka Kushpian. Directed by Tshiuetin Vollant, Wapikoni Mobile, 2001.

Kokom Déménage. Directed by Evelyne Papatie and Vince Papatie, Wapikoni Mobile, 2006.

Le lac Abitibi. Directed by Mélanie Kistabish, Wapikoni Mobile, 2005.

Marceau, Stéphane Guimont. "Le Wapikoni mobile: Conquête d'un nouveau territoire de citoyenneté pour de jeunes autochtones." *ACME: An International E-Journal for Critical Geographies*, vol. 12, no. 3, 2013, pp. 551–75.

Marchessault, Janine. "Amateur Video and the Challenge for Change (1995)." *Challenge for Change: Activist Documentary at the National Film Board of Canada*, edited by Thomas Waugh et al., McGill-Queen's UP, 2010, pp. 354–65.

Marshall, Bill. *Quebec National Cinema*. McGill-Queen's UP, 2000.

Meskano. Directed by Debby Flamand, Wapikoni Mobile, 2012.

Morris, Peter. *Embattled Shadows: A History of Canadian Cinema, 1895–1939*. McGill-Queen's UP, 1978.

Niosi, Laurence. "Odile Joannette succède à Manon Barbeau à la tête de Wapikoni." *Radio-Canada*, 20 Mar. 2018, ici.radio-canada.ca/nouvelle/1090459/odile-joannette- wapikoni-directrice-generale-nomination-manon-barbeau.

Nous sommes. Directed by Kevin Papatie, Wapikoni Mobile, 2009.

Papatie, Kevin. Interview. Conducted by Kester Dyer, 16 Feb. 2014.

Pearson, Wendy Gay. "Detours Homeward: Indigenizing the Road Movie." *The Canadian Journal of Native Studies*, vol. 31, no. 1, 2011, pp. 139–54.

Rien sur les mocassins. Directed by Eden Malina Awashish, Wapikoni Mobile, 2015.

The Romance of Transportation in Canada. Directed by Colin Low, National Film Board of Canada, 1952.

Rosen, Philip. "Border Times and Geopolitical Frames." *Canadian Journal of Film Studies*, vol. 15, no. 2, fall 2006, pp. 2–19.

The Routes. Directed by James McDougall, Wapikoni Mobile, 2014.

Les routes du Québec. Directed by Maurice Proulx, Service de ciné-photographie de la province de Québec, 1951.

Sédillot, Catherine Laurent. "Why Make Movies? Some Atikamekw Answers." *Post Script*, vol. 29, no. 3, summer 2010, pp. 70–82.

Serpereau, Antonin. *Pratiques médiatiques alternatives et espaces publics: Le cas du Wapikoni Mobile.* 2011. Université du Québec, Montréal, doctoral thesis.

Shohat, Ella, and Robert Stam. *Unthinking Eurocentrism: Multiculturalism and the Media.* Routledge, 1994.

Smith, Linda Tuhiwai. *Indigenizing Methodologies: Research and Indigenous Peoples.* 2nd ed., Zed Books, 2012.

Smoke Signals. Directed by Chris Eyre, Miramax Films, 1998.

Starblanket, Noel. "A Voice for Canadian Indians: An Indian Film Crew (1968)." *Challenge for Change: Activist Documentary at the National Film Board of Canada*, edited by Thomas Waugh et al., McGill-Queen's UP, 2010, pp. 38–40.

Trans-Canada Express. Directed by Stanley Hawes, National Film Board of Canada, 1944.

Vers Vancouver. Directed by Bradley Brazeau and Evelyne Papatie, Wapikoni Mobile, 2013.

Le voyage. Directed by Charlotte Poucachiche, Wapikoni Mobile, 2011.

Les Voyageurs. Directed by Bernard Gosselin, National Film Board of Canada, 1964.

Voyageurs. National Film Board of Canada, 1978.

Wapikoni Mobile. *Rapport annuel.* 2005.

———. *Rapport annuel.* 2017.

———. *Rapport annuel.* 2022–23. *Squarespace*, static1.squarespace.com/static/5ceff84615b6f00001ce5366/t/65ef08c0850fc2101426e836/1710164264716/RAPPORT+ANNUEL+WAPIKONI+2022-2023.pdf. Accessed 1 July 2024.

Waugh, Thomas. *The Romance of Transgression in Canada.* McGill-Queen's UP, 2006.

Wente, Jesse. "Debwewin: Truth, Reconciliation and Art." Martin Walsh Memorial Lecture. Film and Media Studies Association of Canada Annual Conference, May 2017.

Wigwas. Directed by Karl Chevrier, Wapikoni Mobile, 2013.

William Arighi

Migrant Literature and the United Nations Convention on Refugees

Jessy Carton argues that "literary studies can contribute to the evaluation of one of the major international law standards of today: the definition [of refugee] that gives access to international protection" (333). In her subsequent analysis of Aleksander Hemon's stories, Carton uses literary methodology to demonstrate the inadequacies of the United Nations Convention Relating to the Status of Refugees of 1951 (also known as the Geneva Convention) as the foundation for international refugee laws. Literary methodology can be used to interpret the convention because the conditions that the convention lays out as necessary to qualify as a refugee require the recounting of biographical details in a narrative form to establish credible fear (Luiselli 11–13; Carton 333). Conversely, the legal nexus that requires a causal relationship be established between life events and present fear provides the basis for many pieces of refugee literature, even beyond memoir. As a result of the narrative work that the convention engenders, assigning it in the literature classroom provides students with both context and stakes for the study of literatures of migration since 1945.

The contemporary system for managing refugee populations and admissions was set up by the United Nations in the wake of World War II. Millions of displaced persons—demobilized military units, concentration camp survivors, persecuted minorities, those fleeing the invading Allies or the Axis powers—were effectively homeless and stateless in areas all across Europe and its imperial territories. Returning them to the homes from which they had been displaced was often not only impractical because of widespread devastation but also undesirable, since many displaced persons now feared the populations alongside whom they had previously lived. As a result, one of the first major pieces of business for the newly formed United Nations was the establishment of rules pertaining to the settling of displaced persons; the United Nations High Commissioner for Refugees (UNHCR) was established by the UN General Assembly in 1950 in order to address this. A year later, the member states of the UN ratified the Geneva Convention to legalize the right of displaced persons to enter and settle in states other than those in which they had previously resided and to ensure that they would not be subjected subsequently to prejudicial mistreatment. The 1951 convention pertains exclusively to those displaced within Europe prior to ratification, but since these limits conflicted with the scope of UNHCR activities, most UN member states adopted the Protocol Relating to the Status of Refugees (also called the New York Protocol) in 1967 (Goodwin-Gill). The 1967 protocol extends the terms of the 1951 convention to all present and future displaced persons outside their country of official belonging, regardless of geography or time frame.

The convention and protocol are simultaneously limited in scope and capacious in principle, and that contradiction is a productive tool for students to develop empathetic reading habits and critical thinking. Since the convention and protocol are meant to address a situation of statelessness brought about through prejudice or war, the definition of *refugee* in article 1A(2) of the convention is broad, covering all those who,

> owing to well-founded fear of being persecuted for reasons of race, religion, nationality, membership of a particular social group or political opinion, is outside the country of his nationality and is unable or, owing to such fear, is unwilling to avail himself of the protection of that country; or who, not having a nationality and being outside the country of his former habitual residence as a result of such events, is unable or, owing to such fear, is unwilling to return to it.
> (United Nations, Convention)

The breadth of the covered characteristics allowed the convention to adjudicate the placement of not only Jewish displaced persons but also the Roma, Catholic, communist, and even homosexual and disabled displaced persons that the Nazi government had deemed enemies of the state. The potential characteristics that allow someone to seek out refugee status overlap significantly with the characteristics protected by antidiscrimination laws in many developed countries and are immediately recognizable to many students.

However, the nexus requirement—"the causal link between the persecution feared and one or more of the five Convention grounds" (Carton 332)—restricts the number of individuals actually covered and provides for the often painful recounting of biography that refugees must perform to be resettled. Additional difficulties in acquiring refugee status include the fact that the individual must be outside the state to which they are counted as belonging, thus precluding mobilization of the UNHCR for internally displaced persons, currently an estimated 62.5 million people ("Figures"), and that refugees are defined as those who cannot return to their country of nationality. Therefore, in the case of individuals with multiple nationalities (i.e., multiple passports or permission to apply for passports), the convention specifically prohibits them from being granted refugee status if they have not sought protection from all their nationalities, or if they do not have a valid reason based on "well-founded fear" not to do so.

Article 1A(2) contains an important ambiguity: namely, the protection of those who have "membership of a particular social group." This condition has been used to argue for an increasing protection of women from patriarchal violence (United States Department of Justice 3), but other potential uses have been only fitfully successful, such as its use to protect transgender individuals and those with stigmatized disabilities or long-term illnesses.[1] Another particularly difficult area of adjudication arises from those fleeing organized gangs, a problem that affects many seeking asylum in the United States (United Nations High Commissioner, "Guidance Note" 1). One reason that this can be so difficult is that while article 1A(2) of the convention provides protection to members of "a particular social group," article 1F(b) excludes those who have committed "a serious non-political crime outside the country of refuge prior to his admission to that country as a refugee" (United Nations, Convention). Since many who flee gangs were themselves once affiliated with gangs—often for survival—these matters can prove difficult to resolve (United Nations High Commissioner, "Guidance Note" 6).[2]

The 1951 convention also contains numerous provisions for the treatment of refugees once they are resettled in a new state, including access to housing and the right to work. All provisions are meant to ensure the security of the refugee, and member states of the UN are bound to honor these provisions (United Nations, Convention). But the reality is not nearly so straightforward as the convention stipulates, and the lived experiences of refugee groups, as well as the literature that represents them, can reveal "the intersection of domestic and foreign political interests and the limits of neoliberal policies in providing the socio-economic freedoms they promise," as Heyang Julie Kae has noted (139).

Three fundamental principles underpin the 1951 convention: nondiscrimination (refugees shall not be excluded based on their identity), nonpenalization (refugees shall not be penalized for violating immigration laws as a part of their flight from persecution), and nonrefoulement, whereby the signatories shall not "expel or return ('refouler') a refugee in any manner whatsoever to the frontiers of territories where his life or freedom would be threatened" based on the conditions for which they are seeking asylum (United Nations, Convention). In practice, this has meant the creation of large refugee camps in countries bordering those suffering from societal collapse, and currently, sixty-nine percent of all refugees are hosted in neighboring countries, while seventy-five percent of all refugees are hosted in low- and middle-income countries ("Figures"). Currently, Türkiye (which, interestingly, does not recognize the geographic expanse of the 1967 protocol) is home to the largest number of refugees in the world, most from neighboring Syria, while Bangladesh's camps house over 900,000 of the over one million refugees from across the border in Myanmar ("Annex 1").

Students in the United States may need help understanding the distinction between a "refugee," as defined by the 1951 convention, and an "asylum seeker," as understood in the context of the US legal code. Though the same experiences apply for both "refugees" and "asylum seekers" under US law, the latter are those who are already in the United States or who request asylum at a US port of entry ("Refugees"). Refugees, meanwhile, may be in any country other than their own and petition for resettlement in the United States from there. The distinction primarily affects how the individual encounters immigration authorities, but, particularly with the heightened attention paid to immigration over the past thirty years, such a distinction may have psychological and material consequences that are visible in the representation of journeys along land routes to the United States and those routed through official refugee agencies from elsewhere.[3]

Another distinction separates "the exile" and "the refugee," both of whom have left their countries because of persecution or governmental edict. Timothy K. August has highlighted that the distinction between "exile" and "refugee" is largely one of representativity, noting that the figure of the exile stands apart for its solitariness and its refusal to be a part of its "new land" (71). The figure of the refugee, with its affinity toward those persecuted for belonging to particular groups (as outlined in the 1951 convention) and its emphasis on the "refuge" of resettlement, more closely resembles other forms of migrant literature than the literature of exile, according to August (72).

Literature that depicts the experiences of this particular subset of migrants, whether refugees or asylum seekers, can benefit from being taught alongside the UN convention and protocol. The productive ambiguity of the definition of *refugee* can help students see the high stakes involved in the recounting of traumatic episodes; aside from the psychological well-being a refugee may experience through the process of self-narration, refugee literature can mean the difference between resettlement and refoulement. Indeed, Valeria Luiselli's *Tell Me How It Ends: An Essay in Forty Questions*—a memoir that juxtaposes the ease with which Luiselli applies for a green card as a creative professional with the credible fear interviews she volunteers to translate—centers the ethical dilemmas involved in translating for Spanish-speaking asylum seekers. The UN convention and protocol help contextualize literary texts like Luiselli's within the practical constraints of bureaucracy that media accounts of immigration tend to ignore, underscoring her own ethical concerns as a migrant trying to be faithful to other migrants and to her outside responsibilities.

If storytelling offers the refugee certain legal protections, though, it also risks homogenizing and sentimentalizing the refugee's story. The publication and marketing of refugee literature often depends on a set of circumscribed conventions that encourage empathetic feeling. As Bishupal Limbu remarks, "If the notion of human rights as storytelling is to have much traction, it must involve primarily a very specific sort of story, the sort that . . . falls within the genre of sentimental fiction with its scenes of suffering" (78). This can be seen in popular contemporary refugee narratives such as Edwidge Danticat's *Brother, I'm Dying* and Thi Bui's *The Best We Could Do*, which foreground experiences of loss and nostalgia as central to the migratory subject in the United States.

While there is a danger in reducing refugee stories to the sentimental tropes of novelistic practice, the production of empathy can also be a powerful tool for teaching critical thought. As Eric Leake points out, developing empathy as a habit of mind can produce "not a suspension of critical engagement but of suspending rejection prior to understanding." Leake discusses empathy in relation to assignments that task students with taking on another person's perspective, but the contrast of the pathos of refugee narratives and the prescriptive conditions for admittance in the convention and protocol may produce a similarly "suspend[ed] rejection" in students who might otherwise dismiss the purely sentimental appeal. The dual appeal to students' understanding—the heart and the head—can be enhanced through prompts that require them to apply the convention and protocol to literary texts in perspective-taking assignments such as those Leake assigns.[4]

Focusing student attention on narratives of and by refugees and placing them within a critical framework of refugee experience can also expose "the costs of US imperialism and destabiliz[e] the primacy of the nation-state by centrally locating refugees within interconnected matrices of colonialism, militarism, and globalization" (Schlund-Vials 201). This approach, called critical refugee studies, can disrupt the facile assimilation of narratives of movement into stories of "becoming American" and encourage students to examine critically their own complicity with structures of exclusion. The UN convention and protocol, which structure refugee admittance to the United States but which are inadequate to enforce the UN's provisions within the territories of its member states or to require its member states to admit specific numbers of refugees, are crucial documents for students to understand the legal and logistical barriers that influence narrative form and rhetorical convention.

I have tried to maintain throughout this essay a distinction between the figure of the refugee and other migrant figures. Nonetheless, I should emphasize that to invoke a singular figure of "the refugee" may perform a universalization that accords neither with the lived experiences of many refugees or with the immensely different texts of, say, Ben Rawlence's *City of Thorns*, a multiperspectival journalistic account of the refugee camp complex in Dadaab, Kenya, and Clemantine Wamariya and Elizabeth Weil's *The Girl Who Smiled Beads*, a first-person memoir of Wamariya's flight from the Rwandan genocide.[5] Despite differences in terms of date, perspective, and structure, such texts coincide in ways that can expose for students the fundamental importance of such institutions as the UN High Commissioner for Refugees and its abject failure to secure for everyone the basic freedoms and rights that we would like to take for granted. As Vinh Nguyen has argued, "While refugees may seem exceptional, as told though some spectacular stories of success, there is nothing singular or unique about the ways in which the state attempts to assimilate them into the nation's capitalist 'melting pot'" (111). Though not all migrant literature will depict the particulars of an asylum interview, modern literatures of migration, like refugee literature, articulate global networks of movement and solidarity within the lived experiences of global racial capital. As the legal underpinning of how one's movements will be categorized in their new home—whether as requiring assistance and supervision or offering skills and capital—the UN convention and protocol offer a clear but frustrating framework for the exploration of refugee rights and a complex entryway into the literatures of migration.

Notes

1. In 2012, the UN High Commissioner for Refugees acknowledged that "the application of the refugee definition remains inconsistent" in regards to LGBTI individuals (United Nations High Commissioner, "Guidelines"). The agency also recognizes refugees with disabilities as having particular concerns in addition to those of refugees without disabilities (United Nations High Commissioner, "Need").

2. Carton summarizes and references many other difficulties in the legal and political history of, and in the administration of, the 1951 convention (331–33).

3. See, for example, the formerly undocumented Salvadorean American poet Javier Zamora's experiences as narrated in an interview by Deborah Paredez.

4. Prompts that ask students to be advocates for the refugees of the narratives, rather than judges or refugees themselves, may be more effective in this regard, since they neither place students in a position of authority over the refugees or in a position to co-opt their experiences. See Golden on perspective-taking pedagogies. Thanks to Dan Fraizer and the Writing Fellows Program at Springfield College for helping me develop an assignment using this framework.

5. See Goyal for how the genre of the "refugee novel" decontextualizes the particular historical conditions that structure individual refugee experiences.

Works Cited

"Annex 1—Populations Protected and/or Assisted by UNHCR by Country/Territory of Asylum." *UNHCR*, 13 June 2024, www.unhcr.org/refugee-statistics/insights/annexes/trends-annexes.html?situation=1.

August, Timothy K. "Re-placing the Accent: From the Exile to Refugee Position." *MELUS: Multi-ethnic Literature of the United States*, vol. 41, no. 3, fall 2016, pp. 68–88, https://doi.org/10.1093/melus/mlw028.

Bui, Thi. *The Best We Could Do.* Abrams Books, 2017.

Carton, Jessy. "Complicated Refugees: A Study of the 1951 Geneva Convention Grounds in Aleksandar Hemon's Life Narrative." *Law and Literature*, vol. 30, no. 2, pp. 331–47, https://doi.org/10.1080/1535685X.2018.1429994.

Danticat, Edwidge. *Brother, I'm Dying*. Knopf, 2007.

"Figures at a Glance." *UNHCR*, 13 June 2024, www.unhcr.org/en-us/figures-at-a-glance.html.

Golden, Paullett. "Contextualized Writing: Promoting Audience-Centered Writing through Scenario-Based Learning." *International Journal for the Scholarship of Teaching and Learning*, vol. 12, no. 1, 2018, https://doi.org/10.20429/ijsotl.2018.120106.

Goodwin-Gill, Guy S. Introduction. *Protocol Relating to the Status of Refugees. United Nations Audiovisual Library of International Law*, Aug. 2008, legal.un.org/avl/ha/prsr/prsr.html.

Goyal, Yogita. "'We Are All Migrants': The Refugee Novel and the Claims of Universalism." *Modern Fiction Studies*, vol. 66, no. 2, 2020, pp. 239–59.

Kae, Heyang Julie. "Collateral Narratives: Neoliberal Citizenship, Juvenile Delinquency, and Cambodian American Refugee Youth in *A.K.A. Don Bonus*." *MELUS: Multi-ethnic Literature of the United States*, vol. 41, no. 3, fall 2016, pp. 133–52, https://doi.org/10.1093/melus/mlw022.

Leake, Eric. "Writing Pedagogies of Empathy: As Rhetoric and Disposition." *Composition Forum*, vol. 34, 2016, compositionforum.com/issue/34/empathy.php.

Limbu, Bishupal. "The Permissible Narratives of Human Rights; or, How to Be a Refugee." *Criticism*, vol. 60, no. 1, 2018, pp. 75–98.

Luiselli, Valeria. *Tell Me How It Ends: An Essay in Forty Questions*. Coffee House Press, 2017.

Nguyen, Vinh. "Refugeetude: When Does a Refugee Stop Being a Refugee?" *Social Text*, vol. 37, no. 2, June 2019, pp. 109–31, https://doi.org/10.1215/01642472-7371003.

Rawlence, Ben. *City of Thorns: Nine Lives in the World's Largest Refugee Camp*. Picador, 2016.

"Refugees and Asylum." *U.S. Citizenship and Immigration Services*, 12 Nov. 2015, www.uscis.gov/humanitarian/refugees-and-asylum.

Schlund-Vials, Cathy J. "The Subjects of 1975: Delineating the Necessity of Critical Refugee Studies." *MELUS: Multi-ethnic Literature of the United States*, vol., 41, no. 3, fall 2016, pp. 199–203, https://doi.org/10.1093/melus/mlw019.

United Nations, General Assembly. Convention Relating to the Status of Refugees. Resolution 429, 28 July 1951. *United Nations Office of the High Commissioner for Human Rights*, www.ohchr.org/en/instruments-mechanisms/instruments/convention-relating-status-refugees.

———. Protocol Relating to the Status of Refugees. Resolution 2198, 16 Dec. 1966. *United Nations Office of the High Commissioner for Human Rights*, www.ohchr.org/en/instruments-mechanisms/instruments/protocol-relating-status-refugees.

United Nations High Commissioner for Refugees. "Guidance Note on Refugee Claims Relating to Victims of Organized Gangs." Mar. 2010. *UNHCR*, 31 Mar. 2010, www.refworld.org/docid/4bb21fa02.html.

————. "Guidelines on International Protection No. 9: Claims to Refugee Status Based on Sexual Orientation and/or Gender Identity within the Context of Article 1A(2) of the 1951 Convention and/or Its 1967 Protocol Relating to the Status of Refugees." 23 Oct. 2012. *UNHCR*, www.unhcr.org/ 509136ca9.pdf.

————. "Need to Know Guidance: Working with Persons with Disabilities in Forced Displacement." 2019. *UNHCR*, www.refworld.org/docid/ 5ce271164.html.

United States Department of Justice, Executive Office for Immigration Review, Board of Immigration Appeals. *Brief of* Amicus Curiae*: The United Nations High Commissioner for Refugees in Support of Respondents. UNHCR*, 21 Nov. 2012, www.refworld.org/pdfid/50b5c2a22.pdf.

Wamariya, Clementine, and Elizabeth Weil. *The Girl Who Smiled Beads: A Story of War and What Comes After*. Crown, 2018.

Zamora, Javier. "*Unaccompanied*: An Interview with Javier Zamora." Conducted by Deborah Paredez. *Poets.org*, 1 Oct. 2017, poets.org/text/ unaccompanied-interview-javier-zamora.

Alexander Dawson

Disability in Narratives of Migration

The popular image of migration, that of a line of people carrying as many of their belongings as possible, walking endlessly to an unseen destination, suggests that all migrants are able-bodied. In the Global South, home to "the majority of the world's displaced people" (Crock et al. 115) and an estimated eighty percent of all people with disabilities (Grech 52), this is not the reality. The migrants with disabilities depicted in both the literatures and the films of the Global South attest to this. These characters, who often trouble the unstable boundaries of economic migrant, asylum seeker, or refugee, foreground the physical journey within which the disabled body figures centrally.[1] Migrating within or away from postcolonies, their mobility is informed by the violence of civil war and structural impoverishment that are legacies of colonial conquest (Berghs 443; Grech 56; Barker, "'Radiant Affliction'" 105). When such figures and environments are portrayed in literature and film, they invoke a complex ethics of representation of concern to scholars of both postcolonial studies and disability studies. By reading migrants with disabilities through an intersectional lens of postcolonial disability studies, we emphasize their multifaceted subjectivity. Such an approach is derived from theories that center the racialized and embodied experiences of marginalized communities. Through this framework, we can excavate the social and geopolitical construction of disability and migrancy and thus extend and nuance conceptions of both migrants and people with disabilities.

Disability is a theoretically capacious and fluid term used to denote one's physical or cognitive deviation from an anticipated norm. Disability is produced when an impairment overlaps with a situational "failure to accommodate, to adapt, and assist" either structurally or attitudinally (Crock et al. ix). This definition registers the shift from locating disability in the individual (medical model) to locating it in one's environment (social model), a move that frames society as the entity in need of change (Siebers 72–73). The cultural model, a lens that still factors in the role of social environment but, unlike the social model, also takes into account the materiality of the body, has been critiqued for not being contextually specific enough when considering disability in the postcolony (Mitchell and Snyder, *Cultural Locations* 10; Barker, *Postcolonial Fiction* 25). Herein lies the difficulty of crafting a transnational approach to disability studies that accounts for migrants with disabilities. It is necessary to adopt an interdisciplinary approach that combines disability, migration, and postcolonial studies, one that advances a more diverse understanding of migrant subjectivity and the embodied nature of migration. Such a methodology emphasizes the historical and cultural contexts that differentiate migrants because it foregrounds the mutually reinforcing origins of migration and disablement. In so doing, it extends the scopes of migration and postcolonial studies, both of which have been critiqued for eliding disability from their purview.[2]

Literature and film that portrays the migration of postcolonial subjects with disabilities is invaluable not just because it depicts an often overlooked material reality but also because it provides new points of entry into studying postcoloniality and its relationship to the body. Depending on how we approach them, the potential of such works is manifold. In some instances, they counter reductive assumptions that pair migrancy and disability with dependence (Dawson); in others, they demonstrate how the injury acquired through colonial violence morphs into the disability produced by the newly elected government. However, the depiction of disability across these narratives raises ethical concerns when it is deployed as "an opportunistic metaphorical device" (Mitchell and Snyder, *Narrative Prosthesis* 47). A common technique in postcolonial literature is to allegorize the body politic through a character's disability or to translate a postcolonial environment of dysfunction and disorder (an environment of civil war or decolonization, for instance) through the "negative affect" of a character (Barker, "Disability" 102; Quayson 128, 142). The issue with such portrayals is that they perpetuate harmful stereotypes about disability in lieu of articulating the lived experience of a person with disabilities. That said, an uneasy tension arises in the fact that colonization is a project of "mass disablement, and that the *acquisition* of disability may be tied into wider patterns of dispossession" (Barker and Murray 69). In this way, postcolonial disability scholars have looked to rejuvenate reading disability as metaphor through a "situated reading" that questions how metaphors would be read within the specific community being portrayed (72).

Such a methodology reveals the complex depiction of disability in the mid-journey portrayal of migrants with disabilities who serve as beacons of hope for their able-bodied migrant peers. The disabilities of these characters act as a "friction" (Cresswell 109, 113) that, while inhibiting mobility in characters with disabilities, incites a spark that motivates their able-bodied migrant peers to endure the difficult journey. Abdulla in Ngũgĩ wa Thiong'-o's novel *Petals of Blood*, a character who loses his leg after he is shot fighting in the Mau Mau rebellion against British colonizers in Kenya, is one such example. Abdulla is denied a job by the government on account of his disability in the wake of political independence. His missing limb thus comes to symbolize the "cost and the disillusionment of independence" (Barker, "Disability" 105). Simultaneously, it inspires those traveling with him by foot from Ilmorog to Limaru to persist despite the difficulty of the journey, for to them, his disability signals stoicism and the historical sacrifice he made as a freedom fighter. Abdulla's "stump" transforms before them into "a badge of courage indelibly imprinted on his body," a metaphorical transformation predicated on inaccurate ableist assumptions of what they think Abdulla is capable of achieving (Ngũgĩ 168). This scene preserves a common but misguided line of reasoning that frames disability as an adversity to be overcome by the heroic individual. Such reasoning follows that those unable to overcome their disability be deemed failures when, in reality, the failure should be located in the environment and society that disable. However, Ngũgĩ's portrayal of disability is more complex than this, for his narrativization of Abdulla simultaneously conveys the myriad kinds of dispossession (political, occupational, personal) that Abdulla endures as a person with disabilities in the neocolonial aftermath of independence.

A similar scenario plays out in Moussa Touré's film *La Pirogue* (*The Pirogue*), in which Aziz, a transfemoral amputee who boards a pirogue with other desperate migrants hoping to reach Spain from Senegal, serves as a beacon of hope who motivates those around him to continue their journey. Halfway across the Atlantic, Aziz agrees on the need to stay positive, stating, "The glass is half full, like my leg" (00:48:06–00:48:08). The optimistic proverb puts the minds of his companions at ease because it simultaneously conceals, through simile, a sinister reading of disability as lack or emptiness in that Aziz is "half full," or incomplete. While this encourages the migrants to persist in their dangerous undertaking, their optimism is subverted when another migrant solemnly fishes one of Aziz's crutches from the water remaining in the pirogue after the storm that kills Aziz. Like the character of Abdulla, however, the character of Aziz testifies to a specific material circumstance of disability in the postcolony in that his purpose in reaching Spain is "to find a device for my leg" (00:36:07–00:36:10), a fact that subtly gestures to the difficulty he faces in trying to receive, or perhaps afford, adequate medical care in Senegal or his unnamed point of origin.

A situated reading of disability extends the cultural model of disability by questioning the constructed nature of bodily normativity and interrogating how conceptions of disability are culturally and situationally informed. In so doing, it subverts a Western bias in disability studies that elides the unique context environing characters in non-Western spaces (Grech; Barker, "'Radiant Affliction'" 114; Barker and Murray). Migrants in flight from persecution, for example, might not ascribe to the kind of able-bodied normativity that thrives in a place of relative safety. Crises that give rise to flight, such as conflict or natural disaster, render injury "more common and more visible than elsewhere" and thus increase the likelihood that disability is more norm than not (Barker, *Postcolonial Fiction* 24). Under such conditions, one might experience what Jasbir K. Puar theorizes as a state of "debilitation" rather than disablement, wherein populations under attack are targeted through a "biopolitics of debilitation" intended to prolong the event of impairment while concealing the transition to disability (xiii). Given the mobility that characterizes migrancy, migrants with disabilities flow across and between spaces and thus continually adjust their situational contexts. This means that disability is perpetually in flux, a phenomenon that must be considered when undertaking an analysis of literature and film.

The situatedness of disability for migrants is well documented in the journey of Jeebleh in Nuruddin Farah's novel *Links*, a text that employs disability to represent the very real consequences of violent conflict as well as the uncanny nature of migrant return. Returning to the Somali capital of Mogadishu, a city now fraught with clan conflict, after having lived twenty years in exile in the United States, Jeebleh is confronted by a multitude of local Somalis who have visible injuries and ailments stemming from the violence and socioeconomic conditions of their surroundings. Throughout these interactions, Farah portrays disability, or in this case debility, in order to underscore Jeebleh's unbelonging on account of his being able-bodied, a point inflected by the fact that he feels "alienated from himself" and "ill at ease" after having been in exile for so long (42). Such encounters between the able-bodied Jeebleh and the debilitated local population are indicative of an "aesthetic nervousness" wherein "the dominant protocols of representation within the literary text are short-circuited in relation to disability" (Quayson 15). As Jeebleh reckons with the "radical contingency" of his own body and personhood (17), he locates the stigma of disability in the bodies of those around him, who, in reality, understand disability to be the norm. This difference in perspective between returnee and local parallels how Jeebleh's Westernized view of the city casts it as a failed state, a point destabilized only once he himself becomes temporarily disabled toward the novel's conclusion and finds, to his shock, that he is in fact no different than those waging battle around him. Thus, while we might read *Links* as a novel that frames the disabilities of Mogadishans as metaphors for "the wider body politic" and symbols of a failed state (Masterson 283), we uncover a much more intricate representation of disability when we take an intersectional approach to migration, postcoloniality, and disability. The flawed methodology of an outsider who attempts to intervene without first taking into account cultural context or, in the words of Farah, "the clumsiness of American attitudes towards complex situations" now becomes legible ("Witnessing" 337).

A similarly informed reading of context in Uwem Akpan's novella "Luxurious Hearses" demonstrates that, in reading migrants with disabilities, we can excavate how postcolonial refugeehood and disability derive from the cartographic violence of colonialism. Fleeing religious conflict after Sharia law is proclaimed over Khamfi in northern Nigeria, Jubril, a sixteen-year-old boy, is forced to conceal the wound of his recently amputated hand from the eyes of other passengers on the bus with whom he is riding south to presumed safety. Having willingly offered his hand to be cut off after he was caught stealing, the devout Muslim is painfully aware that the revelation of his limb will be a dead giveaway to those around him who abhor his religious beliefs. Thus, he passes as both Christian and able-bodied to avoid the suspicion and terror he anticipates from them. Having been baptized in the South but raised Muslim in the North, the complicated and "mangled story of [Jubril's] religious identity" is conveyed through his having to flee Khamfi because he appears Christian while also having to disguise himself on the bus to avoid being read as Muslim (Akpan 320). When Jubril steps onto the bus, he thus shifts into a space in which his wound takes on a new religiously inflected stigma of disability. While the wound might be read as a symbol for both his deracination and the fractured nation, a situated reading of its material existence conveys the contemporary consequences of Nigeria's colonial history. The geographic division of the nation based on ethnic and religious identity, an outcome of British colonial rule, politically destabilized Nigeria and led in the long term to the kinds of conflict and religious tension that Jubril now flees. Jubril's intersecting identities of internally displaced person and person with disabilities are thus social constructs years in the making.

Finally, migrants with disabilities are figures who demonstrate that both disability and migration are constructs that can be mutually reinforcing. We see this in J. M. Coetzee's novel *Life and Times of Michael K*, in the migration of Michael and Anna K, characters who flee Cape Town to Prince Albert during a fictionalized civil war in apartheid-era South Africa. Anna K's limbs, swollen from dropsy (edema), complicate her ability to flee without the support of her son, who, denied a wheelchair by the hospital, pushes her in a stolen wheelbarrow.[3] Michael, who himself was born with a cleft lip, learns the stigma of disability from a young age, when he is withdrawn from school and institutionalized "because of his disfigurement and because his mind was not quick" (Coetzee 3). He is thus segregated based on a physical deviation that is incorrectly associated with lower intelligence, an act that negates his access to the kind of formal education that would invalidate such presumed unintelligence. The long-term consequences of this are his social discomfort and "endemic silence," traits that lead those around him to further ostracize him and literary scholars to diagnose him as having autism spectrum disorder (Quayson 172). The Kafkaesque difficulty he has in obtaining travel permits to leave a Cape Town under threat of siege is due in large part to both his and his mother's disabilities. The police, responsible for issuing permits, view him as an "idiot" as they stare at his lip and refuse to help, and he is informed by a train clerk not only that his mother's physical condition does "not constitute special grounds" for a travel permit but also that he should "not . . . mention her condition at all" if he wants a permit (Coetzee 9, 20). These events heavily insinuate that the delay in receiving permits is based on the fact that both he and his mother have disabilities.[4] In this way, their migration is thwarted by the stigma of disability, which, in turn, becomes physically disabling once they flee (without permission) by means of the wheelbarrow. His cleft lip and her dropsy are conditions that become disabling because of the societal expectations of able-bodied normativity within their social environment. Simultaneously, this same environment produces their migranthood through the civil war that displaces them. The experiences of these migrants with disabilities thus expose the nature of disability and migrancy as mutually reinforcing social and geopolitical constructs.

Migrants with disabilities provoke comprehensive examination of how migration and disability intersect; when a reader analyzes the causes of migration, they practice a methodology that echoes that which should be used to interrogate the production of disability. These characters simultaneously foreground the embodied experience of migration, the precarious nature of the journey, and the vulnerability, desperation, and hope of those who undertake it. In postcolonial narratives, these material consequences of the colonial legacy are made evident through a reading practice that remains attentive to the nuances of disability as metaphor and the cultural-historical context of the narrative.

Notes

1. The analysis I offer in this essay focuses on a specific kind of migrant and migration and says little about the journeys undertaken by the economically stable, documented, encamped, or detained, nor does it encapsulate the experiences of migrants with invisible disabilities (such as neurological impairments). While this is a result of the heightened visibility in migration narratives of physical disability in displaced populations, these elided examples remain reality for people the world over.

2. On migration studies eliding disability, see Pisani and Grech, "Disability" 422–23; Crock et al. 115; Duda-Mikulin et al. 2. On postcolonial studies eliding disability, see Barker, *Postcolonial Fiction* 3; Barker and Murray 61; Quayson xii–xiii.

3. The scene of a migrant with disabilities in flight from violent conflict being pushed in a wheelbarrow, a common image in African literature (Dongala; Mohamed), signifies the desperation and ingenuity of fleeing migrants as well as the insufficient systems of institutional support for people with disabilities.

4. The extent to which race plays a role in their mistreatment—Michael K is identified as a "CM" (short for "colored male") in apartheid South Africa (Coetzee 70)—remains ambiguous in the novel.

Works Cited

Akpan, Uwem. "Luxurious Hearses." *Say You're One of Them*, by Akpan, Little, Brown, 2008, pp. 187–322.

Barker, Clare. "Disability and the Postcolonial Novel." *The Cambridge Companion to the Postcolonial Novel*, edited by Ato Quayson, Cambridge UP, 2015, pp. 99–115.

———. *Postcolonial Fiction and Disability: Exceptional Children, Metaphor, and Materiality*. Palgrave Macmillan, 2011.

———. "'Radiant Affliction': Disability Narratives in Postcolonial Literature." *The Cambridge Companion to Literature and Disability*, edited by Barker and Stuart Murray, Cambridge UP, 2017, pp. 104–20.

Barker, Clare, and Stuart Murray. "Disabling Postcolonialism: Global Disability Cultures and Democratic Criticism." *The Disability Studies Reader*, edited by Lennard J. Davis, 4th ed., Routledge, 2013, pp. 61–73.

Berghs, Maria. "Disability and Displacement in Times of Conflict: Rethinking Migration, Flows and Boundaries." Pisani and Grech, *Disability*, pp. 442–59.

Coetzee, J. M. *Life and Times of Michael K*. Penguin Books, 1985.

Cresswell, Tim. "Friction." *The Routledge Handbook of Mobilities*, edited by Peter Adey et al., Routledge, 2014, pp. 107–16.

Crock, Mary, et al. *The Legal Protection of Refugees with Disabilities: Forgotten and Invisible?* Edward Elgar Publishing, 2017.

Dawson, Alexander. "Stasis in Flight: Reframing Disability and Dependence in the Refugee." *Disability Studies Quarterly*, vol. 39, no. 1, 2019, dsq-sds.org/index.php/dsq/article/view/6285/5186.

Dongala, Emmanuel. *Johnny Mad Dog*. Translated by Maria Louise Archer, Picador, 2006.

Duda-Mikulin, Eva, et al. "Wasted Lives in Scapegoat Britain: Overlaps and Departures between Migration Studies and Disability Studies." *Disability and Society*, 2019, pp. 1–25.

Farah, Nuruddin. *Links*. Penguin Books, 2005.

———. "Witnessing Contemporary Somalia from Abroad: An Interview with Nuruddin Farah." Conducted by Minna Niemi. *Callaloo*, vol. 35, no. 2, 2012, pp. 330–40.

Grech, Shaun. "Disability and the Majority World: A Neocolonial Approach." *Disability and Social Theory: New Developments and Directions*, edited by Dan Goodley et al., Palgrave Macmillan, 2012, pp. 52–69.

Masterson, John. *The Disorder of Things: A Foucauldian Approach to the Work of Nuruddin Farah*. Wits UP, 2013.

Mitchell, David T., and Sharon L. Snyder. *Cultural Locations of Disability*. U of Chicago P, 2006.

———. *Narrative Prosthesis: Disability and the Dependencies of Discourse*. U of Michigan P, 2000.

Mohamed, Nadifa. *The Orchard of Lost Souls*. Farrar, Straus and Giroux, 2013.

Ngũgĩ wa Thiong'o. *Petals of Blood*. 1977. Penguin Books, 2005.

La Pirogue. Directed by Moussa Touré, Les Chauves-Souris, 2012.

Pisani, Maria, and Shaun Grech, editors. *Disability and Forced Migration*. Special issue of *Disability and the Global South*. Vol. 2, no. 1, 2015.

———. "Disability and Forced Migration: Critical Intersectionalities." Pisani and Grech, *Disability*, pp. 421–41.

Puar, Jasbir K. *The Right to Maim: Debility, Capacity, Disability*. Duke UP, 2017.

Quayson, Ato. *Aesthetic Nervousness: Disability and the Crisis of Representation*. Columbia UP, 2007.

Siebers, Tobin. *Disability Theory*. U of Michigan P, 2008.

Hsuan L. Hsu and Rebecca H. Hogue

Climate Migration and Deranged Realism in Amitav Ghosh's *Gun Island*

Instead of representing climate migration as a condition of the dystopian future, Amitav Ghosh's *Gun Island* situates it in the present and past, as both a common condition and a generative myth for rethinking global modernity at scales that extend beyond liberalism's privileged units of the human and the nation-state. The novel layers climate migration in time and space through the revelation of the voyages of three protagonist units: Deen, an antiquarian bookdealer residing in the United States who returns to Bangladesh and decides to research the seventeenth-century legend of the Bonduki Sadagar, or "Gun Merchant," at a temple in the low-lying coastal region of the Sundarbans; Tipu and Rafi, two young men who migrate to Italy after becoming lovers in the Sundarbans; and the legendary Gun Merchant himself. The storylines initially converge in Bangladesh, then diverge for years before the novel's central characters are reunited in the Mediterranean at the novel's conclusion.

The novel's climate migrants—including both human (primarily Bangladeshi) migrants and numerous nonhuman migrants (spiders, sea snakes, bark beetles, and river dolphins, all shifting their geographic range in response to climate shifts)—inhabit a world whose unpredictability and precarity cannot be reduced to bourgeois regularity. In passages that draw on both media sources and firsthand interviews that Ghosh conducted with Pakistani and Bangladeshi migrants in Venice, individual climate migrants—Rafi, Tipu, and numerous Bangladeshi migrants living in Venice—share their migration stories with the narrator, Deen. Presented through a series of interpolated monologues, the novel's migration stories offer an important counterpoint to Deen's worldview. Tipu and Rafi's journey from the Sundarbans to Venice, for example, is characterized by both careful planning and a series of improvisations when those plans fall apart; it culminates with a woman identified as "the Ethiopian," who appears to liberate a group of enslaved migrants through a series of miraculous events. Deen's research into the legend of the Gun Merchant repeatedly draws him into proximity with climate catastrophes (the gradual flooding of the Sundarbans, California wildfires, a boat filled with migrants in the Mediterranean) that challenge his conviction that "nothing was outside the range of the probable" (Ghosh, *Gun Island* 201). In this essay, we contextualize the novel's formal idiosyncrasies—and, in particular, its efforts to extend realism beyond the scope of "the probable"—as efforts to address the narrative challenges posed by climate migration. Drawing on readings from criticism, climate literature, and social science that we find especially productive in orienting classroom discussions of *Gun Island*—as well as ideas generated in the course of our conversations with students—we both characterize and critique Ghosh's approach to representing the vulnerability and resilience of climate migrants.

We teach *Gun Island* in connection with Ghosh's own philosophical manifesto concerning literary representations of climate change, *The Great Derangement: Climate Change and the Unthinkable*. In this book, published three years prior to the novel, Ghosh sets out to explain what he sees as the failure of literary form to adequately interrogate and represent the climate crisis ravaging the planet. Ghosh takes particular issue with the genre of climate fiction, pointing out that climate change is often treated in speculative fiction, magical realism, or even surrealist genres. Ghosh argues that "to treat [climate change events] as magical or surreal would be to rob them of precisely the quality that makes them so urgently compelling—which is that they are actually happening on this earth, at this time" (*Great Derangement* 27). With the term "derangement"—literally, "To disturb or destroy the arrangement or order of (something); to disarrange" ("Derange")—Ghosh reframes the Anthropocene as an epoch marked by profound and ongoing disturbances in the conventions and forms that orient everyday life. Ghosh supports a realist approach to

climate change, but it must be a realism deranged from its generic structures of bourgeois regularity and everydayness. Climate change, he argues,
has removed the veneer of bourgeois banality explored in realism because
"there is no place where the orderly expectations of bourgeois life hold
unchallenged sway" and "the age of global warming defies both literary
fiction and contemporary common sense: the weather events of this time
have a very high degree of improbability. They are not easily accommodated in the deliberately prosaic world of serious prose fiction" (26). Just as
climate change is a compounding problem, so too is our failure to properly
imagine it as it exists in the here and now. For Ghosh, the world and its
climate have become deranged—as have the lives of hundreds of millions of
migrants—in part because literary narrative has failed to reckon with both
the facts and the implications of climate change. What is needed, then, is a
deranged mode of narrative adequate to the exigent improbability of human
and more-than-human catastrophe on a warming planet. Thus, *Gun Island*
juxtaposes realist narratives of climate migration with mythic figures, pro-
phetic visions, and moments of miraculous intervention.

In refusing to adhere to either realist or science fiction conventions in
Gun Island, Ghosh departs from climate fiction's tendency to marginalize actually existing climate migrants. For example, Barbara Kingsolver's
critically acclaimed realist novel *Flight Behavior* includes a family of climate migrants named the Delagados "[who] had lost their world" after
being displaced from Michoacán (103). However, the Delagados quickly
fade from the narrative (although one of them is hired to care for the white
protagonist's children), their vulnerability eclipsed by the anomalous
migration patterns of monarch butterflies. In several widely taught works
of dystopian climate fiction—such as Cormac McCarthy's *The Road* and
Paolo Bacigalupi's *Ship Breaker* and *The Water Knife*—climate migration
is projected into the future as a condition that plagues communities in the
United States that are currently less affected than more vulnerable communities in the Global South. Bacigalupi's climate migrants in these novels originate in coastal Louisiana and drought-ridden Texas; McCarthy
depicts a world "peopled with refugees . . . like migrants in a feverland"
(28). If works like these arguably make it easier for readers to relate to the
precarity of climate migrants (through iconic figures like the butterfly or
putatively universal figures like McCarthy's man and child), they do so by
obscuring the geographically and historically specific conditions of actual
climate migrants, the vast majority of whom have been displaced from
coastal or arid regions in the Global South. Unlike popular dystopian cli-

mate novels that treat the climate migrant as a future subject, Ghosh centers the contemporary climate migrant—for whom temporal, spatial, and ecological regularity are no longer tenable—as the paradigmatic subject of *Gun Island* and of our deranged planet.

Ghosh situates contemporary climate migration amid the deeper timescales of the Anthropocene. The legend of the Gun Merchant draws Deen into a deeper understanding of modernity—one that originates in the series of planetary climate disruptions known as the "Little Ice Age." "During this time," explains a historian who elaborates on this idea at some length in the novel, "temperatures across the globe had dropped sharply, maybe because of fluctuations in solar activity, or a spate of volcanic eruptions—or possibly even because of the reforestation of vast tracts of land following on the genocide of Amerindian peoples after the European conquests of the Americas" (Ghosh, *Gun Island* 135). Spanning from the sixteenth century to the nineteenth century, the Little Ice Age saw a surge in catastrophic weather events, which in turn caused a series of "famines, droughts, and epidemics" and massive political and demographic shifts (135). Deen eventually learns that the Gun Merchant was driven from eastern India to Venice by a series of climate disasters: displaced by "droughts and floods" at home (155), he encounters both ecological catastrophes and the "strange messianic figures" and social unrest that emerge in their wake (156). Thus, the legend of a merchant chased across the globe by the serpent deity Manasa Devi turns out to be an alternative framework for global modernity: Manasa Devi represents the disavowed feminine force of the more-than-human world (both the planet and its multispecies inhabitants), and the Gun Merchant's eventual submission to her demonstrates the untenability of liberalism's vision of a rational human (and implicitly male) subject who can be detached and protected from his environmental entanglements.

Rather than subdue the forces of the earth (a mythical gesture familiar from works that thematize the establishment of a social order, such as the *Oresteia* and *Beowulf*), the Gun Merchant eventually acknowledges Manasa Devi and the planet's more-than-human agencies. As Deen's own journey (which ends with a series of miraculous events occurring not far from Venice) repeats many of the Gun Merchant's experiences, he comes to an understanding of the world that centers not bourgeois regularity but the precarity of migration, the proximity of radical disruptions, and the richness of cultural expressions grounded in these experiences. Among other things, our students are intrigued by how the novel's accounts of the Little Ice Age and the Gun Merchant myth rescale canonical works of literature—for example, the global climate disruption of 1816 that occasioned the writing of *Frankenstein* and "The Vampyre" (Ghosh, *Great Derangement* 67) or the cosmopolitan vision of seventeenth-century Venice afforded by the legend of the "Gun Merchant," which Deen ultimately learns to be just another way of saying "the merchant of Venice." *Gun Island* underscores that climate migration is not just a twenty-first-century phenomenon nor just the stuff of speculative fiction: it has played a vital role in planetary cultural and biological exchanges since at least the sixteenth century.

In addition to discussing with students how the novel reimagines the time and genre of climate migration, we also challenge students to consider the limitations of Ghosh's mode of conceptualizing climate migration. When they note the novel's tendency to center the experiences of male, South Asian migrants, we shift attention to the deus ex machina figure referred to as "the Ethiopian." A Black woman who appears to control the behavior of tornadoes and a range of nonhuman species, the Ethiopian functions as a point of convergence for the novel's numerous departures from realist convention. As a magical figure with no character development, the Ethiopian woman sharply contrasts with characters in Ghosh's other migration narratives, which generally feature carefully researched stories of young Bangladeshi men who "launched their own journeys" in search of a better life (Ghosh, *Gun Island* 304). The Ethiopian—who first appears to Tipu as an angel in a dream—orchestrates the escape of a group of migrants being held by organ traffickers in Egypt and later summons thousands of cetaceans, birds, and bioluminescent organisms to ensure that the migrants are allowed to land in Italy. Like Manasa Devi and the Black Madonna of La Salute (discussed elsewhere in the novel), the Ethiopian is positioned as a mediator "who stands between us and the incarnate Earth, with all its blessings and furies" (243). Although Ghosh alludes to the diversity of contemporary climate migrants ("an unusually motley lot, consisting of Ethiopians, Eritreans, Somalis, Arabs and Bengalis"), the novel's magical representation of the Ethiopian displaces the lived experiences of Black and women migrants (286). Rather than address the intersectional vulnerabilities experienced by Black women and girls, who now make up about half of all migrants from Africa and who "face . . . greater risk of exploitation, abuse and trafficking" (*Women* vii), the Ethiopian obscures them. Given the manifold ways in which anti-Blackness shapes the perception, recognition, and policing of climate migrants (Smythe), Ghosh's reduction of Black migrants' lives to an allegorical figure seems troubling. If Ghosh's derangements of realist narrative are effective in addressing the representational challenges of the Anthropocene, his use of the "magical Negro" trope nevertheless raises critical questions concerning the social, geographic, racial, and gendered locations of seemingly magical or miraculous interruptions of bourgeois regularity.

Ghosh positions the migrant as a paradigmatic figure of both cosmopolitan modernity and the Anthropocene. Refusing a totalizing, global approach to climate change, Ghosh insists on a greater awareness of how rising sea levels will affect the Indian subcontinent and the loss of its traditional ecological knowledges—an important intervention in literary representations of climate crisis and migration. However, the problem of climate migration extends far beyond stories of migration: as Ghosh states in *The Great Derangement*, "[T]he climate crisis is also a crisis of culture" (9). With the shifts in ecosystems comes a concomitant loss of culture, language, storytelling, and ways of knowing that are tied to the environment. In *Gun Island*, the loss of cultural knowledge is presented not as a possibility but as an actuality. The Manasa Devi temple that propels Deen's adventures is ultimately consumed by rising sea levels. Within the diegesis, Deen becomes a remaining vessel of knowledge, while *Gun Island* itself acts as another repository of sorts without interrogating the effects of these losses. While Ghosh's text both represents and is a necessary response to climate migration, we also challenge students to consider what kinds of culture Ghosh presents as valuable by comparing them with other locations facing climate catastrophes. In *The Great Derangement*, for example, Ghosh suggests that the severity of Asia's climate crisis is a matter of comparative populations: "Asia's centrality to global warming rests, in the first regard, upon numbers" (87). He explains that the Sundarban region is one of five million people, whereas Tuvalu, one of the low-lying atolls in the Pacific at greatest risk of being completely under water by 2050, has a significantly smaller population of ten thousand people. Ghosh's argument about "numbers" makes the questionable supposition that numbers are an adequate metric for evaluating loss or cultural impact. What, we might ask, are the implications for less populous Indigenous cultures and their deeply rooted traditional ecological knowledges? While the scenarios in *Gun Island* present stories of loss and subsequent migration, we might also consider the narrative imaginings of what is left behind, and for whom.

While Ghosh's novel offers a compelling demonstration of the power of (deranged) realism as a formal strategy for engaging with the implications of climate migration, its limitations also help underscore the critical importance of other approaches—particularly those innovated by Black and Indigenous women. Thus, our courses read *Gun Island* alongside literary treatments of climate migration and Black and Indigenous futures, such as Octavia Butler's *Parable of the Sower* and Cherie Dimaline's *The Marrow Thieves* as well as poetry by Kathy Jetñil-Kijiner, Jetñil-Kijiner and Aka Niviâna, and Terisa Siagatonu. Although they are not works of realist fiction, these texts share both Ghosh's attention to cosmology as a way of orienting eco-social relationships and his investment in balancing careful attention to histories of migration with a reperiodization of climate crisis as a problem that has been foundational to racial capitalist modernity.

Works Cited

Bacigalupi, Paolo. *Ship Breaker*. Little, Brown, 2010.

———. *The Water Knife*. Knopf Doubleday, 2015.

Butler, Octavia E. *Parable of the Sower*. Grand Central Publishing, 2000.

"Derange, *V.*" *Oxford English Dictionary*, Oxford UP, 2023, www.oed.com/dictionary/derange-v?tl=true&tab=meaning_and_use.

Dimaline, Cherie. *The Marrow Thieves*. DCB, 2017.

Ghosh, Amitav. *The Great Derangement: Climate Change and the Unthinkable*. U of Chicago P, 2016.

———. *Gun Island*. Farrar, Straus and Giroux, 2019.

Jetñil-Kijiner, Kathy. *Iep Jāltok: Poems from a Marshallese Daughter*. U of Arizona P, 2017.

Jetñil-Kijiner, Kathy, and Aka Niviâna. "Rise." *350.org*, 350.org/rise-from-one-island-to-another/#poem. Accessed 10 July 2024.

Kingsolver, Barbara. *Flight Behavior*. Harper Perennial, 2012.

McCarthy, Cormac. *The Road*. Knopf Doubleday, 2006.

Siagatonu, Terisa. "Layers." *YouTube*, uploaded by New Internationalist, 8 Dec. 2015, www.youtube.com/watch?v=7glgz-mUwm0&ab_channel=NewInternationalist.

Smythe, SA. "The Black Mediterranean and the Politics of Imagination." *Middle East Report*, no. 286, spring 2018, pp. 3–9.

Women on the Move: Immigration and Health in the WHO African Region: A Literature Review. World Health Organization, Regional Office for Africa, 2018.

Claudia Sadowski-Smith

Whiteness and Migration Studies

Starting with the work of W. E. B. Du Bois at the end of the nineteenth century, African American authors and activists identified and critiqued the significance of a white racialized identity for the constitution and maintenance of unequal US power structures. The study of white supremacy and institutionalized racism emerged in the US and UK academies in the 1980s and 1990s. The field's particular strength in the United States led to an emphasis on US-specific power structures, ideologies, and practices that have constructed a white racial identity as superior to other racial identities in order to justify racialized systems of inequality with roots in settler coloniality. The field has also aimed to understand the struggles of those racialized as non-white "in order to contribute to the definition and production of analytical frames for antiracist struggles" (Garner, "Surfing" 1585).

The historically largest protest movements in the United States, the Black Lives Matter demonstrations of 2020, moved terms like *white supremacy* and *white privilege* into the public arena. These terms describe how those racialized as white are exempt and benefit from the racial profiling, disproportionate incarceration, and economic injustice inflicted upon African Americans in order to maintain white supremacy.[1] Scholars of whiteness have also analyzed the ongoing mainstreaming of far-right white supremacist ideologies, which were most clearly expressed in the violent and deadly US Capitol insurrection of 6 January 2021. When questions of migration have entered these debates, they have mainly addressed manifestations of white supremacy in the treatment of the currently largest numbers of migrants in the United States, primarily from Mexico and Latin, Central, and South America, who are the target of exclusion, discrimination, profiling, and detention. These debates have also analyzed how Latina/o/x migrants were historically denied access to legal citizenship rights and were subject to violence and discrimination through their racialization as non-white people.

A focus on migration highlights questions of participation in white supremacy, which originated during the time of settler colonialism and grants those racialized as white privileged access to citizenship and associated rights like social status and economic benefits as well as exclusion from state-sponsored racialized violence. The United States was founded on the economic system of chattel slavery, which depended on forced African migration while allowing Europeans, with the initial exception of indentured people, to arrive as settlers and immigrants. As a group, European immigrants and those of immigrant origin were direct beneficiaries of state-sponsored genocidal policies, warfare toward native populations, and the expropriation of Indigenous land. While native people were not considered US citizens until 1924, one of the earliest pieces of US legislation, the 1790 Naturalization Act, granted immigrants who were "free white persons" access to citizenship (United States, Congress), thus excluding European indentured servants, enslaved Africans, and free black people. The act explicitly articulated the concept of a "white" ethnonational identity, defined as a combination of European descent and physiological traits. It also excluded those who arrived through forced forms of migration, such as indentured servitude and slavery, from access to membership in the nation. In the mid-1800s, when European indentured service had largely disappeared as a common labor system in the United States, citizenship was eventually conferred to previously enslaved people and their descendants.

Understood as the main criterion for citizenship, a white ethnoracial identity, in combination with uncoerced arrival in the United States, became further explicitly defined as non-Asian through the late-nineteenth-century exclusion of immigrants from Asia. Considered ineligible for naturalization based on their geographic origin and descent, and their association with "coolie" contract labor migration, would-be migrants from Asia were banned from entering the United States. The passage of the

1882 Chinese Exclusion Act not only barred the entry of Chinese unskilled laborers, considered "coolies," but also prohibited all Chinese immigrants from naturalization, including those exempt from this ban. Novels by Asian American authors such as Amy Tan and Maxine Hong Kingston can help students understand the long-term effects of Chinese exclusion, which continued to influence the formation of Asian American identities, cultures, and families in the United States long after the ban was revoked in 1943. Legal findings in the 1920s extended racial ineligibility for citizenship to immigrants from other parts of Asia, such as Japan and India. The identification of whiteness with European origin also led to the initial exclusion of some immigrants from present-day Syria until the 1915 Supreme Court decision *Dow v. United States*, which stated that "inhabitants of a portion of Asia, including Syria, were to be classed as white persons" and considered eligible for US citizenship (United States, Supreme Court).

A subfield of whiteness studies on the historical construction of whiteness has examined how large-scale turn-of-the-twentieth-century European migration, primarily from Ireland, Italy, and the Russian Empire,[2] decoupled the right to naturalization from access to various other social and economic citizenship rights, all the while continuing to exempt the new immigrants from the kind of institutionalized racial violence suffered by African Americans. Scholarship by historians of whiteness like Eric Goldstein, Thomas Guglielmo, and David Roediger, which is suitable for undergraduate classrooms, has revealed the complex racial dynamics experienced by these immigrants. Guglielmo describes them as "white on arrival," primarily because of their legal access to naturalization and exemption from institutionalized racial violence. James Barrett and Roediger, however, characterize them as "inbetween peoples," highlighting how these groups were initially considered racially ambiguous, encountered limited access to other rights, and faced selective exclusion from admission under 1920s quota acts. These conflicting systems placed the new immigrants ambivalently within the US ethnoracial hierarchy, which divides native-born and more established immigrant Europeans from populations that are considered non-white.

While some barriers to the admission of European immigrants had already been imposed in the nineteenth century—such as associating Italian migration with contract labor—the passage of quota acts in the 1920s marked a significant change. The acts exemplified a shift from an understanding of a white ethnonational identity as a mixture of physiological traits, geographic origin, and uncoerced mobility to more complex eugenics-inspired ideas about genetic differences among various European nationalities. A system of numerical annual quotas allowed greater numbers of arrivals from northern Europe while selectively restricting immigration from southern and eastern Europe and further barring Asian migration. Eastern and southern European migrants faced social stigma, including occasional exclusions from schools, public accommodations, labor unions, and elite social institutions and were concentrated in ethnic ghettoes. Italians in particular experienced occasional noninstitutionalized racialized violence that included lynching (T. Guglielmo 10, 36; J. Guglielmo 11). Many eastern European Jewish immigrants worked as peddlers or in the Jewish-dominated garment industry (Diner 37; Godley 51), and other new immigrants were confined to unskilled occupations where they earned less than native-born white individuals (Garner, "Uses" 265; Schreuder 134). As the right to naturalization became separated from access to other citizenship rights, the term *color* (which today would be called *race*) came to denote generalized geographic origins in Europe. Meanwhile, immigrants' background origins in certain European nations considered genetically inferior were regarded as a form of "race" (which would later be termed *ethnicity*).

When Chinese and European migration declined in the 1920s and 1930s, the treatment of growing numbers of arrivals from Mexico complicated the association between physiological traits, European origin, and freedom of mobility, which had previously been linked to a white ethnonational identity that guaranteed naturalization and access to citizenship rights. While Mexican immigrants were eligible for naturalization because citizenship had been conferred on residents of the part of Mexico that was incorporated into the United States under the 1848 Treaty of Guadalupe Hidalgo, they were also considered non-white (Fox and Guglielmo 353). As part of a racialized group, they became targets of state-sponsored violence (including lynchings), expropriation, segregation, and the enforcement of existing migration laws (358–64).

For those of European origin, the links between political, social, and economic rights were resutured in the notion of a white pan-European identity. After World War II, eastern and southern European immigrants, and especially their children, who had up to this point been considered both white and not quite white, had achieved upward mobility, becoming more fully integrated into the labor market, moving from urban ethnic ghettos to suburbs, and benefitting disproportionally from the unequal distribution of expanded social rights under New Deal legislation (T. Guglielmo 147–48).

This historical inequity led to the kind of residential and educational segregation that still characterizes much of the United States, while the intergenerational transfer of inherited wealth to succeeding generations helped solidify white economic privilege in the contemporary moment (Lipsitz 14).[3] As the concept of a pan-European whiteness came to conflate European origin and descent with upward mobility, it also reconsolidated the exemption of those racialized as white from institutionalized state and public violence. Fictionalized and autobiographical texts by first- and 1.5-generation immigrant writers such as Mary Antin, Abraham Cahan, and Anzia Yezierska, who came from the Pale of Settlement in the Russian Empire, laid the foundation for a literature of immigrant assimilation to a pan-European white racial identity through upward mobility.

Since the elimination of racialized legal exclusions from US admission on the basis of geographic or national origin and prohibitions against contract labor in the 1960s, the largest numbers of US migrants, who come from Central, Latin, and South America; Mexico; and Asia, are generally racialized as non-white and are categorized as part of the so-called model minority or the Latina/o/x diaspora. In cultural productions by contemporary 1.5- and second-generation immigrant authors such as Junot Díaz, Jhumpa Lahiri, and Viet Thanh Nguyen, which are increasingly taught in college classrooms, inquiries into questions of whiteness primarily address the workings of an institutionalized system of supremacy and privilege from which immigrants who are racialized as non-white are excluded or with which they need to contend.

While whiteness studies scholars have examined the current mainstreaming of anti-immigrant politics in support of ongoing efforts to recuperate white supremacy (Garner, "Surfing" 1590), neoliberal changes in the role of a white ethnonational identity that supposedly guarantees immigrants racialized as white access to citizenship rights have remained understudied. A focus on migration from the former Soviet Union and Eastern European countries, which has grown since the demise of most state socialisms in the late 1980s, reveals how the notion of upward mobility in particular has become uncoupled from its post–World War II association with a pan-European racial identity and expanded to include Asian Americans and Asian immigrants. Gary Shteyngart's novel *Super Sad True Love Story* explores similarities in the construction of Jewish migrants from the former Soviet Union and Asian Americans, who are incorporated as so-called honorable whites through the model minority concept, though their inclusion is always contingent and revocable, as manifested in surging anti-Asian violence during the COVID-19 pandemic. While turn-of-the-twentieth-century Chinese immigrants were regarded as Asian "coolies," and Europeans were considered immigrants who supposedly lifted themselves up by their bootstraps to achieve the American dream, today both groups are linked to the myth of upward mobility. This narrative continues to largely exclude African Americans, Indigenous people, and large segments of Latina/o/x populations, a heterogeneous ethnic group.

Other cultural productions fictionalize how the growing diversity of post-Soviet migrants, in terms of their legal and class status and their origins in various post-Soviet nations, further questions their wholesale association with a pan-European whiteness that was created in the context of a growing postwar welfare state. Sana Krasikov's *One More Year* and Anya Ulinich's *Petropolis* represent ethnically and racially diverse protagonists from Russia, Georgia, and Uzbekistan who arrive in the United States on nonimmigrant visas and become undocumented migrants. Already constructed as "other" in their home regions and countries, some are also racialized as non-white (i.e., as African American and Asian) in the United States. The two novels emphasize fictionalized post-Soviet migrants' experiences of diminished access to legal options for admission to the United States and the labor market in the context of a disappearing welfare state and a well-functioning economy that had brought prosperity to an earlier generation of working-class European immigrants and their children.

Contemporary representations of post-Yugoslav and Romanian migration similarly highlight migrants' diminished access to legal forms of entry and economic rights while also pointing to non-US-specific forms of racialization and othering that shape migrants' understanding of their identities in the United States. Natasha Radojčić's *You Don't Have to Live Here* fictionalizes a Yugoslav protagonist of mixed Muslim and Roma descent who becomes a sex worker in the United States, where she refuses her racialization as white by emphasizing her Romani origin and nomadic sensibilities (Bijelić 114). Saviana Stănescu's plays *Lenin's Shoe* and *Aliens with Extraordinary Skills* represent Russian, Moldovan, and Romanian migrants whose low socioeconomic or lack of legal status complicates the notion of their privileged access to political, economic, and social rights that is embodied in the notion of a pan-European whiteness (Popescu-Sandu 177).

The restructuring of connections between national identities, power regimes, and citizenship rights under neoliberal conditions has also shaped the emergence of long overdue globalized lenses on questions of whiteness as a system of power and set of rights and privileges. The field of whiteness studies has moved beyond its origins in the United States and the United Kingdom to the study of settler-Indigenous relationships in settler colonies such as Canada, Australia, and South Africa. In addition, work on the constructed whiteness of northern European countries has complicated the myth of their racial neutrality, progressivism, and egalitarianism, showing how this ideal reproduces structural inequalities by projecting the nations' colonial legacies onto various groups (Loftsdóttir and Jensen 7–8). Responses to the Black Lives Matter movement and to increases in global human movement will likely lead to further inquiries into the linkages between national identities, power regimes, and citizenship rights as well as to studies of the ongoing racialization of migration from the Global South—and the "Global East" (Müller)—in the ethnoracial regimes of Global North countries that grant access to legal, economic, political, and social citizenship rights.

Notes

1. Pioneering twentieth-century texts on whiteness include the work of W. E. B. Du Bois, James Baldwin, Theodore W. Allen, and Toni Morrison. The literature of "white confession" of the 1980s by writers such as Peggy McIntosh and Ruth Frankenberg exemplifies early academic work on whiteness, which argues that white feminists had overlooked the importance of race in connection with gender inequality because they were largely unaware of their own privileges as white (largely middle-class) women.

2. While turn-of-the-twentieth-century eastern Europeans came from various regions, including Romania and the Austro-Hungarian Empire, most were Jewish and arrived from the Pale of Settlement in the Russian Empire, whose borders included much of present-day Lithuania, Belarus, Poland, Moldova, Ukraine, and Russia.

3. Descendants of immigrants selectively borrowed elements from disparate European immigrant backgrounds at a time when these cultural and national distinctions had only a minimal impact on their daily lives to argue that the hardships experienced by their turn-of-the-twentieth-century immigrant ancestors were comparable to those experienced by contemporary immigrants.

Works Cited

Allen, Theodore W. *The Invention of the White Race: The Origin of Racial Oppression in Anglo America*. Verso, 1997.
Antin, Mary. *The Promised Land*. Houghton Mifflin, 1912.

Baldwin, James. *The Fire Next Time*. Dial Press, 1963.

Barrett, James R., and David Roediger. "Inbetween Peoples: Race, Nationality and the 'New Immigrant' Working Class." *Journal of American Ethnic History*, vol. 54, no. 3, 1997, pp. 3–44.

Bijelić, Tatjana. "Between Homeland and Hostland: Representations of Women Migrants' Agency in US Post-Yugoslav Novels." *Twentieth-Century Literature*, vol. 65, nos. 1–2, Mar. 2019, pp. 97–120.

Cahan, Abraham. *"The Imported Bridegroom" and Other Stories of the New York Ghetto*. Houghton Mifflin, 1898.

Díaz, Junot. *The Brief Wondrous Life of Oscar Wao*. Riverhead Books, 2007.

Diner, Hasia R. *Roads Taken: The Great Jewish Migrations to the New World and the Peddlers That Forged the Way*. Yale UP, 2015.

Du Bois, W. E. B. *Darkwater: Voices from within the Veil*. Schocken Books, 1969.

Fox, Cybelle, and Thomas A. Guglielmo. "Defining America's Racial Boundaries: Blacks, Mexicans, and European Immigrants, 1890–1945." *American Journal of Sociology*, vol. 118, no. 2, 2012, pp. 327–79.

Frankenberg, Ruth. *White Women, Race Matters: The Social Construction of Whiteness*. U of Minnesota P, 1993.

Garner, Steve. "Surfing the Third Wave of Whiteness Studies: Reflections on Twine and Gallagher." *Ethnic and Racial Studies*, vol. 40, no. 9, 2017, pp. 1582–97.

———. "The Uses of Whiteness: What Sociologists Working on Europe Can Draw from US Research on Whiteness." *Sociology*, vol. 40, no. 2, 2006, pp. 257–75.

Godley, Andrew. *Jewish Immigrant Entrepreneurship in New York and London, 1880–1914*. Palgrave, 2001.

Goldstein, Eric L. *The Price of Whiteness: Jews, Race, and American Identity*. Princeton UP, 2006.

Guglielmo, Jennifer. "White Lies, Dark Truths." Introduction. *Are Italians White? How Race Is Made in America*, edited by Guglielmo and Salvatore Salerno, Routledge, 2003, pp. 1–16.

Guglielmo, Thomas A. *White on Arrival: Italians, Race, Color, and Power in Chicago, 1890–1945*. Oxford UP, 2003.

Kingston, Maxine Hong. *The Woman Warrior: Memoirs of a Girlhood among Ghosts*. Vintage Books, 1989.

Krasikov, Sana. *One More Year*. Spiegel and Grau, 2009.

Lahiri, Jhumpa. *Interpreter of Maladies*. Houghton Mifflin, 1999.

Lipsitz, George. *The Possessive Investment in Whiteness: How White People Profit from Identity Politics*. Temple UP, 1998.

Loftsdóttir, Kristín, and Lars Jensen. "Nordic Exceptionalism and the Nordic 'Others.'" Introduction. *Whiteness and Postcolonialism in the Nordic Region: Exceptionalism, Migrant Others, and National Identities*, edited by Loftsdóttir and Jensen, Ashgate, 2012, pp. 1–12.

McIntosh, Peggy. *White Privilege and Male Privilege: A Personal Account of Coming to See Correspondences through Work in Women's Studies*. Wellesley College, 1988.

Morrison, Toni. *Playing in the Dark: Whiteness and the Literary Imagination.* Harvard UP, 1992.

Müller, Martin. "In Search of the Global East: Thinking between North and South." *Geopolitics*, vol. 25, no. 3, 2020, pp. 734–44.

Nguyen, Viet Thanh. *The Refugees.* Grove Press, 2017.

Popescu-Sandu, Oana. "Staging the Post-socialist Woman: Saviana Stănescu's Alternative 'Trans-nations.'" *Twentieth-Century Literature*, vol. 65, nos. 1–2, Mar. 2019, pp. 167–86.

Radojčić, Natasha. *You Don't Have to Live Here.* Random House, 2005.

Schreuder, Yda. "Labor Segmentation, Ethnic Division of Labor, and Residential Segregation in American Cities in the Early Twentieth Century." *Professional Geographer*, vol. 41, no. 2, 1989, pp. 131–43.

Shteyngart, Gary. *Super Sad True Love Story.* Random House, 2010.

Stănescu, Saviana. *Aliens with Extraordinary Skills.* Stănescu, *New York Plays,* pp. 260–368.

———. *Lenin's Shoe.* Stănescu, *New York Plays,* pp. 156–259.

———. *The New York Plays.* NoPassport Press, 2010.

Tan, Amy. *The Joy Luck Club.* Putnam, 1989.

Ulinich, Anya. *Petropolis.* Penguin Books, 2008.

United States, Congress. An Act to Establish an Uniform Rule of Naturalization. *United States Statutes at Large,* vol. 1, US Government Publishing Office, 1790, pp. 103–04.

United States, Supreme Court. *Dow v. United States.* 14 Sept. 1915. *Vlex,* case-law.vlex.com/vid/dow-v-united-states-885459875.

Yezierska, Anzia. *How I Found America.* Persea Books, 1991.

Part II

Geopolitical and Pedagogical Contexts

Lisa Dolasinski

Hip-Hop-Based Education and Italian Studies: A Culturally Responsive Approach to Teaching Migration and Contemporary Italy

Researchers and educators alike see value in hip-hop as a pedagogical resource and methodology. Advocating for a hip-hop-based education, they identify rap lyrics as appropriate and engaging curricular resources for fostering critical thinking skills, teaching media literacy, and shaping an inclusive learning community (Dimitriadis; Runell and Diaz; Hill; Hill and Petchauer). Experienced practitioners of hip-hop pedagogy, such as Alastair Pennycook and Emery Petchauer, maintain that hip-hop is more than a product and should in fact be designated an "aesthetic cultural form" that produces "organic epistemologies" (Petchauer 28), which, in turn, reshape "the mainstream discourse of the academy" (Pennycook 150). Global hip-hop is a set of stylized aesthetics that derives from the socially conscious brand of rap music that developed in the 1980s. Born out of multicultural exchanges among members of disenfranchised, low-income communities—African American teens and the children of immigrants from countries in the Caribbean—hip-hop culture provided an alternative to the gang violence that had plagued the Bronx and other US urban areas since the 1960s. By the 1990s, hip-hop had not only asserted itself as a dominant force in popular American culture but also established itself as a preferred medium for challenging global sociopolitical inequities (Mitchell

186–87; Harris 17, 49; Osumare; Terkourafi 5, 19–21, 44–46, 98). Over the last five decades, Italian rap artists have created an original style that addresses issues specific to the *bel paese*, or "beautiful country." More recently, changes in Italy's demographics—in particular, increasing numbers of immigrants and second-generation citizens—have altered the form, sound, and themes of Italian rap and popular Italian culture more generally.

Italian studies programs in the US academy have responded to these demographic shifts by expanding their curricula to include courses, learning modules, and enrichment activities on immigration to Italy and modern Italian society. Drawing on what Joquetta Johnson refers to as the "culturally responsive pedagogy" of hip-hop-based education, I have designed original courses that deepen students' understanding of contemporary migration flows and their impact on Italy's evolving (trans) national identity. In the sections that follow, I highlight key texts and activities in two learning modules: the first module is titled Italian Citizenship and Rap Activism, and the second module is titled Second-Generation Italians and Global Hip-Hop. The examples I propose require intermediate proficiency in Italian. However, they could be modified to support students' acquisition of similar learning objectives in parallel courses where the target language or nation of study (e.g., France, Denmark, Germany) corresponds with a thriving global hip-hop community of immigrant and second-generation rappers. Furthermore, as I illustrate, utilizing hip-hop-based education to teach migration necessitates embracing a culturally, ethically, and ideologically informed pedagogy. Indeed, this particular method not only shapes understandings of the cultural and political dynamics of migration from within (through primary texts of second-generation Italians) but also responds to the psychosocial needs of an increasingly diverse student population by interrogating complex issues through accessible and inclusive modalities.

Module 1: Italian Citizenship and Rap Activism

The first learning module introduces and contextualizes ongoing debates on Italy's citizenship law through assignments centered on the raps and political activism of Amir Issaa. Issaa, a rapper of Roman and Egyptian origin, uses his public platform to champion the social and legal acceptance of second-generation Italians. Since the release of his debut solo album, *Uomo di prestigio* (*Man of Prestige*), in 2006, the rap artist has mobilized music to express his personal struggles with identity formation and belonging and to address broader issues of xenophobia, discrimination, and racism in Italy. It was in the early 2010s, however, when Issaa became increasingly engaged in rap activism. In addition to collaborating with nonprofit organizations that combat racism and sponsor social justice initiatives (e.g., Save the Children, Centro Astalli, Ufficio Nazionale Antidiscriminazioni Razziali), Issaa regularly facilitates rap workshops that promote diversity, multiculturalism, and acceptance in Italy.

Autobiography and Rap Analysis

The introductory activity pairs an excerpt from Issaa's autobiography, *Vivo per questo* (*I Live for This*), with his rap "Caro Presidente" ("Dear President"). To begin, students read and respond to questions on "Il melting pot delle seconde generazioni" ("The Melting Pot of the Second Generation" (Issaa 185–97). This passage describes Issaa's collaboration with *Change.org* in a 2012 campaign aimed at reforming Italy's citizenship legislation. In tandem with an online petition signed by more than 75,000 supporters, Issaa released "Caro Presidente." This rap, which is assigned after a discussion of "Il melting pot delle seconde generazioni," challenges the validity of Italy's current immigration and citizenship policies. Issaa maintains that certain politicians' resolve to maintain *jus sanguinis* (right of blood) legislation is not only antiquated but also, in light of contemporary migration flows to Italy, inappropriate, racist, and exclusionary. In the lyrics and music video to "Caro Presidente," the rap activist addresses President Sergio Mattarella directly; he calls on the political authority to intervene and grant the children of immigrant parents born in Italy Italian citizenship through *ius soli* (right of the soil).

Class Twitter Feed

The second assignment serves as preparation for an interactive class discussion. Working collaboratively, students analyze the lyrics to one of Issaa's singles ("Straniero nella mia nazione" ["Foreigner in My Own Nation"], "Non sono un immigrato" ["I Am Not an Immigrant"], "Ius Music"). Each group crafts a 280-character tweet in which they synthesize the significance of the assigned rap, hashtag key themes, and tag Issaa. In the following session, students refer to content published in the class *Twitter* feed to spark discussion on recurring themes of racism, stereotypes, and the integration of immigrants. With the guidance of the instructor, students may also draw connections between Italy's history of colonization and contemporary migration flows from North Africa.

Rap Workshop

The third and final activity is a rap workshop facilitated by Issaa. This workshop begins with Issaa explaining his creative process for writing a rap. Along with educating students on conventions of the rap music genre (i.e., structure and form), Issaa describes the autobiographical components that influence the content of his compositions. Next, students craft and share their original raps. In the final part of the workshop, Issaa leads a discussion on the history of rap and hip-hop culture in Italy, commenting in particular on how this genre has evolved and grown since he began rapping in the 1990s.

Module 2: Second-Generation Italians and Global Hip-Hop

The second learning module exposes students to Italy's evolving (trans) national identity through creative activities that engage with the global hip-hop of second-generation musicians, in particular Mahmood and Ghali. Both Mahmood and Ghali are the children of immigrant parents and absent fathers, and both grew up in impoverished urban areas. Historically, these qualities have been perceived as undesirable, inferior, and detrimental to an idealized and exclusionary perception of national Italian homogeneity. Yet, rather than attempt to erase or minimize their biographies, Mahmood and Ghali accentuate their multiethnic heritages in song lyrics, music videos, interviews, fashion choices, and social media activity (Ardizzoni; Dolasinski). The young men's eclectic urban style and resolve to remain authentic has proven commercially viable in mainstream Italy and transnational contexts. Accordingly, Mahmood and Ghali have utilized their popularity and social capital to shore up an unprecedented movement toward multiculturalism, diversity, and affirmative otherness in contemporary Italian society.

Music Video Viewing Guide

This module opens with a three-part viewing guide on Mahmood's music video for "Soldi" ("Money") or Ghali's video for "Cara Italia" ("Dear

Italy"). Part 1, the pre-viewing portion, provides useful context. First, students research the selected hip-hop artist's biography (i.e., heritage, upbringing). Next, students skim the rap lyrics, noting keywords, themes, and linguistic practices. Part 2 of the viewing guide is completed while watching the music video (Mahmood, "Mahmood—Soldi"; Ghali, "Ghali—Cara Italia"). In addition to noting the storyline, students list striking visual (i.e., mise-en-scène, cinematography, editing), acoustic (i.e., genre, form, arrangement), and symbolic elements. Part 3, the post-viewing portion, promotes critical thinking. Students connect their observations to the social, political, and cultural landscape of present-day Italy. For example, in the music video for "Soldi," they may examine the juxtaposition of Italian and Egyptian imagery (a Virgin Mary figurine [00:16–00:17], a photograph of a desert landscape [01:09–01:10]), or they may comment on the integration of unconventional sounds for an Italian audience (the interlude in Egyptian Arabic, the sampling of a Middle Eastern musical ensemble known as the *takht*). For "Cara Italia," students may analyze the intermingling of diverse icons, fashion styles, and social practices that signal different cultures and ethnic groups (i.e., a narghile, embroidered tunics, a belly dancer, a tambourine, colorful ponchos, and beaded sombreros), or they may reflect on the video's symbolic conclusion, in which Ghali envisages a more inclusive, multicultural Italy (Dolasinski 131).

Blog Post

The blog entry, which should be between two hundred and three hundred words, complements, and expands on, the viewing guide. It requires students to research, synthesize, and reflect on the broader discourses of heritage, identity, and belonging surrounding the music and far-reaching influence of Mahmood or Ghali. As a follow-up activity to the viewing guide on "Soldi," students focus on the controversy that resulted from Mahmood's 2019 victory at the Sanremo Music Festival. More precisely, the activity asks students to summarize the cultural and historical significance of the festival, respond to social media posts written by Italian politicians of an anti-immigrant persuasion that call into question Mahmood's claims to Italian identity, and hypothesize about the potential for global hip-hop to facilitate the social and legal acceptance of immigrants and second-generation citizens in Italy. In addition to directing students to the social media profiles of Matteo Salvini and Luigi Di Maio, the instructor could invite students to read corresponding articles published by the Italian media (Cursi; Fascia), watch the indirect exchange between Salvini and Mahmood on episodes of the Italian television program *Le Iene* (*The Hyenas* ["Salvini"; "Sanremo"]), and view Mahmood's interview on the Italian talk show *DiMartedì* ("Mahmood: 'Solo'"). The blog post on Ghali and "Cara Italia" requires students to draw connections between the significance of the song's lyrics and Ghali's broader artistic philosophy and to evaluate the effectiveness of hip-hop and social media as pedagogical tools for stimulating positive change in an increasingly global Italy. Key resources for this assignment include Ghali's open letter on "Cara Italia" ("Ghali, il nuovo singolo"), a recent interview with Ghali conducted by the Italian journalist and writer Roberto Saviano (Ghali, "Ghali, il ragazzo"), and the episode of *YouTube* series *The Performers: Act II* featuring Ghali ("Performers").

Class Playlist and Radio Broadcast

The final activity is a collaborative project that could serve as an alternative midterm or final assessment. Working in pairs, students select a second-generation hip-hop artist to research (e.g., Issaa, Mahmood, Ghali, Tommy Kuti, Abe Kayn, Chadia Rodríguez, Maruego, Hell Raton, Laïoung, OG Eastbull, Rancore, Slava, Zanko El Arabe Blanco). Using the information gleaned from their research, each pair scripts a five- to eight-minute radio segment that includes the following components: a one-minute profile on the selected artist (i.e., their biography, recurring themes in their music); one rap that is representative of the artist's signature style; and a two-minute explanation of the selected rap that integrates themes studied in class (i.e., issues of immigration, racism, multiculturalism, and diversity in Italy). Once students have edited and finalized their respective segments, the class decides on a program order and runs a live broadcast on the university radio station.

This activity allows for enrichment through extended learning opportunities. Prior to the broadcast, students can advertise the event on social media, inviting the broader campus community to tune in and live-tweet questions, observations, and comments. The instructor may also opt to add additional criteria to the radio show assignment, such as intercultural connections and comparisons with global hip-hop outside Italy. For example, students presenting on Issaa may address how his newest single, "Non respiro" ("I Can't Breathe"), written in collaboration with David Blank and Davide Shorty (Issaa et al.), corresponds with the Black Lives

Matter movement and the work of the Black Lives Matter Global Network Foundation. Lastly, following the live broadcast, students can be asked to submit a one-page reflection on this experience.

Hip-hop-based education is a culturally responsive pedagogy for teaching immigration, citizenship, and (trans)national Italian identity. This expressive medium is engaging and accessible to diverse groups of students with different educational backgrounds and experiences. Hip-hop also challenges educators to diversify and decolonize traditional university curricula. Defined broadly, decolonizing pedagogy is a progressive, ethically oriented practice that consciously unsettles "monolithic, mono-cultural, and mono-epistemological academic traditions" (Biermann 386). The implementation of a decolonial approach to teaching and learning actively seeks to reconceptualize what counts as knowledge, through which modes and mediums knowledge can be disseminated, and how shifts in knowledge reflect ongoing shifts in power and access. Thus, in practice, this type of pedagogy validates the contributions of authors, artists, and activists who complicate or counter canonical texts and authorial voices of a particular discipline, and it is responsive to the needs of diverse, traditionally underserved student populations. With regard to the adoption of a decolonial approach to teaching in Italian studies more specifically, this has involved incorporating texts of migrant and second-generation Italians into regular course offerings. Ultimately, then, hip-hop is a cultural aesthetic of resistance and empowerment that can be used to shed light on the often intertwined social, cultural, ethnoracial, and political disparities experienced by marginalized migrant communities in Italy and beyond.

Works Cited

Ardizzoni, Michela. "On Rhythms and Rhymes: Poetics of Identity in Postcolonial Italy." *Communication, Culture and Critique*, vol. 13, no. 1, 2020, pp. 1–16, academic.oup.com/ccc/article/13/1/1/5801059.

Biermann, Soenke. "Knowledge, Power and Decolonization: Implication for Non-Indigenous Scholars, Researchers and Educators." *Indigenous Philosophies and Critical Education: A Reader*, special issue of *Counterpoints*, vol. 379, 2011, pp. 386–98.

Cursi, Veronica. "Sanremo 2019, scontro tra giurie e televoto: Mahmood è un caso politico." *Il Messaggero*, 10 Feb. 2019, www.ilmessaggero.it/televisione/sanremo_2019_mahmood_vincitore_voto_giuria-4290677.html.

Dimitriadis, Greg. *Performing Identity / Performing Culture: Hip-Hop as Text, Pedagogy, and Lived Practice.* Peter Lang Publishing, 2001.

Dolasinski, Lisa. "'In Between' Ethnic Heritage and Italian Identity: The Global Hip-Hop of Mahmood and Ghali." *The Italianist*, vol. 42, no. 1, 2022, pp. 119–38.

Fascia, Claudia. "Sanremo 2019, Mahmood e le polemiche: 'Sono italiano al 100% faccio Marocco-pop.'" *Agenzia ANSA*, 12 Feb. 2019, www.ansa.it/sanremo_2019/notizie/2019/02/11/sanremo-2019-mahmood-e-le-polemiche-sono-italiano-al-100-faccio-marocco-pop-_bf2f355d-9438-4351-b5a2-57d4fa77c25c.html.

Ghali. "Ghali—Cara Italia." *YouTube*, uploaded by Ghali, 27 Jan. 2018, www.youtube.com/watch?v=z3UCQj8EFGk.

———. "Ghali, il ragazzo della via rap che canta l'Islam e i migrate." Interview conducted by Roberto Saviano. *La Repubblica*, 30 Apr. 2020, www.repubblica.it/spettacoli/musica/2017/06/04/news/ghali_il_ragazzo_della_via_rap_che_canta_l_islam_l_isis_e_i_migranti-167196276/.

"Ghali, il nuovo singolo è 'Cara Italia.'" *Rolling Stone Italia*, 26 Jan. 2018, www.rollingstone.it/musica/news-musica/ghali-il-nuovo-singolo-e-cara-italia/399795/.

Harris, Travis. "Can It Be Bigger than Hip Hop? From Global Hip Hop Studies to Hip Hop." *Journal of Hip Hop Studies*, vol. 6, no. 2, 2019, pp. 17–70.

Hill, Marc Lamont. *Beats, Rhymes, and Classroom Life: Hip-Hop Pedagogy and the Politics of Identity.* Teachers College Press, 2009.

Hill, Marc Lamont, and Emery Petchauer, editors. *Schooling Hip-Hop: Expanding Hip-Hop Based Education across the Curriculum.* Teachers College Press, 2013.

Issaa, Amir. "Caro Presidente." *YouTube*, uploaded by Amir Issaa, 15 Jan. 2013, www.youtube.com/watch?v=2EsRiiID6bE.

———. "Ius Music." *YouTube*, uploaded by Amir Issaa, 1 July 2014, www.youtube.com/watch?v=ZHUw8zd0FrY.

———. "Non sono un immigrato." *YouTube*, uploaded by Amir Issaa, 1 Jan. 2022, www.youtube.com/watch?v=Eg1DJgQZu4o.

———. "Straniero nella mia nazione." *YouTube*, uploaded by Amir Issaa, 13 May 2020, www.youtube.com/watch?v=xSMsBMXQr_8.

———. *Vivo per questo.* Chiarelettere Editore, 2017.

Issaa, Amir, et al. "Non respiro." *YouTube*, uploaded by Amir Issaa, 1 July 2020, www.youtube.com/watch?v=GB4MngjiiBY.

Johnson, Joquetta. "Culturally Responsive Teaching: Sparking Engagement with Hip-Hop." *Edutopia*, 1 May 2017, www.edutopia.org/blog/sparking-engagement-hip-hop-joquetta-johnson.

Mahmood. "Mahmood—Soldi." *YouTube*, uploaded by Mahmood, 5 Feb. 2019, www.youtube.com/watch?v=22lISUXgSUw.

———. "Mahmood: 'Solo dopo Sanremo ho scoperto di essere straniero nel mio paese.'" Interview conducted by Giovanni Floris. *DiMartedì*, 19 Mar. 2019, www.la7.it/dimartedi/video/mahmood-solo-dopo-sanremo-ho-scoperto-di-essere-straniero-nel-mio-paese-19-03-2019-266413.

Mitchell, Tony, editor. *Global Noise: Rap and Hip Hop outside the USA*. Wesleyan UP, 2001.

Osumare, Halifu. "Beat Streets in the Global Hood." *Journal of American and Comparative Cultures*, vol. 24, nos. 1–2, 2009, pp. 171–81.

Pennycook, Alastair. *Global Englishes and Transcultural Flows*. Routledge, 2007.

"The Performers Act II." *YouTube*, uploaded by GUCCI, 26 July 2019, www.youtube.com/watch?v=O_hd0vOudCQ.

Petchauer, Emery. "'I Feel What He Was Doin': Urban Teacher Development, Hip-Hop Aesthetics, and Justice-Oriented Teaching." *Schooling Hip-Hop: Expanding Hip-Hop Based Education across the Curriculum*, edited by Marc Lamont Hill and Petchauer, Teachers College Press, 2013, pp. 28–46.

Runell, Marcella, and Martha Diaz. *Hip-Hop Education Guidebook*. Vol. 1, Hip-Hop Association, 2007.

"Salvini come Baglioni: Presenta l'italiano vero di Mahmood." *Le Iene*, 19 Feb. 2019, www.iene.mediaset.it/2019/news/salvini-baglioni-mahmood-italiano-vero_307038.shtml.

"Sanremo, fine alle polemiche: Salvini presenta il vincitore Mahmood." *Le Iene*, 19 Feb. 2019, www.iene.mediaset.it/video/sanremo-salvini-presenta-mahmood-vincitore_307363.shtml.

Terkourafi, Marina, editor. *The Languages of Global Hip Hop*. Continuum, 2010.

Eszter Zimanyi

_____

Orban Wallace's *Another News Story*: Media Coverage of the "Migrant Crisis" in Europe

Two inflatable rafts, carrying far more refugees than they can safely handle, sway precariously as they find their way toward the rocky beach of Lesbos. Volunteers rush to help the new arrivals disembark, throwing life rings to those who have tumbled into deceptively shallow waters. As men, women, and children stumble onto land, some smile and cheer in celebration, while others break down in tears.

We have seen these images before. Since 2015, media coverage of Europe's so-called migrant crisis has inundated global audiences with heart-wrenching and horrifying footage of dangerous sea crossings, overcrowded makeshift camps, and clashes at border zones between refugees and police. The scene I describe above appears in the opening ten minutes of the documentary *Another News Story*, the feature film debut of the British director Orban Wallace. Yet despite its familiarity, the sequence is not memorable for the emotionally charged arrival of refugees that it depicts. Rather, it is the number of cameramen that appear in Wallace's frame that captures our attention. Unlike much of the media coverage of the crisis, Wallace's film does not train the camera solely on refugees. Instead, *Another News Story* places journalists front and center, emphasizing the lengths to which news correspondents will go to capture gripping images for distant audiences.

Another News Story joins several documentaries about the "migrant crisis" released to critical acclaim between 2015 and 2025. These films have ranged in style and documentary mode, from observational films such as *Fire at Sea*, directed by Gianfranco Rosi, and *4.1 Miles*, directed by Daphne Matziaraki, to the stunning *Midnight Traveler*, directed by the Afghan filmmaker and refugee Hassan Fazili and made up entirely of cell phone footage taken by Fazili and his family members. Like *Another News Story*, Ai Weiwei's sprawling meditation on migration, *Human Flow*, is notable for its self-reflexivity and awareness of migration as a process of mediation. But if *Human Flow* brings our attention to the artifice of filmmaking (Ai and his crew appear consistently throughout the film), *Another News Story* goes one step further, emphasizing the competitive environment in which that artifice is staged. Wallace's observations of journalists and filmmakers interacting with refugees not only remind us of the seemingly endless number of news reports, human interest stories, and artistic treatments of the "migrant crisis" available at our fingertips. They also confront us with the uneven and often exploitative relationship between refugees and media makers who—in seeking to both share refugees' stories and monetize audience engagement—demand that refugees repeatedly testify to their traumas and hardships. In doing so, the film makes visible how the "migrant crisis" is produced as a mediated event, one marked by global news media's insatiable hunger for drama.

Another News Story is notable for being entirely crowdfunded, from pre- through postproduction. The majority of the film was shot with a five-person crew across nine countries over a six-week period. Filming took place between September and October 2015, with some additional follow-up footage completed in November 2015, following the Paris terror attacks ("Ethics" 00:12:38–00:13:36, 00:24:09–00:34:14; "*Another News Story*"). The film eschews many of the classic tropes associated with documentary filmmaking. There are no sit-down interviews with experts who provide broader context for the events depicted in the film; there is no voice-over narration promising either detached objectivity toward, or a diaristic reflection about, the "migrant crisis." Instead, montages of broadcast news reports from around the world provide the narrative framing for Wallace's *cinéma vérité* footage of refugees and journalists alike.

The film often shifts seamlessly between these two modes, as the tele-vised news packages showing journalists reporting live on location melt into Wallace's behind-the-scenes images of the same journalists delivering their reports. These editorial decisions work to demystify and defamiliar-ize the news media as well as Wallace's own filmmaking practice. For exam-ple, in one of the film's opening scenes, we watch NBC's televised footage of its chief foreign correspondent, Richard Engel, reporting live from the Serbian-Hungarian border. It is half past midnight, and Engel stands among numerous pitched tents in which refugees try to sleep. He informs viewers that "frustration is growing among the refugees and migrants because Hungary is detaining them but doesn't even have a place to put them" (00:01:18–00:01:35). Engel sounds incredulous, but his on-screen demeanor is calm and controlled. His delivery suggests that this live report is in fact pre-scripted and invites us to consider how broadcast news relies on the ideology of liveness to communicate authenticity and immediacy to viewers at home (Feuer; Rangan).[1]

Partway through Engel's report, the film cuts from NBC's footage to Wallace's. Suddenly, the diegetic sound of generators threatens to over-whelm Engel's voice. Two large stage lights illuminating his surroundings appear in the frame, along with a boom mic and multiple crew members. The reveal of NBC's equipment and crew reminds us that the news, even when it is reported live, is a process of mediation, with myriad decisions being made about what to place within the camera's frame. After pausing a few moments to make sure they are no longer on-air, Engel's producer informs the crew that they can "switch everything off, break down, and pack up." Engel turns to his crew and jokes: "That was it? All that, for all that money and the jacket, for this? Ten seconds?" (00:01:35–00:01:55). We hear a baby crying in the distance, and as the NBC news team noisily deconstructs its set, we are left to wonder how any of the refugees can sleep through this televised intrusion (00:01:55–00:03:38).

By making the production of news media visible to viewers, Wallace's film prompts students to consider the narrative and aesthetic tropes that journalists, photographers, filmmakers, and refugees themselves rely on in their attempts to make forced migration and humanitarian emergency legible and urgent issues for viewing publics. Beyond asking how these tropes shape our understandings of migrants and refugees, *Another News Story* helps students approach the topic of migration and media from mul-tiple perspectives—those of the subject, the producer, and the consumer—and reevaluate their practices of looking. The film asks students to consider the ways these relational and overlapping subject positions sustain the event of crisis in global media discourses and to reflect on the political and ethical stakes of consuming images of crisis. As such, it is an essential text for teaching migration through nonfiction media. In the rest of this essay, I reflect on my experience teaching *Another News Story* in a graduate seminar at the University of Southern California.[2] Focusing on key scenes from the film and reflecting on class discussions, I consider some of the ways in which instructors can use *Another News Story* as a platform for exploring questions about the mediation of migration.

Visuality at Work; or, Who Has the Right to Look?

Let us return to the scene of arrival that opened this essay. Moments before the two inflatable rafts become visible from shore, Wallace is casually speaking with a pair of young Australian journalists who have been stationed in Lesbos to cover the crisis. The journalists are milling about on one of the island's cliffs overlooking the sea, deliberating where to go next, when we hear someone shout "Look, there's a boat!" from offscreen (00:05:03–00:06:15). At once, the reporters gathered on Lesbos mobilize. A montage shows multiple journalists from different organizations run to their cars, race to the beach, and transfer footage to their employers as quickly as possible. We see news reporters chasing after refugees on foot, aggressively shoving cameras into refugees' faces, and pulling refugees aside for interviews as soon as they disembark (00:06:15–00:08:35). The intensity of the arrival is made all the more disturbing by the film's display of invasive media practices normally hidden from view. Yet what students found most remarkable about this scene is the moment Wallace reapproaches the Australian journalists to ask about their thoughts on the refugees' arrival. When one of the journalists notices that Wallace is still filming her, she becomes agitated: "Why are you filming journalists and not them? They've got way more important stories. . . . If I was you, I'd go film the refugees, not the journalists" (00:08:35–00:09:05).

This is one of several tense exchanges between Wallace and journalists, many of whom appear impatient or irritated with Wallace's insistence on filming them. Prior to viewing the film, I required students to read the preface and introductory chapter of Nicholas Mirzoeff's *The Right to Look: A Counterhistory of Visuality*. Mirzoeff describes visuality as "both a medium for the transmission and dissemination of authority, and a means for the mediation of those subject to that authority" ("Ineluctable Visualities" xv).

Visuality invests the visualizer with authority and makes "that exclusive claim to be able to look" (Mirzoeff, "Right" 2). Vested with the authority to see on the public's behalf, journalists play a significant role in producing migrants and refugees as knowable, surveillable, and containable subjects. In class, I asked students, "How does Wallace unsettle visuality's operations in *Another News Story* by turning the camera back onto reporters?" They remarked that the journalists' resistance to being interviewed on film raises salient questions about who is allowed to look at whom and who has the power to avoid being looked at. These questions are made all the more poignant in another key scene I asked students to discuss where Ali, one of the refugees Wallace interviews, tells Wallace:

> As long as the number of filmmakers increase, a kind of humiliating feeling starts within our, you know, soul. We are like toys, alright, and they're playing with us. This guy is making a movie of me and Europeans at home, they're having their, you know, French fries, or snack, or a beer, watching us. "Okay, pity those Afghans" or Africans or whatever. "Let's go to futbol," or Americans, "Let's go to baseball!" (00:16:50–00:17:45)

Ali's frustration speaks directly to the exploitative nature of news media, which, as he rightly points out, demands refugees participate in the commodification of their own suffering with no guarantee that doing so will benefit their chances of survival. It is not lost on students that *Another News Story* is also engaged in the mediation of refugees; however, by making journalists a central part of the film's narrative, Wallace successfully disturbs the hierarchies of looking that global news media function to maintain and invites students to interrogate their own practices of looking as well.

"Eating Human Stories"

Beyond providing students an opportunity to think critically about practices of looking, *Another News Story* also challenges students to rethink the narrative and aesthetic tropes we associate with refugees. The second reading I assigned to students was a chapter from Pooja Rangan's *Immediations: The Humanitarian Impulse in Documentary* (61–101). In this chapter, Rangan cogently argues that there are "prescribed testimonial code[s] through which the subjects of humanitarian emergencies become legible to humanitarian audiences," one of which is the demonstration of vulnerability (66).

These codes "mediate the speech of the dispossessed when it is articulated in the form of human rights claims" (100). I asked students, "After reading Rangan's chapter, how do you think *Another News Story* frames refugees' testimonies in comparison to other documentaries about vulnerable subjects that you have seen?" They remarked that the film not only makes visible the performative labor extracted from refugees by journalists but also avoids essentializing refugees as helpless victims. One student was particularly intrigued by Wallace's treatment of Mahasen, a middle-aged Syrian refugee who is traveling alone and hopes to be reunited with her children in Germany. Despite the unthinkable hardships she has lived through, Mahasen does not offer any detailed testimony about her life in Syria. Instead, she speaks about her future: her desire to live a peaceful life, be a "good citizen," and pay her taxes in Germany (01:07:00–01:07:15).

Mahasen is presented as determined, outspoken, and willing to push for her rights. In one memorable scene, she boards an overcrowded train carriage destined for Croatia. The cabin is sweltering; there is no electricity or air conditioning, and the windows are sealed shut. Realizing how dangerous the situation is, Mahasen spends half an hour shouting down reporters and police, demanding the group be moved to a different area of the train. Wallace, however, does not show her in action. Instead, he cuts from the interior of the overheated cabin to the moment the refugees are moved to another area of the train and asks Mahasen to describe how she's feeling after her successful intervention (00:52:57–00:55:36). One student noted that different editing might have made Mahasen seem either more sympathetic or more heroic and felt she instead came across as a person pushing an agenda. This observation opened a wider discussion among students about how we come to understand refugees as sympathetic. Students reflected on how narrative tropes of suffering and aesthetics of vulnerability shape our expectations for refugees' behavior and limit refugees' subjecthood. We are not accustomed to seeing refugees challenge the conditions of their resettlement, and Mahasen unsettles our expectations by refusing to perform the role of the passive, helpless victim awaiting our rescue. At the same time, Wallace's decision not to include footage of her intervention resists heroizing Mahasan as an exceptional character. Through a close reading of this scene, students are encouraged to consider their preconceived notions about refugees as well as their assumptions about the conventions of representation.

Images of crisis no longer seem to pierce through the mundanity of the everyday; rather, they have become a permanent fixture of our lives, mundane in and of themselves. Francisco, an Italian television reporter, echoes this feeling when he describes the current state of news reporting to Wallace: "Human story, human story, human story. . . . We are eating human stories" (00:44:00–00:45:45). As I write this essay in the final weeks of 2020, the COVID-19 pandemic has ravaged most of the globe. Media coverage of hospitals filled to capacity and refrigerated trucks packed with body bags holding the dead has, for the time being, overshadowed reporting on the conditions of migrants and refugees in Europe and elsewhere—even as unauthorized migrants and refugees remain particularly vulnerable to illness. The questions *Another News Story* raises for students about processes of mediation are all the more necessary as the crises of the pandemic, climate change, economic instability, war, and mass displacement intersect and compound one another. It is vital that we continue to interrogate the role media plays in sustaining crisis as our shared condition.

Notes

1. Feuer's influential essay theorizes how an ideology of liveness structures television at large. See Rangan for a specific engagement with how the ideology of liveness structures televised news reporting about humanitarian crises.

2. I thank Professor Anikó Imre for inviting me to guest-lecture in her fall 2020 graduate seminar Media, Nationalism, and Global Crisis and the students in this course for their thoughtful engagement with the film.

Works Cited

Another News Story. Directed by Orban Wallace, Gallivant Film / Wislocki Films, 2017.
"*Another News Story*: A Film by Orban Wallace." Gallivant Film / Wislocki Films, 2017. Press kit.
"Ethics in the News 2: *Another News Story*." *YouTube*, uploaded by Frontline Club, 5 Apr. 2018, www.youtube.com/watch?v=oqUsCGJUYKQ.
Feuer, Jane. "The Concept of Live Television: Ontology as Ideology." *Reading Television: Critical Approaches: An Anthology*, edited by E. Ann Kaplan, University Publications of America, 1983, pp. 12–22.
Fire at Sea. Directed by Gianfranco Rosi, Kino Lorber, 2016.
4.1 Miles. Directed by Daphne Matziaraki, Graduate School of Journalism, U of California, Berkeley, 2016.

Human Flow. Directed by Ai Weiwei, Participant Media, 2017.

Midnight Traveler. Directed by Hassan Fazili, Oscilloscope, 2019.

Mirzoeff, Nicholas. "Ineluctable Visualities." Preface. Mirzoeff, *Right*, pp. xiii–xvi.

———. *The Right to Look: A Counterhistory of Visuality*. Duke UP, 2011.

———. "The Right to Look; or, How to Think with and against Visuality." Introduction. Mirzoeff, *Right*, pp. 1–47.

Rangan, Pooja. *Immediations: The Humanitarian Impulse in Documentary*. Duke UP, 2017.

Kristen Stern

Questioning the Possibility of Return in Francophone Literatures

This essay outlines the goals, curricular objectives, primary texts, and student work of a course I have taught in several different undergraduate French programs at small colleges and at a midsize public university, The Return in Francophone Literatures. While the study of migration in francophone literature and film often focuses on the protagonists' departures or destinations, this course asks students to examine the flip side of that experience: the return to the native land. In so doing, this course asks students to think critically about portrayals of what Chimamanda Adichie might call a "single story" of migration that prevail in popular culture and political discourse. Particularly for students at US universities, the texts and themes studied here lend nuance to students' understanding of global migration flows and individual experiences beyond US contexts and of story arcs that situate European or North American cities as paradisiacal final destinations.

Course Goals and Primary Texts

Conducted in French for students with Intermediate High to Advanced Low proficiency,[1] the course includes foundational and contemporary texts in French in a variety of forms and genres by authors with diverse geographic and cultural roots. In most cases, this course has been students' first exposure to literary studies at the college level and in almost all cases their first exposure to literary studies in French and francophone literatures. The course therefore also introduces the basics of reading and critiquing literary texts (and films) in the target language while building a foundation in the canon of francophone literatures from the Caribbean and the African continent specifically. The course also introduces more contemporary examples of the theme of return that address current issues regarding migration and its representation. The primary materials intentionally include several different genres: poetry, fiction and nonfiction prose, fiction and documentary film, and *bande dessinée* (comics), exposing students to a rich variety of texts from the mid–twentieth century through today in which the themes of the course are addressed.

A cornerstone for the course's theme of return is Aimé Césaire's long poem *Cahier d'un retour au pays natal* (*Notebook of a Return to the Native Land*). While the surrealist imagery, specific vocabulary, and rich historical references pose a challenge to students, they appreciate the importance in the francophone tradition of the recurring image of the "return to the native land." As the semester progresses, they see and hear this image repeated in written texts and even in author interviews shared in class. I choose excerpts to focus their attention on the most crucial elements of the long poem: repetition, the image of dawn, the references to the Haitian Revolution, and Césaire's universal connections to oppressed peoples the world over and particularly in the African diaspora.

Prose is heavily emphasized in the course, both for its familiarity to students and its visibility in literary studies today. The first prose text students read is Dany Laferrière's novel *Pays sans chapeau* (*Down among the Dead Men*). This novel tells the story of a fictionalized version of Laferrière himself, a writer living in exile in Montreal who returns to Haiti to visit his mother and aunt. While there, he questions the existence of a zombie army that his family and friends explain controls the night, while the US Army and other foreign interventionist NGOs control the daylight hours. Students grapple with the novel's ambiguous use of language—for example, the protagonst's mother never names the city of Montreal when she speaks about his exile and only refers to his being "là-bas" ("over there"; 28; my trans.). Ambiguous language like this brings to light both the brutality of the migrant experience, including for those who are left behind, as well as the poetic ways that humans try to speak about unnamable traumas. Students are encouraged to move beyond simply questioning whether the zombie army is real or not and to investigate instead what other questions this imagery might raise concerning the devastating effects of centuries of foreign interventions and the difficulties of using language to express trauma.

Building on a secondary theme of autobiography and writing the self, students also read nonfiction prose extracts from Alain Mabanckou's *Lumières de Pointe-Noire* (*The Lights of Pointe-Noire*), a memoir recounting the author's first return to the city of his childhood in the Republic of the Congo after three decades. The book includes photographs at the end of most chapters, some from the writer's past and some from present of the trip that he takes. Our study of this text raises questions of memory, family interactions, and the rhetorical strategies Mabanckou uses when juxtaposing visual and textual imagery. Specifically, the black-and-white photographs do not always align in grandeur or splendor with the descriptions given by the author in the preceding pages, at times subverting the textual message or at the very least startling the reader and thus leading the reader to question the trustworthiness of the version of the autobiography in their hands.

Following this engagement with the interplay between text and image, we spend significant time understanding how to decode and interpret visual grammar. Two films are studied: a fiction feature film directed by Alain Gomis, *Aujourd'hui (Tey)* (*Today*), and a documentary directed by Jean-Marie Teno, *Vacances au Pays* (*A Trip to the Country*). In Gomis's film, the viewer follows Satché's last day alive as he visits his old friends, family members, and sites in his home city of Dakar, Senegal. The return theme is subtler in this film than it is in other texts in this course, but it is still there: Satché is a returned migrant who has spent significant time abroad in the United States before returning to Senegal with his wife and family in the year preceding the day we follow in the film. I use a sensory approach to teach student strategies for decoding the visual and aural elements of the film, which is particularly productive in a film with many scenes with minimal dialogue. Focusing on the five senses affords students quick access to a concrete understanding of how visual and sound imagery produce meaning in film and specifically how all five senses are activated, while the filmmaker, strictly speaking, has access to only two.

Teno's documentary follows the filmmaker (and offscreen narrator) on a long road trip from the Cameroonian capital city, Yaoundé, north to his childhood village. Returning for a visit after many years in France and traveling abroad for his film career, Teno retraces the same long journey he used to take back home as a schoolboy during vacations from his studies in the capital city. Throughout the nostalgic rediscovery of roadside stops and landmarks he used to know, the filmmaker asks the viewer to question assumptions about modernity and so-called development as they are understood by his interlocutors, many of whom equate development with late capitalist consumerism. Students also make connections between *Vacances au pays* and texts by Mabanckou and Laferrière studied earlier in the semester, raising similar questions about self-writing (self-filming) and the trustworthiness of the narrator. Teno is essentially a one-man show, operating his own handheld camera, conducting the interviews, and providing the postproduction off-camera narration (though the viewer never sees his face). His nostalgic voice-overs describe the past, while the often run-down sites of significance are shown on-screen in the present: his former high school in Yaoundé, now boarded up; a soccer field in his family's hometown, now overgrown with few volunteers to tend it. The contrast in narration and visual imagery somewhat brutally answers the question: no, you can't really go home again.

Finally, students read two texts by authors who narrate their return to Algeria for personal or family reasons: a graphic novel by Olivia Burton, *L'Algérie c'est beau comme l'Amérique* (*Algeria Is Beautiful like America*) and excerpts from Akram Belkaïd's *Retours en Algérie* (*Returns to Algeria*). I assign the graphic novel—a form that students increasingly already have some familiarity with as fans of manga and other styles—in combination with short excerpts of Scott McCloud's *Understanding Comics: The Invisible Art*. (The French translation, *L'Art invisible*, exposes students to the vocabulary of comics and *bande dessinée* in French.) These excerpts invite students to think about the participation of the reader in graphic novels and the reader's role in filling in the literal gaps to create the movement and action of the story.

The reader's complicity with the writer and illustrator is particularly important in Burton's memoir of the experience of a daughter and granddaughter of *pieds-noirs* (white French Algerian settler families who resettled in mainland France following Algerian independence in 1962) who visits the site of the family home for the first time. The protagonist, along with the reader, must come to terms with the roles previous generations of her family played in the colonial occupation and settlement of the country.

In Belkaïd's memoir, we study the first of the multiple return trips recounted in the book (as suggested by the plural *Returns* in the title), in which the author, an Algerian-born journalist living in France, is invited to join a group of French military veterans of the Algerian War (1954–62) who are returning for the first time since the end of the armed conflict with the former colonial power. The exceptional circumstances of Belkaïd's return raise particular questions regarding the possibilities for and limits of reconciliation, repair, and understanding on individual and institutional scales. Like Burton's story in *L'Algérie c'est beau comme l'Amérique*, Belkaïd's story asks students to think critically about who and under what circumstances one can claim some path of return, particularly when feelings of personal or intergenerational ownership of a territory are explicitly born of violent colonial conquest.

The variety of forms and genres studied in the course serves a curricular need, introducing students to the breadth of francophone studies and the variety of methods needed for interpreting prominent genres and forms such as poetry, prose (particularly memoir and autofiction), film (fiction and documentary), and graphic novels. At the same time, students consider an enduring and pertinent theme in these texts through the many ways return stories are told while also contemplating what each form affords its author. The range of the authors' geographic origins and circumstances also eschews overgeneralization of a single migrant narrative.

Assignments and Evaluation

The course alternately zooms out to structural forces at play in a narrator's migration experience and zooms in to the human scale of the narrative. While historical contexts are addressed in class discussion, students also reflect on their own experiences and points of view to anchor their readings. Many students on the mostly residential campuses where I have taught this course are familiar with leaving and returning home; in my current institution in particular, students who are immigrants or children of immigrants themselves also make up a significant portion of learners. While I encourage students to find connections with the protagonists of the texts and films we study, we also discuss the limits of relying on our individual experiences as a lens for reading the authors we study, who may narrate experiences of characters living in exile for decades because of fears for personal safety, for example. This more reflective part of our work is accomplished mainly through weekly journals (individual, low-stakes, short writing assignments with feedback from the instructor) and seminar-style discussion in class. The journals serve as students' personal archives of their reflections on each text and the initial feedback from the instructor that can later be used as a springboard for more sustained reflection in two short essay assignments and a longer final project.

While personal reflection is a significant component of the course, students are also introduced to secondary sources in literary and francophone studies. This work is concentrated in two assignments: first, a collective annotated bibliography assignment completed in the last third of the course and, second, an individual critical essay, which is the course's final project. For the shared annotated bibliography, I preselect a collection of peer-reviewed journal articles and essays related to the authors, texts, and themes of the course that I have assembled (see the appendix). By prescreening these secondary sources, I allow students to focus on reading and understanding the main arguments of these at times challenging academic texts and on how to apply those arguments to the course themes and materials in their final essays. Class time is spent understanding the basics of citation—how to acknowledge, and why it is important to acknowledge, the other scholars we are in conversation with—and the purpose of an annotated bibliography. While their aim in this class is to help their classmates evaluate and select pertinent secondary sources for their final essays, we discuss how at a larger scale this is similar to how scholarly reviews work among communities of researchers. Students each pick one source that they will read in detail and evaluate in writing, the intended audience being their classmates, helping them judge whether a source is pertinent to their research question in the final essay. The articles and essays I curate explore a variety of texts and topics: some are focused on a specific author or text studied in class; others address larger themes of migration, return, or autobiography. We discuss how when conducting research, we may not find resources that speak exactly to our primary sources, but reading around somewhat broader research questions may be necessary and generative, especially when studying topics and authors that have not yet been extensively written about. Supported by the secondary sources in this shared annotated bibliography, students write a final essay, incorporating both elements of personal reflection and a critical reading of one or more primary texts studied in the course, demonstrating proficiency in both approaches. French majors and minors are expected to produce writing of significant length and richness at the advanced level, and the quantity of reflective and critical writing that students produce in this course meets that curricular demand.

Outcomes

Focusing on individual narratives, both fiction and nonfiction, of migrating subjects contrasts with the aggregated statistics or policy discussions that students may encounter in social sciences classrooms or on national news coverage. At the same time, students are pushed beyond initial questions of how they might relate to a protagonist, applying introductory skills in literary and film analysis to decode the nuances of individual works and the effects of certain aesthetic choices. Examining the theme of return also offers a way to trouble the cliché immigrant story in which the northern city is the final, paradisiacal destination. Ultimately, students gain a foundation in francophone studies through material that humanizes the migration experience and asks US-based readers to consider migration flows as more multidirectional than political discourse may portray them. This course demonstrates that curricular needs in a language department— such as the introduction to a field of study and the development of critical skills in writing through specific research- and reflection-driven tasks— can be met through a specific thematic course on migration in literature and film. Such a course prepares students to continue on to more advanced classes in literary studies and in francophone studies in general. At the same time, a theme such as migration, which is both timely and enduring, need not only be found in add-on courses or electives but can and should be part of foundational courses offered to students in modern languages and literary studies.

Notes

I wish to acknowledge the undergraduate students at Bates College, Davidson College, and the University of Massachusetts, Lowell, who were part of different iterations of this course for helping further my understanding of the topic of migration and the texts themselves.

1. This is based on the ACTFL Proficiency Guidelines.

Works Cited

Adichie, Chimamanda Ngozi. "The Danger of a Single Story." *TED*, July 2009, www.ted.com/talks/chimamanda_ngozi_adichie_the_danger_of_a_single_story.

Aujourd'hui (Tey). Directed by Alain Gomis, Screen Media Films, 2013.

Belkaïd, Akram. *Retours en Algérie: Des retrouvailles émouvantes avec l'Algérie d'aujourd'hui.* Carnets Nord, 2013.

Burton, Olivia. *L'Algérie c'est beau comme l'Amérique.* Illustrated by Mahi Grand, Steinkis, 2015.

Césaire, Aimé. *Cahier d'un retour au pays natal.* Présence Africaine, 1939.

Laferrière, Dany. *Down among the Dead Men.* Translated by David Homel, Douglas and MacIntyre, 2012.

———. *Pays sans chapeau.* Éditions Lanctôt, 1996.

Mabanckou, Alain. *The Lights of Pointe-Noire.* Translated by Helen Stevenson, New Press, 2016.

———. *Lumières de Pointe-Noire.* Seuil, 2013.

McCloud, Scott. *L'Art Invisible.* Translated by Dominique Petitfaux, Delcourt, 2007.

———. *Understanding Comics: The Invisible Art.* Kitchen Sink, 1993.

Vacances au pays. Directed by Jean-Marie Teno, Les Films du Raphia, 2000.

Appendix: Secondary Sources for Annotated Bibliography Assignment

Cousins, Helen, and Pauline Dodgson-Katiyo. "Leaving Home / Returning Home: Migration and Contemporary African Literature." *Diaspora and Returns in Fiction,* special issue of *African Literature Today,* no. 34, 2016, pp. 1–11.

DuCournau, Claire. "From One Place to Another: The Transnational Mobility of Contemporary Francophone Sub-Saharan African Writers." Mabanckou and Thomas, pp. 49–61.

Hardwick, Louise. "Thwarted Expectations? Stasis and Change in Haiti in Dany Laferrière's *L'odeur du care* and *Le charme des après-midi sans fin.*" *Childhood, Autobiography, and the Francophone Caribbean,* by Hardwick, Liverpool UP, 2013, pp. 158–80.

Husti-Laboye, Carmen. "D'un certain éternel retour dans la littérature franco-phone actuelle." *Otago French Notes: Cahiers d'études littéraires françaises de l'Université d'Otago,* vol. 3, 2010, pp. 191–204.

Ireland, Susan. "First-Generation Immigrant Narratives." *Immigrant Narratives in Contemporary France,* edited by Ireland and Patrice J. Proulx, Greenwood Press, 2001, pp. 23–43.

Kom, Ambroise. "Il n'y a pas de retour heureux." *Mots Pluriels,* no. 20, Feb. 2002, motspluriels.arts.uwa.edu.au/MP2002ak.html.

Lahens, Yanick. "Exile: Between Writing and Place." *Callaloo,* vol. 15, no. 3, 1992, pp. 735–46.

Mabanckou, Alain, and Donald Nicholson-Smith. "Immigration, 'Littérature-Monde,' and Universality: The Strange Fate of the African Writer." Mabanckou and Thomas, pp. 75–87.

Mabanckou, Alain, and Rokiatou Soumaré. "How to Become Globalized without Losing Your Mind." *World Literature Today*, Sept.-Oct. 2016, pp. 64–66.

Mabanckou, Alain, and Dominic Thomas, editors. *Francophone Sub-Saharan African Literature in Global Contexts*. Special issue of *Yale French Studies*. No. 120, 2011.

Ménard, Nadève. "The Myth of the Exiled Writer." *New Narratives of Haiti*, special issue of *Transition*, no. 111, edited by Laurent Dubois and Kaiama L. Glover, 2013, pp. 53–58.

Naudillon, Françoise. "Autofictionalités francophones: 'C'est moi et ce n'est pas moi.'" *Nouvelles Études Francophones*, vol. 31, no. 1, spring 2016, pp. 1–6.

Prieto, Eric Luis. "The Poetics of Place, the Rhetoric of Authenticity, and Aimé Césaire's *Cahier d'un retour au pays natal*." *Dalhousie French Studies*, vol. 55, summer 2001, pp. 142–51.

Shumsky, Neil Larry. "Return Migration in American Novels of the 1920s and 1930s." *Writing across Worlds: Literature and Migration*, edited by Russell King et al., Routledge, 2002, pp. 198–215.

Toivanen, Anna-Leena. "Uneasy 'Homecoming' in Alain Mabanckou's *Lumières de Pointe-Noire*." *Studies in Travel Writing*, vol. 21, no. 3, 6 Sept. 2017, pp. 327–45, https://doi.org/10.1080/13645145.2017.1360276.

Elizabeth Rich

The Impact of Emigration on Narrativizing the Arab Spring

The Arab Spring of 2011 links a long history of the Middle East's development after colonial contact with complex twenty-first-century global dynamics. Preconceived ideas that students bring to the classroom about immigration, foreign affairs, and the Middle East, such as the belief that violence in the Middle East is spontaneous and constant and that immigrants are a monolithic group, can be adjusted by addressing the historical and material contexts that initiated the Arab Spring[1] and by studying the event and its effects. However, doing so requires being aware of how the Arab Spring is heavily mediated by editors, publishers, and Western institutions. Mediation always involves limitations, yet it also presents an opportunity to advance a critical context and form discussions around how migrants who are writers, filmmakers, activists, journalists, and artists use various outlets to bring the voices of young Arab people to English-speaking audiences. Literature and the Arab Spring, a sophomore-level general education course for non-English majors that I teach, contains three units that each approach the Arab Spring and its contexts by laying out the problematics and promises of globalization; studying expressions about the Arab Spring by writers, documentarians, filmmakers, protesters, and students; and reviewing what writers and critics have to say several years after the events. Additionally, including both migrants who do not necessarily migrate west as well as migrants who live in the West and use publishing houses, government institutions, and other ways of sharing voices from the Arab world challenges static narratives regarding self-determination and personal responsibility.

Without emigrants leaving for the West, the English-language accounts and critical interpretations of the Arab Spring that we read in the second part of the course would not be accessible even in a filtered form. Therefore, unlike most general education courses, this one pays special attention to writing contests, editors, literary blogs, literary festivals, and other ways of producing and promoting cross-cultural texts so that students gain a sense of the human work that goes into building narratives beyond constructs of Western subjectivity and stereotypes about people who cross borders.

Drawing on a materialist critical framework that aims to locate historical and material conditions for social unrest, the first part of the class focuses on understanding structural violence and inequality. The neoliberal terrain of identity politics is an area that can be as reductive as it can be productive. The texts used in this class, I argue, have the potential to open spaces for critical assessments of reductive individualistic views of identity because the emigrants who call for Arab voices also embed key texts with solid critiques of Western notions about the Arab Spring. Texts that ground the first unit of the course give students access to forces that drive migration, such as globalization, interference by Western governments, civil unrest, and economic, environmental, and military involvement. The idea of "poverty" enjoys little critical attention in common parlance because it seems evident to anyone who assumes Western capitalist standards. The film *Garbage Dreams*, directed by Mai Iskander, and the essay "Why Development Creates Poverty," by Edward Goldsmith, pair well to address the material and historical processes by which globalization affects social structures and, thus, the lives and identities of people. Iskander, the daughter of an Egyptian emigrant to the United States, also filmed a documentary entitled *Words of Witness*, which chronicles Tahrir Square's events, events that caused her to fly to Egypt days before the resignation of President Hosni Mubarak. *Garbage Dreams* tells the story of the Zabaleen people of Cairo, who live among heaps of waste and recycle eighty percent of it. Once forgotten and considered useless, the refuse is transformed. The Zabaleen people make it profitable. Their community-based standards create a space of belonging. Their previous displacement from rural herding practices shows how migration is not simply a movement toward the so-called Global North. Globalization creates pockets of poverty and wealth in so-called developing countries by demanding migration from rural to urban areas. The once displaced Zabaleen people set up an urban "Recycling School" (18:07), where children learn math and reading skills and how to be efficient in recycling. While still difficult and dangerous, this work is done with a sense of pride, as a way to earn income, and it shows a capacity to adapt to urban life. Once the Zabaleen people created a productive space, Cairo contracted with Spanish and Italian companies, displacing the Zabaleen people yet again. Students are dismayed as they watch a less efficient process prevail, since the contract requires only twenty percent of the material to be recycled. The film traces a loss of income, a story of displacement set in an urban area that is founded on a much earlier rural-to-urban migration story. Migration in this context recurs because of pressure from economic development.

This film pairs well with Goldsmith's essay. Goldsmith explains how poverty spreads when economic development appears and how, paradoxically, the remedy proposed by proponents of development is additional development (44). Challenging a host of anchored images of migrants, people from the Middle East, and poverty takes reinforcement and a combination of narratives that are both documentary in nature as well as creative. Terms such as *embedded societies*, *disembedded societies*, and *globalization* are useful in encouraging students to think beyond their initial empathetic responses and as a means of emphasizing structural conditions. Goldsmith's essay searches for an equivalent term for *poverty* in embedded societies, societies in which economic and social structures are intertwined rather than separated. The closest term he can find for *poverty* is one that translates to "orphan" (45). The oxymoronic title *Garbage Dreams* speaks to rural-to-urban migrants' desire for belonging and a future in the face of poverty that development created.

In *Garbage Dreams*, "dreaming" signifies hopefulness for the future, a central concept in several other texts. "Dreaming" links these foundational ideas about the context of rising social unrest in the twenty-first century with familiar contexts for English-speaking audiences. The second portion of the course covers the Arab Spring in Tunisia and Egypt from December 2010 through Mubarak's resignation, with an acknowledgment that protests continued in different countries in the following years. The process by which the language of dreaming can draw out and undercut radical aspects of uprisings is a central concern. In their edited collection of memoirs by young Arab people, *Arab Spring Dreams: The Next Generation Speaks Out for Freedom and Justice from North Africa to Iran*, Nasser Weddady, civil rights outreach director for the American Islamic Congress, and Sohrab Ahmari, a former refugee who was born in Iran and is now based in Boston, give ample critical context to the narratives. The text contains a rationale for its title, saying that it is inspired by the "I Have a Dream" speech given by Martin Luther King, Jr., which, in turn, was inspired by Langston Hughes's poem "Harlem." The structure of the introduction aligns with the first part of the course and explains the conditions of "the roots of an explosion" (Weddady and Ahmari, "New Generation" 1). Students tend to be more familiar with King's speech than they are with Hughes's poem, so more time is dedicated to the poem and to the idea of a "dream deferred." The poem's concrete imagery of a "dream deferred" decaying ("dry," "fester," "stink, "crust"), being a physical burden, or something that may "explode" balances inevitable conditions for living things that perish with the hopeful and emotional idea of an implied healthy dream and, implicitly, life (Hughes, "Harlem"). Hughes's language, appropriated by King, arises in the memoirs in *Arab Spring Dreams* and some of the other texts that the course covers, such as "Graffiti for Two," by Alaa Abd El-Fattah and Ahmed Douma. The hybrid nature of the language of the civil rights movement in Weddady and Ahmari's call for expressions from Arab youth gives a rich space to consider questions such as the following: What concerns do young Arab people share with young people in English-speaking countries? What does the language of imagining "dreams" do to capture and critique the state of one's present moment? How can individual expressions of oppression serve larger populations and address systemic problems? What work enables the voices of young Arab people to appear in a US classroom? While the brief essays in Weddady and Ahmari's collection were written prior to 2011, the introduction, "A New Generation of Reformers Speaks Out," and the conclusion, "Our Dream Deferred: Enlisting You in the Mideast Civil Rights Alliance," frame the edition in terms of the Arab Spring.

The editors resourcefully use both the language of civil rights, which has its roots in examining economic inequality, and the institution of the American Islamic Congress, formed in 2001. However, King's message, when reiterated, often loses its radical edge. Similarly, beyond promoting diversity, the American Islamic Congress, which sponsored the contest for short personal essays for Weddady and Ahmari's book, states that it "encourages social and economic prosperity" and aims to "protect the

rights of minorities in the Muslim world" ("About Us"). By considering
the filters, institutions, and processes through which young voices of the
Arab world come to be published, we can examine how identity intersects
with economic and political considerations. Interpreting *Arab Spring
Dreams* takes more than allowing the memoirs to speak for themselves; it
also entails using tools that the editors include, which contextualize the
memoirs. Just as other readings in the course point toward the convenient
term *Arab Spring*, Weddady and Ahmari's introduction locates the term
in the language of current events and the history of the term *spring* in "the
giddy headlines of Marxist magazines from decades ago that would hail the
arrival of a national 'spring' every time socialists won elections" ("New Generation" 12). A headnote prefacing each memoir provides information about
the colonial history of the country where the writer lives; the restrictions or
consequences, if any, that the writer faces; and the writer's identity. In "The
Shredded Exam Card," a twenty-one-year-old Iranian woman who wanted
to be a teacher explains how her family's Baha'i ethnicity caused her father
to lose his job, never to teach again; how her mother could no longer teach;
and how her sister was expelled. The headnotes explain how opportunity
and identity (ethnic, gendered, queer) intersect and show that the results of
political shifts regarding identity bear material consequences. The headnote
to "The Shredded Exam Card" reads as follows:

> A confidential 1991 memorandum signed by Seyyed Muhammad Gol-
> paygani, secretary of Iran's Supreme Cultural Revolutionary Council,
> and approved by the Supreme Leader, spelled out the new regime's edu-
> cation policy toward the Baha'i. The Baha'i, Golpaygani wrote, "must
> be expelled from universities, either in the admission process or dur-
> ing the course of their studies, once it becomes known that they are
> Baha'is." (T. T. 64)

The text concludes with a discussion about what identity politics means
to Arab pro-democracy movements in specific terms, making it, if time is
spent on this portion of the text, impossible to generalize, universalize,
and flatten the text. It contains a glossary of "past mistakes" with expla-
nations, which are useful for the recursive consideration of the memoirs
(Weddady and Ahmari, "Our Dream" 210). The "past mistakes" are interpretive errors in characterizing the Middle East: "Headline Conflicts,"
"Engagement," "Non-Interventionism," "The Authenticity Fetish,"
"Essentialization," and "The Islamist Threat" (211–14). Each refers back
to a specific memoir or common ideas among memoirs in the collection
and encourages a textured review.

The language of dreaming, or visions for the future, takes a collective turn as the unit focuses on tweets related to the uprisings. Nadia Idle, who grew up in Egypt but was living in London in 2011, hurried to Tahrir Square upon hearing of the events unfolding. Idle and Alex Nunns's *Tweets from Tahrir* provides Western students with access to the voices of Arab youth in tweets. Again, ample explanation in the introduction provides context and a brief but essential statement of transparency. The preface reveals the collection's framing devices: "It is important to say that we do not claim that this collection is comprehensive. It is merely a sample of some of the activity that was taking place on Twitter. . . . Neither do we claim to have included all of the key tweeters who took part" (Idle and Nunns, Preface 14). Idle and Nunns's editorial choices privilege giving "a readable, fast-paced account of the Revolution that gives a sense of what was being said on Twitter" (14). In the introduction, the editors make a cogent case for writing against global media portrayals of "the Egyptian uprising" as being a "Twitter Revolution" (Idle and Nunns, Introduction 19). Doing so shows "a certain arrogance [of] the lazy Western description" (21). Such an "arrogance"

> excuses commentators from seeking to understand the deep-seated causes of the uprising—the brutal economic reality for the majority of the population, the imposition of neoliberal policies reducing job security and suppressing wages, the lack of opportunities for educated young people, the sheer vindictiveness of a Western-backed dictator as expressed through his police gangs.
>
> It ignores the role of the urban poor. . . .
>
> It ignores the role of the organized working class, which had been striking since 2006, and whose refusal to go to work in the days before Mubarak resigned finally removed the last plank from under his regime.
>
> And it ignores the years of thankless work by the very activists who made such good use of Twitter. (21–22)

The collection maintains a critical view by interrupting the linear assemblage of tweets with chapter headings and explanatory headnotes. The editorial voice does not absent itself from the representations of events and is even performative by inserting two inked-black pages to indicate the government's shutting down of Internet access, an epilogue that explains that the successes of the uprisings later met greater government oppression, and additional tweets after the epilogue to show the persistence of the activists. Like *Arab Spring Dreams*, the editors use an established publisher (OR Books in this case) to bring an alternative narrative to a Western readership, one that shows how a "sense of international solidarity was forged online that was then taken to the streets" (Idle and Nunns, Epilogue 231). The interplay between thought, text or writing, and action sets up the most hopeful expressions that the course offers, though the long-term effects of the uprisings demonstrate many challenges.

In the third and final unit, the essay "The 'Arab Spring,' Five Years On," by Elisabeth Jaquette and Nariman Youssef, both literary translators, frames the event in the past for the January 2016 issue of *Words without Borders*. The essay defines the Arab Spring as "a Western invention" and yet also as an event that precipitated a prolific response by creative writers. *Words without Borders* is a free digital international publication of literary work formed in 2003 to broaden access to exemplary literature in many languages by publishing works in translation. Based in New York and founded by Alane Salierno Mason, a senior editor at W. W. Norton, this publication invites submissions from writers around the world. Like the American Islamic Congress and OR Books, *Words without Borders* is a vehicle that emigrants from and people living in the Arab world use to share their words and art. The emphasis on translation means that the kind of filters used in *Arab Spring Dreams* and *Tweets from Tahrir* are modified so that works written in English do not crowd out those written in other languages. The January 2016 issue of *Words without Borders* brings together several of the critical views in the course. The international staff members gather writers whose voices may not find outlets and some who have migrated—not always to Western countries. Youssef, one of the translators and a coauthor of the introductory essay, "The 'Arab Spring,' Five Years On," is an Egyptian translator living in London, and Jaquette lived for a time in Cairo. One of the contributors to the issue, Noor Dakerli, migrated from Syria to Lebanon. For two other writers, Alaa Abd El-Fattah and Ahmed Douma, who remained in prison in Egypt for years[2] and whose poem is linked to in the introduction to the issue, a publication like *Words without Borders* is one of the few ways their voices were heard. Their hybrid poem-essay "Graffiti for Two" in parts features the language of hope and dreams. Using "dream" forty-three times, the text reflects on the *midan*, the space where protesters convened; what tensions existed within it; what promises it held; and what consequences it faced. Unable to be discussed at length in this essay are *Beirut 39*, edited by Samuel Shimon, a compendium of thirty-nine Arab writers under the age of thirty-nine, as well as street art and music, like Emel Mathlouthi's "My Word Is Free," which Mathlouthi sang in the 2011 Tunisian protest as well as at the Nobel Concert in 2015. *Politics, Popular*

Culture and the 2011 Egyptian Revolution is a collection of freely available creative texts housed online by the University of Warwick and funded by the Arts and Humanities Research Council (egyptrevolution2011.ac.uk).

While this course examines the conditions that create migrant flows and the intellectual work of emigrants that facilitates access to Arab voices, its primary goal is to challenge dominant narratives about people who migrate. The former binary narrative that rests on "we" who live "here" and "they" who come from "there" falls apart because similar conditions that sparked "the Arab uprising" are apparent across the globe, including in university classrooms in the United States. The emigrants who locate writing, translate it, and publish it make texts available that challenge the misconception that uprisings in other countries have nothing to do with people in the West.

Notes

1. The term *Arab Spring* is understood as a construct, though a useful one, in this essay, as per the discussion of Jaquette and Youssef's essay, "The 'Arab Spring,' Five Years On," below.

2. Alaa Abd El-Fattah was released from prison in 2019. Ahmed Douma was released in August 2023.

Works Cited and Consulted

"About Us." *American Islamic Congress*, 2018, aicongress.org/who-we-are/about-us/.

Adonis. "The Wound." Translated by Khaled Mattawa. *Poetry Foundation*, 2024, www.poetryfoundation.org/poems/55318/the-wound-56d236c8c5ded.

Alemdaroğlu, Ayça. "The APK's Problem with Youth." *Middle East Report*, no. 288, fall 2018, merip.org/2018/12/the-akps-problem-with-youth.

Al-Mousawi, Nahrain. "Literature after the Arab Spring." *Middle East Institute*, 5 Feb. 2016, www.mei.edu/publications/literature-after-arab-spring.

Aquilanti, Alessandra. "Stanford Scholar Sees Revolution in the Literature of the Middle East." *Stanford Report*, 24 June 2013, news.stanford.edu/news/2013/june/literature-arab-spring-062413.html. Accessed 7 Jan. 2019.

Aziz, Basma Abdel. "In Egypt, the Drying Up of Dissent." *Guernica*, 7 May 2018, www.guernicamag.com/in-egypt-the-drying-up-of-dissent/.

———. *The Queue*. Penguin Random House, 2013.

Dakerli, Noor. "I Will Leave, without Lying Down on the Dewy Grass Even Once." Translated by Alice Guthrie. *The Arab Spring: Five Years Later*, special

issue of *Words without Borders*, edited by Elisabeth Jaquette, Jan. 2016, www
.wordswithoutborders.org/article/january-2016-captivity-will-leave-without
-lying-down-on-the-dewy-grass.

Daoud, Chakib. "The Dump." Translated by Elisabeth Jaquette and Nariman
Youssef. *The Arab Spring: Five Years Later*, special issue of *Words without
Borders*, edited by Jaquette, Jan. 2016, wordswithoutborders.org/read/
article/2016-01/january-2016-arab-spring-the-dump.

The Economics of Happiness. Directed by Helena Norberg-Hodge, Local
Futures, 2011. DVD.

Fattah, Alaa Abd El-, and Ahmed Douma. "Graffiti for Two." *MadaMasr*,
25 Jan. 2014, www.madamasr.com/en/2014/01/25/feature/politics/
graffiti-for-two-alaa-and-douma/.

Gamodi, Hawa. "Awaiting a Poem." Translated by Nariman Youssef. *The Arab
Spring: Five Years Later*, special issue of *Words without Borders*, edited by
Elisabeth Jaquette, Jan. 2016, www.wordswithoutborders.org/article/
january-2016-captivity-awaiting-a-poem-hawa-gamodi-nariman-yousseff.

Garbage Dreams. Directed by Mai Iskander, Wynne Films, 2009. DVD.

Ghonim, Wael. "Inside the Egyptian Revolution." TEDX Cairo, Mar. 2011,
www.ted.com/talks/wael_ghonim_inside_the_egyptian_revolution.

Goldsmith, Edward. "Why Development Creates Poverty." *Pacific Ecologist*,
no. 11, summer 2005, pp. 43–47.

Halford, Macy. "They Laughed at Democracy: Naguib Mahfouz on Egypt in
the Twentieth Century." *The New Yorker*, 2 Feb. 2011, www.newyorker
.com/books/page-turner/they-laughed-at-democracy-naguib-mahfouz-on
-egypt-in-the-twentieth-century.

Hamid, Mohsin. *How to Get Filthy Rich in Rising Asia*. Riverhead Books, 2014.

———. "An Interview with Mohsin Hamid." Interview by Robert Repino.
OUPblog, 30 Nov. 2013, blog.oup.com/2013/11/mohsin-hamid-interview/.

Hughes, Langston. "Dreams." *Poetry Foundation*, 2024, www.poetryfoundation
.org/poems/150995/dreams.

———. "Harlem." *Poetry Foundation*, 2024, www.poetryfoundation.org/
poems/46548/harlem.

———. "I, Too." *Poetry Foundation*, 2024, www.poetryfoundation.org/
poems/47558/i-too.

Idle, Nadia, and Alex Nunns. Epilogue. Idle and Nunns, *Tweets*, pp. 231–34.

———. Introduction. Idle and Nunns, *Tweets*, pp. 19–22.

———. Preface. Idle and Nunns, *Tweets*, pp. 13–16.

———, editors. *Tweets from Tahrir*. OR Books, 2011.

Ismat, Riad. *Artists, Writers, and the Arab Spring*. Palgrave Macmillan, 2019.

Jaquette, Elisabeth, and Nariman Youssef. "The 'Arab Spring,' Five Years On."
The Arab Spring: Five Years Later, special issue of *Words without Borders*,
edited by Jaquette, Jan. 2016, www.wordswithoutborders.org/article/
january-2016-captivity-the-arab-spring-five-years-on.

Lindsey, Ursula. "The Novel after the Arab Spring." *The New Yorker*,
8 May 2014, www.newyorker.com/books/page-turner/the-novel-after-the
-arab-spring.

Maarouf, Mazen. "Downtown." Translated by Kareem James Abu-Zeid and Nathalie Handal. *Words without Borders*, 1 Apr. 2014, www .wordswithoutborders.org/article/downtown.

Mahfouz, Naguib. *"The Time and the Place" and Other Stories*. Translated by Denys Johnson-Davies. Knopf Doubleday, 1992.

Mathlouthi, Emel. "Kelmti Horra (My Word Is Free)." *Bandcamp*, 33rpmvoices .bandcamp.com/track/kelmti-horra-my-word-is-free-tunisia. Accessed 24 May 2024.

Mattawa, Khaled. "After Forty-Two Years." *Los Angeles Times*, 25 Oct. 2011, www.latimes.com/opinion/la-xpm-2011-oct-25-la-oe-mattawa-poem-kadafi -20111025-story.html.

Shimon, Samuel, editor. *Beirut 39: New Writing from the Arab World*. Bloomsbury, 2010.

Subin, Anna Della. "The Night Journey of Ahmed Bouanani." *Bidoun*, bidoun .org/articles/the-night-journey-of-ahmed-bouanani. Accessed 24 May 2024.

T. T. "The Shredded Exam Card." Weddady and Ahmari, *Arab Spring Dreams*, pp. 63–66.

Vericat, José. "In Light of the Intellectuals: The Role of Novelists in the Arab Uprisings." *International Peace Institute*, 25 Sept. 2014, www.ipinst.org/ 2014/09/in-light-of-the-intellectuals-the-role-of-novelists-in-the-arab -uprisings.

Weddady, Nasser, and Sohrab Ahmari, editors. *Arab Spring Dreams: The Next Generation Speaks Out for Freedom and Justice from North Africa to Iran*. St. Martin's Press, 2012.

———. "A New Generation of Reformers Speaks Out." Weddady and Ahmari, *Arab Spring Dreams*, pp. 1–12.

———. "Our Dream Deferred: Enlisting You in the Mideast Civil Rights Alliance." Weddady and Ahmari, *Arab Spring Dreams*, pp. 205–23.

Words of Witness. Directed by Mai Iskander, Cinema Guild, 2012.

Jocelyn Frelier and Paige Andersson

Migration and #FamiliesBelongTogether

This essay advocates for including the topic of the family (and the child, as a subset of the family) in courses related to migration. Our choice to focus on the family is dictated largely by the realities of migration as they appear in both policy and cultural texts—to assume that the migrant, refugee, or asylee is a male adult laborer in search of opportunity is to erase the nuance and complexity of the migrant. In contrast, attention to the topics of family and children invigorate classroom discussion on migration. As a point of departure, we make two assumptions: first, that migration is a "wicked problem,"[1] and, second, that it is the charge of the humanities curriculum to engage wicked problems in the classroom and train students to see wicked problems as such. We argue that classroom discussion on the family and the child allows students and instructors alike to visualize the intersections between global migration and other ongoing crises.

The Family and the Child: Pedagogical Stakes

As debates linked to the global migrant crisis surge on an international scale, questions about the family consistently emerge in media coverage and popular culture while also inspiring humanitarian and activist efforts.

These debates also underpin both national and international policy decisions, such as France's 1974 *regroupement familial* (family reunification) policies, which provided immigrants with a mechanism for sponsoring the migration of their overseas family members, or the so-called zero-tolerance policy imposed by the Trump administration in 2017, which separated parents from their children and put them into makeshift or inhumane migrant detention centers.[2] The topic of family, as it relates to migration, has long been a point of consideration, but the #FamiliesBelongTogether social movements of June 2018 highlighted how conversations about family have recently intensified.

As instructors who often teach the topic of migration, we maintain that undergraduate courses on this topic must contain a unit on family. We believe that it is pedagogically useful to ground coursework on migration in a context that is familiar to students and, thus, as instructors who teach in the United States, our overview of this topic includes the US-Mexico border. We also include discussion of migration to France to model comparative pedagogical approaches. Since we both often teach non-English-language classes, we have suggested an array of multilingual resources.

We begin with a comparative analysis of policies that protect certain types of families while leaving others disenfranchised. We then pivot toward the figure of the child, who we argue introduces an important tension in conversations related to migration. When the child is the focus of discussions about migration, the gravity, nuances, and pitfalls of activist platforms like #FamiliesBelongTogether become visible. We urge instructors to raise the following questions in class:

> Who is the architect of "the family" in different historical moments?
> Which families deserve protection, and from whose perspective?
> Are there situations in which families do *not* belong together? If so, how can narratives and policies capture those situations?
> Is the family a contemporary manifestation of neoliberal myths?

We conclude with the suggestion that migration and the family be approached as a wicked problem in the classroom.

The Family and Migration Policy

Educational materials often frame contemporary US immigration policy around the 1965 Immigration and Nationality Act, attributing to it a migration wave made up mostly of individuals from developing nations.

The 1965 act eliminated the racist quota system established by the Immigration Act of 1924, which favored certain European immigrants over all others and especially discriminated against Chinese and other Asian immigrants. Although the 1965 act theoretically leveled the geographic playing field, it still included discriminatory admissibility requirements and instituted an immigration cap for the Western Hemisphere where none had previously existed. The act also gave priority to individuals who had pre-existing familial and professional ties, the assumption being that this would lead to the proliferation of white Europeans on US soil.

However, post-1965 immigration policy (at least with respect to Latin America) may be better understood not as a cause but rather as a reaction to how the United States' imperialist interventions before, during, and after the Cold War created conflicts and environmental and economic hardships from which migrants have fled (Hoffnung-Garskof 128–33). Although asylum and family reunification are two interwoven aspects of a post-1965 order, models based on reunification have waxed and waned with presidential administrations and are intimately tied to US foreign relations. For example, refugees from El Salvador could not be labeled as refugees because the United States formally backed El Salvador's brutal military government in the name of strategic interests and, now, the precarious fate of DACA is inextricably tied to this history. Rather than frame migrant families as part of an invasive wave, historicizing US policies overseas in this way helps students link the more complex, transnational forces at play with respect to migration and the #FamiliesBelongTogether movement.

Educators can use cultural production not only to spur conversations about the relations between the United States and Latin America that have given rise to mass migration but also to organize debates on topics such as border policy, the construct of the family, and the United States' ethical responsibility to provide asylum. The family and the child are at the center of many films, novels, and journalistic pieces documenting migrant realities. For example, films like *Voces inocentes* provide intimate context for the lived realities of migrant children fleeing Central America as a result of US intervention (see also Martínez). Asylees are not only men in search of jobs to support their families but also families and children, who are suspended in a state of limbo, either detained or given statuses that never offer a path to citizenship (Luiselli). Since the 1990s, immigration enforcement tactics have also shifted, making border crossing a longer and more dangerous endeavor, as portrayed in the child-centered film *La jaula de oro* (*The Golden Dream*). Finally, migrant apprehensions and detentions have also risen, the corruption and cruelty of which can be examined through documentaries like *The Infiltrators*.

Across the Atlantic Ocean, policymakers in Europe sponsored legislation intended to protect families by reuniting them on the same side of the Mediterranean. For example, the mid-1970s saw the development of French *regroupement familial* policies, which resulted in a wave of migration from African countries and especially from Algeria. The opening of Yamina Benguigui's film *Inch'Allah Dimanche* (*Sunday, God Willing*) highlights some of the by-products of policies such as these: the film's protagonist leaves Algeria with her children to join her husband in France despite not having seen him in years and not relying on him for affect-based support. The film offers viewers a limiting interpretation of how migration to the West offers women alleged freedoms they cannot access in their home countries, but these opening scenes astutely point out that *regroupement familial* policies forcibly separate extended families in order to realize a French mission of nuclear family "regrouping." In fact, academics have pointed out that these policies were likely designed by politicians to expedite the assimilation of the mostly male immigrant workforce (Higbee 18).

In 2015 a major motion picture featuring a migration story, *Dheepan*, was released in France. The film's main character and namesake, Dheepan, is a former Tamil Tiger who seeks asylum in France after his family is killed in the Sri Lankan civil war, which lasted from 1983 to 2009. To successfully make his way to France, Dheepan assembles an artificial nuclear family with a woman and child who are strangers to him and equally alone in the world. Here, the migratory process requires these individuals to reassess their own ideas about kinship, and the newly created family denaturalizes mainstream constructs related to the naturalness of a kinship arrangement rooted in nuclearity. Dheepan's creation of family raises important questions related to the relationship between migration policy and family: Do so-called host nations look more favorably upon immigrant parents with children? To what extent is the immigration process, based on interactions with opinionated case workers who cannot shed their own values and prejudices, arbitrary?

Each of these examples illustrates the importance of grounding classroom conversation in the relationship between policy and cultural production before turning toward additional layers that continue to complicate discourses of family and migration.

The Child and #FamiliesBelongTogether

A classroom analysis of the figure of the child in migration stories sheds light on how politicians often regard children as exceptional migrants and how the media draws on the public's empathy for childhood innocence. For example, in September 2015, photographs of the lifeless body of Alan Kurdi, a two-year-old Syrian-Kurdish boy, went viral internationally. The toddler, his older brother, and his mother drowned in the Mediterranean Sea after the family left Syria in hopes of reaching Europe. The number of individuals who drown each year after an unsuccessful Mediterranean crossing is unknown, but this child's death captured an international audience.[3]

The power of the child migrant lies partially in their lack of agency regarding their condition. A year after images of Alan Kurdi garnered international attention, the Spanish director and producer Hernán Zin released his documentary *Nacido en Siria* (*Born in Syria*). Zin's documentary focuses on children, who have made up approximately half of all migrants fleeing Syria post-2011. Zin succeeds in his emphasis on the humanitarian concern that underpins child migration stories by depicting these weary child travelers who are simultaneously absorbing the concerns of adults around them and carving out time to play.

The caretakers of these children only rarely receive screen time, but in one notable exception, two men talk while the young brothers who are in their charge play together. The viewer learns that one of the little boys was taken into custody by local authorities because law enforcement suspected child abuse or neglect. This exceptional storyline in Zin's documentary problematizes generalizations about family: Do families belong together if or when they fail to meet the host nation's criteria for child protection? Did local authorities intervene unnecessarily because they assume migrant men are less capable of caring for children than their non-migrant woman counterparts? When activists say that "families belong together," do they really mean that children belong with their biological mothers?[4] If anyone belongs together, might it be the two young brothers, who are living apart in the film's present?

When presented with these stories, students can engage with the following topics: Why do international audiences turn a blind eye to Mediterranean drownings until one specific boy dies? How might the power of that boy's story be related to a family romance, in which desperate parents risked everything to provide futures for their children? At what point do nation-states and immigration policies come to understand children as adults? What happens if we remind ourselves that the adults in Zin's documentary were also born in Syria?

Similarly, photographs of anguished and dead children have been powerful mobilizing forces against child detention and family separation at the US-Mexico border. For example, a picture of a toddler wailing as ICE agents separated her from her distraught mother tugged at the heartstrings of many onlookers in the United States (Hanna). This image compelled members of the public to share #FamiliesBelongTogether on social media platforms, but this generated questions about the limitations of such a campaign: Was the campaign suggesting that if families were detained together, the system would be humane? Or perhaps the hashtag has an unwritten addendum: #FamiliesBelongTogether (and free from cages and prisons).[5]

In another notable example, when photos circulated of Angie and Óscar Ramírez, a father and daughter who drowned in the Rio Grande, criticism shifted not just to US detention practices but also to the inhumanity of the border itself, thus broadening the scope of public demands (Maxouris et al.). It was nearly impossible to argue that these parents and children were hardened criminals, a well-documented government tactic intended to shift the US public's general sympathies for economic migrants or refugees. When instructors pair these news stories with a text like Valeria Luiselli's *Tell Me How It Ends*, whose accounts of two-, three-, and four-year-olds having to defend themselves before a judge render the defenses of children in court absurd, or with a music video like Benny Blanco, Calvin Harris, and Miguel's "I Found You / Nilda's Story," a touching account of a mother and her baby being separated between two US detention centers, students can identify their own biases or lacunae with respect to immigration. These materials also facilitate students' critical reflection on the limits and possibilities of activist initiatives.

The image of the migrant child and their parent or parents is powerful precisely because children are nearly immune from criminalization narratives—after all, all children need guardians and advocates.[6] Nonetheless, many films and immigration accounts muddy these waters, particularly through the figure of the capable child and the adolescent who is on the threshold not only of adulthood but also of criminality. Capable children are depicted as both awe-inspiring and deprived of childhood, and the films that highlight their stories inspire the question, What is to be done with the migrant child with whom the nation presently sympathizes but whose detention-induced trauma may lead to future criminalization? William Lopez's *Separated* is a riveting scholarly account of the relationship between PTSD in children and ICE raids.[7] The telenovela *Reina del sur* (*Queen of the South*; both the original and the *Netflix* reboot) is an example of an unconventional source ripe with transnational connections and problematic aspects to untangle. This series allows students to consider how society, culture, and governments uphold or undo constructions of the family, motherhood, and fatherhood. With questions of family reunification, criminality, race, gender, class, and migration at its heart, the telenovela features Mexico, Spain, the United States, Italy, Russia, and North Africa.

Throughout this essay we have shown how a unit on family might create space in classroom discussion for student engagement with migration as a wicked problem. The family, the child, and #FamiliesBelongTogether underscore the various points of intersection between migration and a variety of other social conundrums ranging from policy history, war, and violence to economic forces and environmental changes. As humanities instructors, we are uniquely positioned to address wicked problems in our classrooms. A unit on family can help us send students into the workforce with the knowledge that it is impossible to be truly pro-immigration or anti-immigration because the very nature of migration is varied, nuanced, and incredibly complex.

Notes

1. Wicked problems are "problems with many interdependent factors making them *seem* impossible to solve. Because the factors are often incomplete, in flux, and difficult to define, solving wicked problems requires a deep understanding of the stakeholders involved" ("Wicked Problems").

2. The US Migrant Protection Protocols also forced many families to remain in shelters on the other side of the US-Mexico border. Despite the Biden administration's stated intentions to reform these and other policies, as of the writing of this essay, the administration's proposed changes have yet to materialize in full. The administration is no longer separating families, but a recent wave of children who arrived alone are being detained in inadequate facilities.

3. Databases like those assembled by the *Missing Migrants Project* (missingmigrants.iom.int) provide yearly estimates but acknowledge that two to three times as many people as estimated may drown each year, their bodies never found. The same applies to border deaths officially reported by the United States Border Patrol, which remain undercounts.

4. #FamiliesBelongTogether, as a social movement, can be read as conservative insofar as it upholds a limiting vision of the family. However, it allows for a "revolutionary motherhood" whereby women and parents can respond collectively to meet community needs and see beyond the siloed nuclear family unit (Sierra Becerra).

5. It should be noted that we advocate for the latter.

6. Instructors may also consider including the topic of transnational adoption on their syllabi. This topic has appeared in recent cultural productions such as the television series *Little Fires Everywhere*, the film *Ixcanul*, and Kelly Kerney's novel *Hard Red Spring*.

7. See also Luiselli's *Tell Me How It Ends* and the film *Ya no estoy aquí* (*I'm No Longer Here*).

Works Cited

Blanco, Benny, et al. "I Found You / Nilda's Story." *YouTube*, uploaded by benny blanco, 4 Jan. 2019, www.youtube.com/watch?v=kxupN5eLS8g.

Dheepan. Directed by Jacques Audiard, UGC, 2015.

Hanna, Jason. "'Crying Girl' Picture Near US Border Wins World Press Photo of the Year." *CNN*, 12 Apr. 2019, www.cnn.com/2019/04/12/us/crying-girl-john-moore-immigration-photo-of-the-year/index.html.

Higbee, Will. *Post-Beur Cinema: North African Émigré and Maghrebi-French Filmmaking in France since 2000*. Edinburgh UP, 2013.

Hoffnung-Garskof, Jesse. "The Immigration Reform Act of 1965." *The Familiar Made Strange: American Icons and Artifacts after the Transnational Turn*, edited by Brooke L. Blower and Mark Philip Bradley, Cornell UP, 2015, pp. 125–40.

Inch'Allah Dimanche. Directed by Yamina Benguigui, Film Movement, 2001.

The Infiltrators. Directed by Cristina Ibarra and Alex Rivera, Oscilloscope Laboratories, 2020.

Ixcanul. Directed by Jayro Bustamante, Cinéart, 2015.

La jaula de oro. Directed by Diego Quemada-Diez, Machete Productions, 2013.

Kerney, Kelly. *Hard Red Spring*. Penguin Books, 2016.

Lopez, William D. *Separated: Family and Community in the Aftermath of an Immigration Raid*. John Hopkins UP, 2019.

Luiselli, Valeria. *Tell Me How It Ends: An Essay in Forty Questions*. Coffee House Press, 2017.

Martínez, Óscar. *The History of Violence: Living and Dying in Central America*. Verso, 2016.

Maxouris, Christina, et al. "A Woman Watched Her Husband and Daughter Drown at the Mexican Border, Report Says." *CNN*, 26 June 2019, www.cnn.com/2019/06/26/politics/mexico-father-daughter-dead-rio-grande-wednesday/index.html.

Nacido en Siria. Directed by Hernán Zin, La Claqueta, 2016.

Sierra Becerra, Diana Carolina. "Harvesting Hope: Building Worker Power at the Pioneer Valley Workers Center." *Meridians*, vol. 19, no. 1, Apr. 2020, pp. 209–36.

Voces inocentes. Directed by Luis Mandoki, Lionsgate, 2004.

"Wicked Problems." *Interaction Design Foundation*, www.interaction-design .org/literature/topics/wicked-problems. Accessed 28 May 2024.

Ya no estoy aquí. Directed by Fernando Frías, Netflix, 2019.

B. Judith Martínez-García

Pedagogical Approaches to Contemporary Latin American Literature: Narco-Narratives and Central American Migrants in Mexico

Central America's current environment continues to be an indication of uneven development as an inherent part of the neoliberal era. Many people in these countries find themselves in a position where they seek only to survive while navigating everyday violence, hunger, and fear. The decision to migrate north is not at all a personal choice to better their lives but a primary instinct to stay alive wherever that is a possibility. Although forced migration is not a new topic, it has gained additional attention in the media. Therefore, it is becoming an increasingly important subject to study, and it draws students from interdisciplinary areas to join courses that address it.

Immigration and drug cartels can be controversial topics, and instructors should be aware of the preconceived ideas students might have that can interfere with a true understanding of texts that explore such topics. Therefore, a brief introductory background helps students build the necessary prior knowledge to objectively analyze the complex situation and equips them with enough information to evaluate the relevance of the texts. It is just as important to utilize a variety of pedagogical approaches to aid them through this process and to create an environment of learning. The purpose of the course is for students to reflect on the role of literature and its narrative. The aim is to generate a space of discussion.

Students reflect on the purpose of the texts, whether they are intended to resist or expose a system of oppression or whether they confirm the configurations of knowledge that are primarily mediated by a narrative of the hegemonic institutions that perpetuate a status quo, which translates to modern forms of violence. To arrive at this dialogue, instructors can provide students with primary and secondary sources in the assigned readings and lectures in order to offer them a multidimensional approach as they analyze the waves of forced migration and narco-narratives. Students can learn to recognize forced migration from Central America and cartel violence in Mexico as complex effects of rapid modernization in a neoliberal economy rather than as an issue of cause and effect that could be solved if the problem were attacked. A short summary of the impact of neoliberal policies in Central America and Mexico is useful in such an approach because it helps students understand how economic practices intertwine with cultural ideology such as class and patriarchy to allow violence to become the norm, the way of life, and the only way to remain alive.

I have selected two primary texts that address the current geopolitical situation of Central American migrants and their journey through Mexico and that emphasize the constant presence of drug lords and criminal organizations: *The Beast: Riding the Rails and Dodging Narcos on the Migrant Trail*, by Óscar Martínez, and *La fila india*, by Antonio Ortuño. These texts depict the systematic violence of the southern and northern border as well as the journey of many Central Americans through Mexico to reach the myth of the American dream. These works portray the border as a lawless land and Mexico as a continuous desert that allegorizes the never-ending situation of the dispossessed, who belong nowhere. Other texts that could be included as optional readings for students are *Tell Me How It Ends: An Essay in Forty Questions*, by Valeria Luiselli; *Unaccompanied*, by Javier Zamora; *Album of Fences*, by Omar Pimienta; and *Among the Lost*, by Emiliano Monge. They can also serve as possibilities for individual projects or outside book clubs. These texts represent various literary genres and styles, and students can be encouraged to read them as a complement to the course content or after the course is over to enhance their knowledge of the content.

Activating Prior Knowledge

I have found some of my students are not familiar with the hardships of the journeys of illegal immigrants. Visual assignments can fill this gap to a certain extent. The Spanish-language news outlet *El Faro* offers a variety of artifacts that provide students with a visual experience of the reality of migrants' journeys—for example, "Escaping Death, Asylum Seekers Surge in Mexico," by Martínez. They can also watch documentaries such as *The Beast*, by Pedro Ultreras; *Fronteras al límite: La frontera de la Bestia*, produced by RTV.es; or similar videos that can be accessed online. Afterward students can write a simple response in an online discussion board to keep them accountable. Students can discuss some of the reasons why these people are choosing to flee from their home countries, the risks and dangers they face in their journey, the role of the authorities, and so on. They can also benefit from reading and responding to other students' responses. It is important to emphasize that the purpose of this activity is not to analyze a film but to activate prior knowledge of the course content. This is also an effective way for instructors to fill in and address some of the existing gaps, myths, or misconceptions students might have that might prevent them from comprehending the texts and, most importantly, the conditions of Central American migrants.

Another important aspect of prior knowledge is an understanding of the geography of Central America and Mexico. Some of the visual artifacts mentioned above offer an introduction to the itineraries of migrants in their journeys to the United States. However, showing students a map of Central America and Mexico with the names of the main points of crossing and cities facilitates their learning as they read the books. It is also helpful to familiarize students with a list of the names of places most migrants travel through in their journeys as well as the routes of the train known as "La Bestia," or "The Beast."

Before we discuss these texts, students need to be familiar with vocabulary that has been developed and adopted as immigration jargon and also narco jargon. Some students might not be fluent in Spanish or might be unfamiliar with these terms if Spanish is not their native language. I provide a list of vocabulary to help them in their reading. I also provide a list of any other vocabulary that might confuse students or make the reading comprehension process difficult because of idiomatic expressions that require additional context. Beyond just translating vocabulary, students need to understand the contexts in which these words emerged. For instance, although Martínez explains in *The Beast* who Los Zetas are, students need to have a prior understanding of this group as one of the main criminal organizations in Mexico, formed by deserters of the Mexican Army Special Forces who once worked as the enforcement arm of the Gulf

Cartel. They are known for their cruelty and sanguinary practices and now profit from the vulnerability of migrants who pass through Mexico.

Theoretical Sources

Although it would be impossible for students to read all the theory instructors might like to incorporate for a more thorough understanding of this complex situation, it is still crucial to acquaint students with some basic concepts. Lectures can be divided into historical background, the texts themselves, and the role of literature, each with respective readings and assignments. Students need to have an overall understanding of the complexity of two key points: first, the way that the system produces violence and waves of migration and, second, the migrant as the embodiment of bare life and, consequently, a potential object of profit for the Mexican cartels. To help students grasp these theoretical frameworks, instructors can briefly introduce theories that address concepts such as violence, neo-liberalism, bare life, undoing of the community, and the co-belonging of literature and violence. Although it would not be feasible to have students read all the theory necessary to be able to deeply master such a complex topic as Central American migrants and the drug violence in Mexico, instructors can provide enough of a theoretical framework for students to comprehend the systemic violence. Works by authors such as Saskia Sassen, Zygmunt Bauman, David Harvey, Giorgio Agamben, Sergio Villalobos-Ruminott, and Jacques Rancière can provide a strong foundation for students. These critical theories offer a wider perspective on the dynamics of economic policies that are contributing to the dehumanization of populations in specifics parts of the world. They can also challenge the general perception students might have of Central American migrants. Once students have a background on the neoliberal practices and contemporary forms of violence that marginalize people from the community and drive them into a lawless land, they can then begin to dismantle the myth of the American dream. Through these sources, students are able to partially enter and view the complicated and detrimental location or dislocation of somebody who is uprooted from their home and the susceptibility of a particular group to becoming the merchandise and property of Mexican cartels as they cross through Mexico.

Students can learn to differentiate between migration and forced migration by understanding the immigration journey from Central America as one that is often undertaken by migrants who are pushed to leave their countries because of violence or extreme poverty. This is where I incorporate the theories of Sassen and Bauman: both critics explain that the current systems function by expulsing or evicting people (Sassen 79) who are not able to participate in the "economic flow" (Bauman 58). These concepts can open up a discussion of the economic policies that most Central American countries have adopted under neoliberal practices.[1] Harvey's *A Brief History of Neoliberalism* is helpful in explaining this idea. Students need to have at least a basic understanding of neoliberalism in order to understand its relationship with violence and poverty, since poverty and violence have grown exponentially because of the lack of state intervention to protect its people.[2] Before or as students begin to read, instructors should highlight the impossibility of including everyone in a community. Therefore, undocumented migrants begin this journey not as a choice but as a last resort in order to survive.

Bare Life and Central American Migrants

Bare life is a key concept to Agamben. He explains it as the "figure of archaic Roman law, in which human life is included in the juridical order . . . solely in the form of its exclusion (that is, of its capacity to be killed)" (8). This enhances students' comprehension of the figure of the migrant and its relationship as an inherent part of a system that allows for this type of violence to be possible. The migrant precisely represents victims that can be killed without anyone to hold accountable for their killing. A basic understanding of bare life provides students with a background on the possibility of countless deaths within our legal systems. This lecture also reinforces the discussion of lives that matter and those that do not. Students need to be familiar with the concept of bare life to be able to arrive at the conclusion Agamben proposes and thus understand that Central Americans "live . . . in the ban of a law and a tradition that are maintained solely as the 'zero point' of their own content, and that include men within them in the form of a pure relation of abandonment" (Agamben 51).

It is necessary to emphasize how Ortuño throughout his fiction reinscribes the atrocities Central Americans go through as they enter a lawless land, without an identity, being called the NNs (no names). Ortuño's narrative presents the figure of a migrant as the embodiment of a precarious life, which relates to Agamben's theory of the *homo sacer*. The following quotation argues this point, the wording referring more to an animal than to a human: "carne en su expresión más frágil y baja . . . incapaz de animar el menor deseo o servir para más cosa que asestar dolencias . . . bestias arruinadas, . . ." ("flesh in their most fragile and lowest expression . . . unable to animate the least desire or serve to anything but to deal with pain . . . ruined beasts, . . ." (Ortuño 28; my trans.). Students should be able to discern through both narratives the argument that the Central American migrant constitutes a life that does not appear to have the same value as others.

Students should also be prompted to think about and assess the role of the narco in today's society. Drug lords are portrayed in both texts as part of criminal organizations with clear chains of commands and hierarchies. However, the key concept to focus on is the organizational component. Drug lords and their cartels have an objective profit and power. They work to benefit the legal and illegal circles of power indistinctively. In *The Beast*, Martínez describes an organized system, not the old idea of a thief dressed in cowboy regalia but a transnational corporation that feeds itself with any kind of illegal or criminal activity. Thus, migrants trespassing borders seeking pure survival become an easy target. Drug trafficking is now merely a branch of the cartels, and migrants, as Martinez describes in his chronicle, are becoming a new form of profit. Students should have an opportunity to compare how new forms of transnational economy are similar to the ways the narco world currently operates. In other words, the narco has established an industry that imitates transnational enterprises. By the end of these discussions, students understand the narco either as an antagonist of the state, as part of the state, as working for the state, or all of the above while operating jointly or partially at different levels and moments.

The Role of Aesthetics

The previous classwork leads to a discussion of the role of aesthetics as a space to disrupt the narrative or as an accomplice of a discourse. Students should ponder the question of what the texts are able to accomplish. This is where I incorporate sources such as Rancière and Villalobos-Ruminott. Students should be introduced to the different techniques the authors use in their texts and to the tension between literature and violence. On the one hand, Ortuño chooses to create fictional characters that reflect the reality of the real world. He creates characters with and without names to argue the mistreatment of Central American migrants as they enter Mexico. He creates a narrative, a language to present reality through a literary lens. He links the theory of the body of the migrant to neoliberal violence.[3] On the other hand, Martínez chooses to tell a story based on testimonies, statistics, and arguments taken from archives that can be proven and reflect a journalistic review. Students realize that even though the story utilizes real statistics and facts to describe the events, most characters need to be protected and remain anonymous, while others are in fact unable to be tracked. Martínez develops a voice and narrative to support his argument and to present an uncomfortable reality the reader wishes was fiction. It is important to point out to students the different writing styles and genres of these works, one being a chronicle, and the other fiction. However, both books attempt to accomplish similar goals. Class assignments can focus on the similarities of the texts' goals and the different ways each author seeks to convey a message that might prompt action. Students should be able to reflect on the unique methods each writer uses to engage the reader. Instructors can guide a discussion that allows students to observe, analyze, and learn from their different reactions to the texts, which certainly vary depending on a student's personal context. Students gather knowledge from the diverse insights of their peers that result from reading the same narratives, and that is another level of learning that differs from class to class according to the demographics and experiences of students. *The Beast* and *La fila india* present a reality that appears to be fiction and a fiction that seems to be the reality of the current crisis we face in our global community. I believe that bringing this discussion into the classroom is already a subversive act that intends to resist the official narrative of inclusion and invites a rethinking of human rights policies. As the semester progresses, we read similar works, not only to learn about the reality for Central American migrants but also to promote and amplify the disruption of the discourse of the state that the authors have begun. This is our very own form of resistance, which provides a political space in our classrooms that seeks to reclaim the rights of and a place for Central American migrants. As Rancière points out, politics consists of making visible what was not, of listening to those who can speak and those who cannot (15), and this is precisely what students need to realize aesthetics is trying to accomplish in the case of the works read in class.

By the end of the semester students should be able to produce a critical assessment of the texts in two senses: one acquired from the information the texts offer, whether through a fictional perspective in *La fila india* or Martínez's journalistic approach, and the other derived from the political work performed by each text. Students should be able to provide a comparison that demonstrates awareness of the different genres while considering the similarities of the goals of each text. Both books attempt to account for the mistreatment of Central American migrants as they enter Mexico, reflecting in a significant manner the intensity of the waves of forced migration of Central Americans. By this point, students should be able to realize that the difficulty of this issue is precisely the impossibility to target a single responsible party. They should arrive at an understanding that we face a form of systematic violence permeated by neoliberal practices, a narco state, and a cultural ideology that foster the naturalization of violence. The readings, lectures, reflections, and commentaries should be pedagogical practices that guide students to recognize the representation of the precarious lives that Martínez and Ortuño depict in their work through the main character of the Central American migrant. In addition, students should be able to produce a dialectical analysis of the texts, identifying the disruption of the official narrative they offer by constructing an aesthetic work that strives to reclaim a voice for those who are invisible and powerless in our global community.

Notes

1. Sassen, for instance, explains that "the move from Keynesianism to the global, era of privatizations, deregulation, and open borders for some, entailed a switch from dynamics that brought people into dynamics that push people out" (211).

2. According to Harvey, in a neoliberal system the "anarchy of the market . . . generates a situation that becomes increasingly ungovernable. It may even lead to a breakdown of all bonds of solidarity and a condition verging of social anarchy and nihilism" (82).

3. Villalobos-Ruminott has suggested that the new forms of law are "inscribed in the bodies and the corpses reappear in literature" (7).

Works Cited

Agamben, Giorgio. *Homo Sacer: Sovereign Power and Bare Life.* Stanford UP, 1998.
Bauman, Zygmunt. *Wasted Lives: Modernity and Its Outcasts.* Polity, 2004.
The Beast. Directed by Pedro Ultreras, Venevision International, 2010.

Fronteras al límite: La frontera de la Bestia. RTVE.es, 13 May 2015, www.rtve.es/ play/videos/fronteras-al-limite/fronteras-limite-frontera-bestia/3126663/.

Harvey, David. *A Brief History of Neoliberalism.* Oxford UP, 2005.

Luiselli, Valeria. *Tell Me How It Ends: An Essay in Forty Questions.* Coffee House Press, 2017.

Martínez, Óscar. *The Beast: Riding the Rails and Dodging Narcos on the Migrant Trail.* Verso, 2013.

———. "Escaping Death, Asylum Seekers Surge in Mexico." *El Faro*, 17 Feb. 2017, www.especiales.elfaro.net/en/migrants/mexico/.

Monge, Emiliano. *Among the Lost.* Translated by Fran Wynne, Scribe US, 2019.

Ortuño, Antonio. *La fila india.* Conaculta, 2013.

Pimienta, Omar. *Album of Fences.* Translated by Jose Antonio Villarán, Cardboard House Press, 2018.

Rancière, Jacques. *Sobre políticas estéticas.* Translated by Manuel Arranz, Museu d'Art Contemporani de Barcelona, 2005.

Sassen, Saskia. *Expulsions: Brutality and Complexity in the Global Economy.* Belknap Press, 2014.

Villalobos-Ruminott, Sergio. "Ontología y vida: Notas sobre el corpus literario." *Kaleidoscopio*, 30 Oct. 2013, U of Arkansas.

Zamora, Javier. *Unaccompanied.* Copper Canyon Press, 2017.

Spencer R. Herrera

Dual Citizenship: Migration and the Imagined Borderlands Community in Three Chicano-Themed Films

The Mexican-American War ended in 1848 with the signing of the Treaty of Guadalupe Hidalgo. The terms of the treaty called for Mexico to cede half its territory, including present-day California, Arizona, New Mexico, Colorado, Utah, Nevada, and parts of Oklahoma, Kansas, and Wyoming. Mexico had already lost Texas in its battle for independence, which was later annexed by the United States in 1845 and then officially ceded by the treaty. The newly acquired land mass was not void of people when it became a part of the United States. The 525,000 square miles of annexed land came with an estimated population of 100,000 Mexicans who, per the treaty's conditions, became US citizens overnight. This number does not include Indigenous peoples who had been living in this region since time immemorial. Article IX of the treaty stipulates that these new US citizens were guaranteed "the enjoyment of all the rights of citizens of the United States, according to the principles of the Constitution" ("Treaty"). However, article X, which protected the validity of Mexican and Spanish land grants, was stricken from the treaty. In this light, Mexico not only lost half its territory, Mexican Americans also lost ownership of the vast majority of their communal land grants. Mexican Americans thus became, as the noted historian David Weber calls them, "foreigners in their native land." Chicano-themed border films dealing with migration show us how this geographic area that Mexico lost is part of a larger space that transcends borders and creates, in Benedict Anderson's terms, an "imagined community" of a borderlands nation.

It is common to view the United States and Mexico as places of monolithic culture, history, and ethnic identity, especially as portrayed by the mass media and in literature. The United States and Mexico have large populations, each of which has a dominant language, a hegemonic social identity forged through normative institutions (e.g., government offices, schools, churches, etc.), and a national political system. But within those vast geographic spaces, there are ethnic communities where those shared dominant cultural values intersect with other sets of values and experiences. These ethnic, linguistic, and historical culture clashes, referred to as "contact zones" by Mary Louise Pratt, have existed since the inception of borders as a method to distinguish national boundaries.

With territory that has been historically shared or disputed, the more politically or economically dominant group will sometimes view those who do not belong to that group as immigrants, while those who are othered by the dominant group may see their presence there as a natural migration within their historic homeland. This has often been the case with the United States and Mexico, which share a border defined by the Rio Grande, miles of fencing, and 276 border markers. Despite this, the borderlands space that transcends this border on both sides with thousands of square miles and millions of inhabitants creates a borderlands nation that defies political borders. Even so, sometimes the hardest border to cross is not a physical one but the one our minds create when we imagine these places as fixed instead of as spaces that have historically been and will continue to be fluid so long as there is movement among people between places within a larger traditional homeland.

Three border films that show how Mexicans and Mexican Americans engage with ideas of borders and borderlands through migration are *Born in East LA*, *Lone Star*, and *The Three Burials of Melquiades Estrada*. Each film takes a different approach to narrating the migration experience, but all convey that migration is not just a movement from south to north (Mexico to United States). It can also be a movement from north to south or back and forth within this "Greater Mexican" borderlands nation (Paredes). The idea of an imagined "Greater Mexico" was coined by the Chicano scholar Américo Paredes in the mid-1970s. Paredes defined "Greater Mexico" as "all the areas inhabited by people of Mexican descent—not only within the present limits of the Republic of Mexico but in the United States as well in a cultural rather than a political sense" (xiv). The idea of migrating within a Greater Mexican nation is key to understanding the migration of people who call the US-Mexico borderlands home. To appreciate this point from a broader perspective and not solely a geographic one, we can consider the United Nations' definition of a migrant as "any person who is moving or has moved across an international border or within a State away from his/her habitual place of residence" ("Migration"). Movement across the US-Mexico border takes place in all three films. But each film also grapples with something more complex than a straightforward physical movement across an international border or within a sovereign state. Anderson's concept of imagined communities, which aligns with Paredes's notion of a "Greater Mexico," helps us analyze the deeper complexities at play regarding migration in these three border films.

In his groundbreaking work *Imagined Communities*, Anderson defines the nation as "an imagined political community—and imagined as both inherently limited and sovereign. It is *imagined* because the members of even the smallest nation will never know most of their fellow-members, meet them, or even hear of them, yet in the minds of each lives the image of their communion" (6). With regard to forging a Greater Mexican nation, many of the approximately 37 million Mexican Americans in the United States, especially those who live in the Southwest, help form part of this imagined community by seeing themselves as culturally, linguistically, and historically connected to Mexico. However, the lack of sovereignty is where this idea of a Greater Mexico differs, something that these films indirectly reference. But what this imagined nation lacks in sovereignty, it makes up for in its inhabitants' acknowledgment of their compatriots' existence, even if they have never or will never meet those compatriots. In essence, they exist in a space that they share and collectively call home. In these three films we get a glimpse of how different people, including Mexican Americans, Mexicans, and even Anglo-Americans, form a citizenry that belongs in this Greater Mexican imagined community.

Before viewing the films, students can read the Treaty of Guadalupe Hidalgo ("Treaty"). They will notice that article X was stricken from the document. Students should then locate article X online, read it, and debate why they believe it was stricken from the treaty. Students can then review the map, available on the National Archives website ("Map"), that was created in 1848 and discuss how the redrawn US-Mexico boundary might have affected Mexicans and Indigenous peoples who were already living in the newly acquired territory. After viewing a film, students can then explain how history, borders (of all kinds), languages, and cultures help create imagined communities in the borderlands or where they live (which may be one and the same).

Born in East LA is an eighties-themed genre film that utilizes comedy to covertly criticize US immigration history and policy through the story of Rudy Robles, a Mexican American who gets deported to Mexico when he cannot prove his US citizenship during an immigration raid. It is no coincidence that the film was released one year after the 1986 Immigration Reform and Control Act, which the then president, Ronald Reagan, pushed to grant amnesty for all undocumented immigrants who could prove residency in the United States since 1982. Immigration from Mexico to the United States and subsequent repatriation is a major theme of the film. However, it was not a recent phenomenon that began in the 1980s. It is estimated that in the aftermath of the Great Depression, the United States deported up to 1.8 million Mexicans and Mexican Americans who could not prove citizenship (Little). Later, in 1954, the United States conducted "Operation Wetback," which was designed to deport Mexicans from the southwestern United States. The recession of the early 1980s, the worst since the Great Depression, once again triggered the pattern of scapegoating Mexicans in the United States as a result of the country's economic woes, thus targeting them for deportation. Cheech Marin, who doubles as the film's director and protagonist, reminds the viewer that this space (east LA and the surrounding borderlands) once belonged to Mexico, thus showing that question of history and borders is too complex to be answered by seemingly simple questions (e.g., Where were you born?). Marin effectively uses comedy as a tool to ridicule how people in authority get to decide who has the right to live in the United States and claim citizenry. As such, the film calls into question who gets to call themselves an "American citizen."

The film begins when Rudy goes to a factory to pick up his cousin. Immigration officials arrest Rudy because he does not have any identification to prove his identity. After being deported to Tijuana, he quickly gets in line to return to the United States. Although he goes by "Rudy Robles," he tells the immigration agent his full name is Guadalupe Rodolfo Robles. The agent informs Rudy that, according to their records for that name, he has been apprehended and deported nine times. Now it will be ten. Rudy is then dragged away by immigration officers while yelling "I'm an American citizen, you idiots" (*Born* 19:36) and promptly returned to Tijuana. Without any money or anyone at home to answer his collect calls, Rudy attempts to cross the border illegally numerous times, each time ending in failure.

This notion of ethnicity and belonging is pertinent to the message of *Born in East LA*. For what is at play here is that members of a nation can imagine other members of their nation without ever meeting them. In the same vein, members of another nation can view others as not belonging to their nation just by looking at them and noting their differences. This is especially true for Rudy, who, although Mexican American, has assimilated into "American"[1] culture and thus speaks Spanish poorly. However, to the immigration officials he does not look "American" but Mexican because of what they perceive to be Mexican physical markers. The idea of looking the part is taken one step further when Rudy is offered a job to help him pay for a coyote to take him back to the United States. The job is to teach a group of Asian immigrants living in Tijuana how to blend in while in East LA so that they are not suspected of being undocumented. Rudy responds "all you gotta to do to blend in in East LA is look brown" (*Born* 45:05). He then gives them a few lessons on how to walk with attitude, properly wear a bandana, and use several Chicano slang expressions, giving them the look of a stereotypical cholo.[2] The message is clear: to be part of the Greater Mexican nation, at least in East LA, you just have to look brown, talk the talk, and walk the walk.

In this sense, to be a part of an imagined community is not just about how you see yourself but also about how others see you. Rudy is not seen as an "American," and he has no way of proving it at the time of his apprehension. Despite the fact that he, his parents, and his grandparents were all born in East LA, he looks like a "bean in a beanbag," according to the arresting immigration officer (*Born* 11:21). This act of othering and of deciding who belongs in the "American" imagined community and who belongs in the Mexican imagined community, vis-à-vis forced deportation, has been happening for well over a century. In *Born in East LA*, the border is a clear dividing line that separates citizens from noncitizens. In reality, borders are messy spaces that defy clear demarcations of nationhood. This is Marin's point with the film, its title, and its theme song, Marin's own "Born in East LA." Rudy was born in East LA, a part of the United States, and that's where he belongs. For Mexican Americans like Rudy, it is an old but true adage: they did not cross the border; the border crossed them.

For these imagined communities, the idea of a borderlands space is more appropriate, which can be seen in the film *Lone Star*, directed by John Sayles. This film also takes place on both sides of the US-Mexico border, along the South Texas border. It is a film with a serious tone that delves into history and examines how individuals can remember shared memories differently. Sam Deeds, the newly elected sheriff of Rio County, the son of the renowned sheriff Buddy Deeds, is attempting to solve the decades-old murder mystery of Sheriff Charlie Wade, who preceded Buddy Deeds as sheriff. Sheriff Wade was highly unpopular because he terrorized the county through his rampant abuse of power.

Although *Lone Star* deals with migration and geographic space, it is more interested in examining the borders of time and memory. To accomplish this, Sayles combines two film techniques, camera panning and close-ups. In one scene, Hollis, the mayor of Frontera, reminisces about how Buddy came to be the sheriff of Rio County after Buddy and Sheriff Wade got into an altercation. Sheriff Sam asks Hollis to tell his version of the story. The camera then closes in on Hollis, creating the sense that what he is about to say is key to the film's storyline. Hollis leans into the table where he is having lunch, at the same Mexican restaurant where the incident took place. As he begins to say "It started over a basket of tortillas . . . ," the camera pans over to the basket of tortillas and then zooms in over a hand reaching inside the basket, and as the camera zooms out, the viewer is transported to the same place but roughly forty years prior, to the time of the incident (*Lone Star* 8:50–12:58). The old-timers love hearing this story, and each of them has a different memory of what took place and when. People around town fondly remember the days when Sheriff Buddy Deeds was in charge because it marked the end of an ugly period of Sheriff Wade's cruel dealings. But the film also delves into deeper themes of what place means, whose history counts, and how we marry different historical accounts and interpretations.

These more complex ideas begin to unfold when a second theme develops, the rekindling of an old romance between Sheriff Sam and Pilar, who dated as teenagers. As Sheriff Sam unravels the murder mystery, he tries to understand why he and Pilar were forbidden to see each other by his father and her mother. They always thought it was because Sam was white and Pilar Mexican and because they were so young (fourteen years old at the time) and developing an inappropriate sexual relationship. Sheriff Sam eventually uncovers what his father and Pilar's mother were hiding: Sheriff Buddy Deeds (Sam's father) and Mercedes (Pilar's mother) had an affair, and Pilar was their love child, which made Sam and Pilar half-siblings.

In the closing sequence, Sam and Pilar meet at an abandoned drive-in movie theater, the same place where they were caught as teenagers in the back seat of a car by Sam's father and his deputy. It is there, as middle-aged adults, that Sam reveals the truth that connects them, which his father and Pilar's mother hid from them for so many years. Naturally, Pilar is taken aback by the news, however she is not deterred. She responds by asking Sam, "So that's it, you're not going to want to be with me anymore?" (*Lone Star* 2:10:34). Sam replies, "If I met you for the first time today, I'd still want to be with you" (2:10:43). Pilar, the history teacher, although in shock, is cognizant of the complex situation. She realizes that if they are to make their relationship work, they'll have to rewrite their personal narrative together, stating, "Let's start from scratch, all that other stuff, all that history, to hell with it, right?" (2:10:58). While staring at the faded blank movie screen, she then remarks, "Forget the Alamo" (2:11:15). This brilliant closing line also shows the need to rewrite our public historical narrative, allowing for our imagined communities to be reimagined. *Lone Star* examines how borders of all kinds allow viewers to see the complex and overlapping layers of our multiple, interconnected histories and cultural *mestizaje*.[3]

The Three Burials of Melquiades Estrada continues this trend of broadening the scope of migration and place. *Three Burials* recounts the circumstances that surround the death and three burials of Melquiades Estrada, a Mexican ranch hand who travels on horseback from his village in Coahuila, Mexico, in search of work in West Texas. It is a complex film that wrestles with the construct of time and space across the United States and Mexico and forces the viewer to question their limited understanding of borders and replace it with an imagined borderlands community.

For Tommy Lee Jones, the film's director, and Guillermo Arriaga, the screenwriter, space, time, and memory all collide in this borderlands place, which they call "our country" ("On Story" 3:08). Jones and Arriaga collaborated on this film by exploring "the concept of the border between two countries where the borders may not exist all the time and sometimes it may" (2:42). This starting point of looking at the physical border led to other questions about the "borders between the heart and the mind and desire and reality" (2:53). These questions about borders and home space make for a compelling storyline because, as Jones notes, "I'm a Texan, he's a Mexican, and we wanted to make a movie about our country" (3:05). Jones's comment concerning "our country" is insightful because the film is not about the United States, Texas, or Mexico. Instead it focuses on a psychological and emotional space that exists in our minds and memories. In this case, the borderlands that traverse both countries.

As the title of the film suggests, the plot centers around the three burials of Melquiades. The first occurs when a border patrol agent, Mike Norton, buries Melquiades in a shallow grave after killing him. County officials later rebury him in a pauper's grave without attempting to locate his next of kin or notify his good friend Pete Perkins. Thereafter, acting as a vigilante, Pete kidnaps Norton as revenge for Melquiades's death and forces him to travel on horseback to rebury Melquiades in his hometown of Jiménez, Coahuila. Jones and Arriaga transport the viewer between the different time periods of the three burials but do so in a nonlinear fashion, which requires viewers to suspend their normal perception of time.

In the second burial scene, in which county officials rebury Melquiades's body, the viewer begins to see how the film unveils the idea of nationhood. After the tractor operator flattens the loose dirt over the plot, he takes a simple white wooden cross and black Sharpie and asks how to register it (*Three Burials* 24:05). A county deputy replies, "Write down Melquiades" (24:14). He marks the cross with his first name and state and country of origin (24:24). It is a simple migrant's grave. In an interesting comparison, Anderson contends that "[n]o more arresting emblems of the modern culture of nationalism exist than cenotaphs and tombs of Unknown Soldiers. The public ceremonial reverence accorded these monuments precisely *because* they are either deliberately empty or no one knows who lies inside them" (9). I argue, however, that these poorly marked migrant graves, and even more so the thousands of unmarked final resting places of migrants who died crossing the borderlands, better reflect this idea of an imagined borderlands nationhood. These migrants died not in their hometowns but within their larger imagined community.

Pete, Melquiades's good friend, takes it upon himself to see that Melquiades's body is properly returned and buried in his hometown of Jiménez. Pete is white but speaks the regional Spanish dialect of the US-Mexico border. He is also a cowboy, like Melquiades, who feels comfortable in the high desert landscape on both sides of the border. These borderlands reflect an imagined community that people like Melquiades and Pete can cross in either direction. Borders, with their checkpoints and armed guards, represent artificial boundaries. People—their language, culture, and histories—are what define this Greater Mexican imagined borderlands community.

As a consequence of the Mexican-American War, Mexico lost the vast territory that became the southwestern United States, and a nation was split. But its people remained in their traditional homeland. Now, over

175 years later, we continue to grapple with issues of migration and questions of who belongs in the United States. These films remind us that migration is a natural and long-standing phenomenon. The development of the United States as a nation was dependent on migration. The question then becomes, Who do we see as belonging in our community? The answer is as inclusive as we allow ourselves to imagine it.

Notes

1. I use the term "American" in quotation marks to refer to the culture and citizens of the United States. Technically, however, anyone born in North, Central, or South America is an American.

2. A cholo is mostly distinguished by his dress: khaki or baggy pants, a flannel shirt or white muscle T-shirt, and dark sunglasses.

3. *Mestizaje* refers to the mixing of bloodlines, cultures, and languages.

Works Cited

Anderson, Benedict. *Imagined Communities*. Verso, 1983.

Born in East LA. Directed by Cheech Marin, Universal Pictures, 1987.

Little, Becky. "The US Deported a Million of Its Own Citizens to Mexico during the Great Depression." *History.com*, 12 July 2019, www.history.com/news/great-depression-repatriation-drives-mexico-deportation.

Lone Star. Directed by John Sayles, Columbia Pictures, 1996.

"Map of the United States including Western Territories, December 1848." *National Archives*, www.archives.gov/legislative/features/nm-az-statehood/us-map.html. Accessed 30 Oct. 2024.

"Migration." *United Nations*, www.un.org/en/sections/issues-depth/migration/index.html. Accessed 26 Oct. 2020.

"On Story: 511 Tommy Lee Jones: Bringing *The Three Burials of Melquiades Estrada* to Life." *YouTube*, uploaded by Austin Film Festival, 27 June 2015, www.youtube.com/watch?v=QrHBGGXRe2U.

Paredes, Américo. *A Texas Mexican Cancionero: Folksongs of the Lower Border*. U of Illinois P, 1976.

Pratt, Mary Louise. *Imperial Eyes: Travel Writing and Transculturation*. Routledge, 1992.

The Three Burials of Melquiades Estrada. Directed by Tommy Lee Jones, Sony Pictures Classic, 2005.

"Treaty of Guadalupe Hidalgo (1848)." *National Archives*, www.archives.gov/milestone-documents/treaty-of-guadalupe-hidalgo. Accessed 27 Oct. 2020.

Weber, David. *Foreigners in Their Native Land: Historical Roots of the Mexican Americans*. U of New Mexico P, 1973.

Manuel Chinchilla

Beyond Empathy:
Teaching Central American Migration
through Film and Literature

Migration presently generates an abundance of discourse both within and beyond academia. Yet it also presents particular problems for teachers wishing to guide their students toward a complex perspective on the topic. Cultural production about Central American migration can respond to that challenge by offering an archive from which to build a critical approach to migrancy. Central American migration to the United States has been framed through polar opposites: either a crisis-ridden narrative that criminalizes migrants or a portrayal of vulnerability in search of empathy. The task is not to find an objective middle ground within this binary but to problematize migrancy's representation by moving from empathetic engagement to a deeper critique of migrants as vulnerable yet empowered subjects. The primary works I use to construct such a critique are Marc Silver's documentary *Who Is Dayani Cristal?*, Valeria Luiselli's *Tell Me How It Ends*, and Javier Zamora's *Unaccompanied*.

In *Distant Suffering*, Luc Boltanski focuses on a spectatorship of suffering that divides fortunate spectators from unfortunate sufferers, whereby the shock of viewing pain on the part of the fortunate ones leads to a mixture of sensations, such as surprise or indignation, and possible responses, such as expression or political activism (11). This dynamic is also at work

202

in Silver's *Who Is Dayani Cristal?*, which links a paternalistic view of migrancy and the empathetic response it seeks to encourage. The documentary is based on the discovery of a dead Honduran migrant, Yohan Martínez, in the Sonoran Desert, and its combination of reportage and reenactment leads the viewer to an emotional identification with the protagonist and empathy toward migrants. The reenactment achieves its empathetic effect in a straightforward manner, since Gael García Bernal breaks the fourth wall while playing Yohan and addresses the audience directly. In his voice-over, he emphasizes the difference between himself, a famous actor traveling while making a film, and the real migrants taking on a dangerous journey. Although the documentary's main strategy of recounting migrant life as individual plight fulfills Boltanski's conception of a paradigmatic experience extrapolated to general circumstances, conforming "a politics of pity" that groups the suffering of several people (12), Silver allows viewers both to create a general perspective on migration through empirical and anecdotal data and to engage in an empathetic identification with Yohan when played by García Bernal.[1]

In the opening scene, García Bernal recites "The Migrant's Prayer," which equates Christ's life to the migrant's journey, in a sequence that alternates between the actor's image and a crucified Christ.[2] The scene concludes when we hear the name "Yohan" and García Bernal joins a group of migrants aboard a van headed for the border (*Who* 1:30–2:16). This prologue is fully immersed in the reenactment's fictional world and fosters identification with the character, and the analogical vision of Christ's martyrdom and the migrant's journey cements the notion of witnessing someone's suffering. The film then shifts to less curated images of officers removing a body from the Arizona side of the Sonoran Desert and delivering it to the medical examiner's office in Tucson (5:27–7:54). From then on, the documentary alternates between the reenactment of the journey and the investigation of the body's identity, using both narratives to persuade the viewer to empathize with migrants. A useful approach for discussing the film with students is to ask them to compare these two strands, the narrative versus the documentary, and to assess how each affects their understanding of and empathy with the migrant's journey. Highlighting this distinction greatly enhances discussion of the film's ethical dimension.

The discovery of Yohan's body sheds light on the regime of surveillance and death operating in the Sonoran Desert, what Sandro Mezzadra and Brett Neilson call "border governmentality," the combination of technologies of surveillance and defense that constitute a modern border

(183). Jason De León engages border governmentality by examining prevention-through-deterrence policies in place since the mid-1990s. De León's *Land of Open Graves* details how the Sonoran Desert is taken up by border governmentality to produce a state of exception that, following Giorgio Agamben's theorization, produces blameless migrant deaths, since the killer is the desert itself. The expression of such governmentality is the production of "bare life," individuals without rights rendered "killable" and "erasable" (De León 68–69). For De León, prevention through deterrence actively seeks the production of unaccounted deaths and enacts exclusion not just from a territory but also from the very idea of humanity: "Looking at the bodies left at the border reveals what the physical boundary of sovereignty and the symbolic edge of humanity look like" (84). Silver's documentary addresses prevention through deterrence in interviews with the forensic anthropologist Bruce Anderson and with Robin Reineke, coordinator for the Missing Migrants Project, an initiative that identifies deaths and disappearances resulting from the intersection of US border governmentality and the Sonoran Desert's lethality. Anderson informs the viewer about the desert's death toll—an average of two hundred a year since 2001—and criticizes the hypocrisy of the US government for categorizing migrants as disposable when near the border and as advantageous cheap labor once part of the country's economy.[3] Reineke describes the difficult work of identifying bodies, tracing them back to their families, and having to break the news to them (*Who* 23:00–24:00). This portion of the film can be used in class to inform students about the work of many organizations in repatriating bodies, preventing deaths at the border, and advocating for better treatment of migrants. The interviews are intertwined with images of corpses being examined and cataloged, a repetition of anonymous and abandoned bodies that evokes that "edge of humanity" De León mentions. Yet these deaths also provide a visual index and a semblance of life to the numbers accounting for migrant fatalities. The documentary achieves this by displaying objects and mementos carried by migrants: clothing, documents, discarded food items, and in the case of Yohan, the migrant's prayer and the tattoo with his daughter's name—Dayani—that are key to establishing his identity. But it is of course in the reenactment of a life that the film produces a most intimate effect of closeness.

For Bill Nichols, the impact of the reenactment has to do with its "fictionalized repetition," which carries a "fantasmatic element" that enfolds the viewer (35), enabling a "vivification" that projects desires onto past events: "Reenactments contribute to a vivification of that for which they stand. They make what it feels like to occupy a certain situation, to perform a certain action, to adopt a particular perspective visible and more vivid" (49). Despite the fact that this is a trip whose tragic ending is known, García Bernal's reenactments generate expectations in the viewer and become even more complex when the actor encourages others to interact with him in a collaborative theater where real migrants play themselves. In the most striking scene, García Bernal impersonates Yohan on a bus surrounded by migrants while talking to them about traveling north, speaking of his dreams and the family he leaves behind, and accepting a migrant's reciprocal account of his own hopes. García Bernal admits in a voice-over, "They sometimes let me play the role" (*Who* 25:30–25:40), making clear the assumption of their role-playing. Another important reenactment takes place in the Hermanos en el Camino (Brothers on the Road) shelter run by Father Alejandro Solalinde, who reenacts the gifting of "The Migrant's Prayer" later found among Yohan's belongings (1:01:20–1:01:50). In these exchanges, we follow Yohan and build our own hopes and desires about him as he learns skills useful for his journey. The documentary, however, employs two parallel narratives running in opposite directions. One sets up identification with a protagonist fulfilling a journey and builds emotional empathy toward him, while the forensic investigation travels back to Yohan's village, El Escanito, and offers an explanation of the push-and-pull factors behind Central American migration.

Even though *Who Is Dayani Cristal?* manages the difficult task of creating empathy toward migrants, the film still falls into paternalistic condescension. The restitution of Yohan's body to family and friends involves a long sequence through airports, a village procession, a tearful vigil and funeral, and a final image of Yohan's loved ones posing for the camera with his best friend holding his picture. This cathartic sequence is followed by a last reenactment of Yohan walking across the desert, as García Bernal's voice summarizes his life. Then the camera drifts off, focusing on the landscape and fenced border, letting the final credits roll. The documentary depicts Yohan and his family through conceptions of vulnerability and victimization that effectively ask the viewer to empathize with their plight, but it also reinforces the idea of their extreme lack of power. The family's mourning over Yohan's body, and the last image of him as he walks across the desert toward certain death, work to move the viewer once again to a feeling of pity toward Yohan in particular and migrants in general, fashioning them as precarious subjects in need of aid.

The portrayal of migrant precariousness can be countered through Judith Butler's concept of the "critical image." The "critical image" cancels out marketable and moralistic commodification by interrupting a "triumphalist image" that allows the liberal subject's recognition of their own power vis-à-vis others. Silver's documentary, in my view, falls short of this breakthrough because of its reliance on images of victimization that end up reinforcing migrant precariousness by concentrating exclusively on deaths along the US-Mexico border and rarely touching on life on the American side. Instead of the perfect circular narrative of Yohan's death conveying a sense of fatality about migrant life, Butler's strategy would disrupt reification through a failure of representation, "for representation to convey the human, then, representation must not only fail, but it must show its failure" (144). The objective would be to show several views and potentials beyond the victimized subject. Didier Fassin similarly criticizes a humanitarianism reason that "pays more attention to the biological life of the destitute and unfortunate, the life in the name of which they are given aid, than to their biographical life, the life through which they could . . . give a meaning to their own existence" (254). Likewise, Pooja Rangan, in her reassessment of documentary filmmaking, criticizes mediatized framings of "emergencies"—like the one at the US-Mexico border—that replace the political in favor of mere compassion (10) and argues for conceiving human beings as open subjects capable of existing beyond a politics of pity (7–8). Following these arguments, I believe that a film like *Who Is Dayani Cristal?* must be complemented by works that directly confront liberal representation and create a more complex view of migrancy.

In *Tell Me How It Ends*, Luiselli uses the forty questions from the federal court questionnaire for unaccompanied child migrants to structure a response to her daughter's anxiety about such children. The essay recounts Luiselli's life from 2014 to 2015, when she was applying for a green card and volunteering as a court interpreter for The Door, an organization helping migrant children achieve residency in the United States. The essay surpasses the humanitarian imperative and represents migrant subjects beyond victimhood. An important element is the parody of intolerant language aimed at migrants by the US government and media. Luiselli mocks the green card questionnaire for feeling "like the grainy Cold War films we watched on VHS" (10) and news depicting child migrants like a "biblical plague" (15). She later muses over the word *alien* and its absurd, and comic, view of migrants as extraterrestrials excluded from humanity (16–17).

Most notably, Luiselli confronts the need for narratives of victimization regarding children, since answers proving past trauma are advantageous in court.

The essay's central story is that of Manu López, a sixteen-year-old Honduran who, unlike the migrants in *Who Is Dayani Cristal?*, is at first quite distrustful. Manu nonetheless warms up to Luiselli and, despite narrating how he was the object of gang violence, shows that he is in control of his own narrative and that he wants a new life. The conclusion of his story is positive: he is awarded a Special Immigrant Juvenile visa, begins studying English, and finds a welcoming community. More importantly, the coda informing the reader about Manu's new life in 2017 avoids the traps of a fixed migrant identity, leaving us with a "critical image" that opens up to the future and portrays Manu's youth as a source of joy rather than victimization.

The final words in the essay are accompanied by three photos of Manu jumping on a trampoline and practicing, as he tells Luiselli, "the art of flight" (106). To keep his identity hidden, his face and body appear as shadows, a critical reminder that full belonging is not yet possible, but Manu's playful silhouette already signals a way of defining migrants beyond pity. A fruitful in-class exercise is to ask students to contrast how Yohan and Manu are depicted, the differences and similarities of their stories, and how each narrative ending, despite their common trope of a fade-out, creates a different view of the migrant.

The essay's coda fits well with Thomas Nail's rethinking of political philosophy from the point of view of the migrant rather than the citizen. In *The Figure of the Migrant*, Nail avoids conferring a fixed being to the migrant, choosing instead the concept of a "figure" that "is not an unchanging essence [but] a social vector or tendency" (16). For Nail, the migrant propels progress and change: "the figure of the migrant is a socially constitutive power. It is the subjective figure that allows society to move and change" (13). Manu's figure, his silhouette taking flight, exceeds and overcomes the trauma of his story.

I would like to conclude by reviewing two poems by Zamora from his book *Unaccompanied*. Zamora migrated on his own at the age of nine from El Salvador to California, crossing the Sonoran Desert to reunite with his parents. In his poetry, El Salvador, the journey, the border, and his present life are never separate but appear interwoven. I find Nail's theories useful also for understanding Zamora's poetry. Nail's *Theory of the Border* conceives the border as more than a separation producing inclusion and exclusion, favoring an understanding related to the circulation of people and their continuous rearrangement: "Borders are never done including someone or something. . . . [B]orders regularly change their selection process of inclusion such that anyone might be expelled at any moment" (7). Nail mentions the status of undocumented immigrants to illustrate how "the frontier is not always outside. It is both an internal and external process of disjunction" (41). Zamora's poems grapple with this sense of belonging that could at any point reach a safer status (permanent residency or citizenship) or a negative outcome (deportation, a life in the shadows).

In "Second Attempt Crossing," Zamora remembers a raid at the border and pays homage to Chino, a former gang member who had managed to escape but returned to protect and save Zamora before helping him make a final, successful crossing: "So I wouldn't touch their legs that kicked you, / you pushed me under your chest" (9). The poem is moving because it depicts the loyalty of a man who in most contexts would be criminalized, his nickname turned into a solemn apostrophe, the gang affiliation a rhythmic cadence lengthening and delaying a reluctant farewell: "Beautiful Chino—/ the only name I know to call you by—/ farewell your tattooed chest: the M / the S / the 13" (9). Zamora then tells of Chino's death in Alexandria at the hands of the gang that provoked his migration from El Salvador. The last verses attest to the paradoxical legacy of their joint border crossing, portraying life in the United States as a constant threat. Still, Chino's strength, his care, exceed both trauma and time: "Farewell / your brown arms that shielded me then, / that shield me now, from La Migra" (10).

In Zamora's "Let Me Try Again," another failed crossing is treated as a sign of migrant perseverance. The poem begins by discounting the setting—"I could bore you with the sunset" (61)—and avoids dramatizing the fact that only four migrants out of forty made it to the other side. The crossing ends with the small group's being detained by a border patrol officer who acts in solidarity with them: "He must've remembered his family / over the border, / or the border coming over them, because he drove us to the border" (62). The border, as Nail points out, is harnessed by the state but not under its control (*Theory* 7), and so the enforcer of the law becomes an ally instructing migrants on how to succeed in their next crossing. The poem's last verses are at once timeless and tied to the current context of Central American migration: "He knew we would try again / and again, / like everyone does" (Zamora, "Let" 62). An interesting way to approach this cycle of works in class is to ask students to consider not just the differences in sensibility and purpose of each work but also how different instances of closeness are embodied in their makers, from the committed film director to the foreign yet privileged writer to the child turned adult poet who recounts the memory of his own border crossing.

Just like Luiselli, who reimagines joy and potentiality in Manu and undoes the condescending triumphalism of liberal superiority, Zamora alters the regime of representation that sets migrants into specific types in order to elevate their character and struggle. But such critical stances need to be discussed alongside upfront, empathetic works like *Who Is Dayani Cristal?*, which is able to lay the foundation required for an open and critical discussion of migrant experiences.

Notes

1. Shifting focus between strong protagonists and groups of migrants is a constant trope in works about Central American migration. Some examples are *Sin nombre* (*Nameless*), directed by Cary Joji Fukunaga, in which a former Honduran gang member tries to escape his gang by migrating to the United States; *La jaula de oro* (*The Golden Dream*), directed by Diego Quemada-Díez, in which three young Guatemalans, each representing a racial or socioeconomic minority, travel through Mexico; and Óscar Martínez's *The Beast*. In all these works, migration begins as the activity of a group (a family, a clique of friends, a group of nationals) and ends with only a few individuals, often only one, making it across the US-Mexico border. Of course, *El Norte*, directed by Gregory Nava, is an important work in this regard.

2. "The Migrant's Prayer" is an important detail in the documentary's plot, and the film reproduces it in its entirety. For versions in English and Spanish, see "Oración."

3. As of 28 October 2024, the Missing Migrants Project reported 362 dead or missing migrants along the US-Mexico border in 2023 (missingmigrants.iom.int).

Works Cited

Boltanski, Luc. *Distant Suffering: Morality, Media, and Politics.* Translated by Graham D. Burchell, Cambridge UP, 1999.
Butler, Judith. *Precarious Life: The Powers of Mourning and Violence.* Verso, 2006.
De León, Jason. *The Land of Open Graves: Living and Dying on the Migrant Trail.* U of California P, 2015.
Fassin, Didier. *Humanitarian Reason: A Moral History of the Present.* U of California P, 2011.

La jaula de oro. Directed by Diego Quemada-Díez, Animal de Luz Films / Castafiore Films / CONACULTA / Eficine / Estudios Churubusco Azteca / IMCINE / Kinemascope Films / Machete Producciones, 2013.

Luiselli, Valeria. *Tell Me How It Ends: An Essay in Forty Questions.* Coffee House Press, 2017.

Martínez, Óscar. *The Beast: Riding the Rails and Dodging Narcos on the Migrant Trail.* Verso, 2014.

Mezzadra, Sandro, and Brett Neilson. *Border as Method; or, The Multiplication of Labor.* Duke UP, 2013.

Nail, Thomas. *The Figure of the Migrant.* Stanford UP, 2015.

———. *Theory of the Border.* Oxford UP, 2016.

Nichols, Bill. *Speaking Truths with Film: Evidence, Ethics, Politics in Documentary.* U of California P, 2016.

El Norte. Directed by Gregory Nava, American Playhouse / Channel 4 Films / Independent Productions / Island Alive / PBS, 1983.

"Oración del migrante—The Migrant's Prayer." *World Prayers,* www .worldprayers.org/archive/prayers/adorations/the_journey_towards_you_ lord_is_life.html. Accessed 4 June 2024.

Rangan, Pooja. *Immediations: The Humanitarian Impulse in Documentary.* Duke UP, 2017.

Sin nombre. Directed by Cary Joji Fukunaga, Scion Films / Canana Films / Creando Films / Primary Productions, 2009.

Who Is Dayani Cristal? Directed by Marc Silver, Pulse Films / Canada Films / Canana USA / Candescent Films / Rise Films, 2013.

Zamora, Javier. "Let Me Try Again." Zamora, *Unaccompanied,* pp. 61–62.

———. "Second Attempt Crossing." Zamora, *Unaccompanied,* pp. 9–10.

———. *Unaccompanied.* Copper Canyon Press, 2017.

Part III

Pedagogical Approaches and Methods

Weixian Pan

Border Migrants:
A Comparative Pedagogical Approach

Teaching about any transborder migration and its mediation often entails tremendous efforts to lay out the specific historical, social, and political conditions. Yet is there still a way to encourage students to compare migratory experiences that are geographically distant? This question has spurred educators and media researchers working from different cultural regions to be in conversation with one another and to share knowledge on some of the most common migratory paths across the world: labor forces who migrate from rural to urban regions or across national borders in search of work or students from underprivileged regions searching for high-quality education in North America and Europe. More importantly, a comparative approach reveals that searching for migratory connection between countries of the Global South goes beyond tracing geographic linkages. As educators, our task could also entail efforts to emphasize that, in most global migratory experiences, formal and informal movements occur in relation to one another, and together, they shape the experience of border crossing and social mobility of those who lived in countries of the Global South.

Making such comparative analysis an aspect of a general topics course such as Global Media or Transnational Media, I scaffold a seminar where students are guided to compare the material and affective mediation of crossing the US-Mexico border and the mainland China–Hong Kong border. In preparation for a three-hour discussion-based class (with a twenty-minute break halfway through), I assign one text and one film to students to read and watch in advance: Shannon Mattern's essay "All Eyes on the Border," which unpacks the material apparatus and sensing technologies along the US-Mexico border under Donald Trump's presidency, and the film *The Crossing*, by the Chinese director Xue Bai. The film portrays the layers of social, economic, and sexual desires activated through the everyday crossing of the mainland China–Hong Kong border. At first glance, the juxtaposition might seem odd, but Mattern's reflection on border surveillance and the mundane desire of social mobility in Bai's film, when juxtaposed, make for an interesting conversation about techno-specificity and affective economy in transborder movements.

At the beginning of class, I often use a collaborative task as a way for students to reflect on their own border-crossing experiences. For a class of twenty, I break students into four to five smaller groups and give each group about fifteen minutes to exchange ideas and make notes. The prompt allows students to lean into their diverse cultural backgrounds and also guides them to collect these personal anecdotes as one kind of shared knowledge of global migratory practices. The prompt normally includes concrete tasks that students are asked to complete together, such as the following:

> List all the objects that you would put into your backpack (i.e., those that you think are essential) were you to travel across borders and through customs.
>
> Recall a border or customs hall in a quick sketch, including as many spatial, visual, and technological details as possible.
>
> Map the emotional changes that you experienced during border crossing, especially when unexpected situations happened (describe those situations).

I find that students are very motivated to share some of their memories of and stories about border crossings in this activity. Each of these tasks requires them to reflect on the process of border crossing as challenging both physically and mentally. Certainly, the results of this activity change for each class group, but students are often surprised to discover the material and emotional complexity associated with our movement across national borders, however mundane they may seem (e.g., making sure that one has access to water and battery power and wears comfortable clothes).

After the brainstorming activity, I ask students to compare these initial attempts to recall their border-crossing experiences (in sketches and unorganized lists and maps) with the more systematic and hyper-technologized mediation of the zone along the US-Mexico border demonstrated in Mattern's writing. Students growing up outside the United States were first struck by the richness and accessibility of media on border movements. From journalistic media, aerial photography, and surveillance footage to applications and satellite maps, these imageries and data are consistently circulated as public knowledge of the US-Mexico cross-border migration. These reflections remind us that the mediated knowledges of migration vary as a result of students' different cultural positions—where borders are more likely kept away from public scrutiny. But when exposed to such differences, students can also begin to pay attention to what Camilla Fojas calls "border optics," referring to "a visual archive and the optical infrastructure of borderlands that constitute the cultural technologies of borderveillance" (2–3).

I then break the class into groups of two to do close readings of Mattern's essay, following and extending the provocations she lays out. Here are some sample discussion questions:

> What does Mattern mean when she writes that "we must first train ourselves to recognize the border itself, which is not a fence or a wall but a security apparatus whose powers extend deep into the interior"? What, then, could become "a border"?
> With the intricate and layering optical and surveillance infrastructures, why does she emphasize the "failures to see and be seen" as the prevailing political crisis?

When students regroup and share discussion notes, I notice how their focuses pivot from seeing the border as a fixed object or space to finding new vocabularies to articulate the cultural operations well beyond the physical presence of a border and how their analytical scope exceeds the geography of the United States and Mexico. For example, Chinese students might scrutinize their personal credit score from Alipay, China's largest e-commerce and mobile payment platform, as an unrecognized border technology through which the state and society determines a person's social status, credibility, and sense of mobility (e.g., high credit scores are advantageous in visa applications for countries such as Canada, the United Kingdom, and Japan). Students who grew up in South and Central America might discuss forms of linguistic and racial segregation that continue to play a role in their search for an education and career. Acknowledging the harsh policing and techno-surveillance along the US-Mexico border (detention centers and physical violence), students slowly extend the logic of border optics to reflect on their more immediate geographic and social experiences. The global proliferation of borders and transborder migration, pieced together through students' situated knowledge, shows startlingly similar characteristics in social and racial differentiation, politics of recognition, and spatial management.

The second part of the class shifts attention to everyday migratory practices, especially border crossing, as involving the mediation of desires and affect. I begin by introducing the broader cultural contexts to which Bai's *The Crossing* responds. Crossing the mainland China–Hong Kong border, whether as an everyday migratory practice or an imagined mobility on screen, invokes layers of historical anxiety, social division, and geopolitical tension (Yau). For example, the crime classic *Long Arm of the Law*, directed by Johnny Mak, shows that border crossing in the 1980s meant risking one's life but was also full of economic promises; in many films by the Hong Kong director Wong Kar-Wai, the romanticized and nostalgic reminiscences of mainland China appear repetitively in his portrayal of Hong Kong; and more recently, the controversial speculative anthology film *Ten Years* presents a dystopian, semiautonomous territory of Hong Kong in 2025, after the Chinese government tightens its governance across the border. We can see from these cinematic imaginations that crossing the mainland China–Hong Kong border has been charged with cultural and political meanings over the past few decades. As a young mainland Chinese director, Bai received much criticism for portraying "[a] depoliticized perception of Hong Kong" in *The Crossing* (Zeng).

The Crossing features a distinct migratory population that crosses the mainland China–Hong Kong border daily. These everyday border crossers may be parallel traders,[1] businessmen, truck drivers, or service workers, but the film's protagonist—a sixteen-year-old high school student named Peipei—represents the daily cross-border schoolers who often have complex family relations on both sides of the border. Peipei's mother, who lives in Shenzhen, was distanced from her daughter because of gambling and irresponsible behavior; Peipei's father, a regular working-class Hong Konger, remarried and refused to acknowledge Peipei in front of his new family. For Peipei, the everyday practice of border crossing is part of her coming-of-age journey. This journey is aspirational at times and dangerous at others, such as when she accidentally gets involved in the cross-border smuggling of iPhones and weapons.

With these contexts in mind, I then play the film's trailer to refresh students' memory and set up the last exercise for the day. This exercise asks students to untangle the intricate desires and emotional tensions associated with the mainland China–Hong Kong border and to focus in on each of the social worlds Peipei encounters in her daily migratory practice. To differentiate these social worlds, I use five still shots from the film as the anchor points in each group's discussion. For example, the scene of Peipei crossing the metal detector and the busy Shenzhen–Hong Kong border signals her relationship with the state and the border apparatus (*Crossing* 11:22–11:37). Students quickly situate Peipei in relation to Mattern's vocabularies: she is exposed to border optics that include various surveillance technologies, the questioning and searching from border patrols, and the dual political systems. But at the same time, students point out that in this scene, Peipei becomes almost invisible to these border optics because of her status as a seemingly trustworthy, innocent-looking cross-border high schooler. Her ability to move across the border under the radar later becomes an asset for the smuggling business.

Another film still directs attention to Peipei's complex friendship with her best friend. In this scene, Peipei and her friend stand on the rooftop, dreaming of going to Japan together at Christmas to see snow (*Crossing* 4:45–6:21). While they share the same aspiration to escape their everyday reality, unlike her best friend, who comes from a rich family, Peipei needs to find ways to save up and thus temporarily bypass their class differences to make this trip happen. One question that often comes up in class discussion is "Why Japan?" The question is never addressed in the film. Some students suggest that Japan seems to be an empty signifier for the two schoolgirls. It is a place that seems relatively easy to reach, but all they can imagine is the empty landscape of snow they see in magazines and on television. Other students also bring up a crucial point to consider: the influence of Japanese popular culture in this generation's transborder imagination of the world and Asia. One advantage of these scene-by-scene discussions is to allow students to carefully articulate the social aspirations in each of Peipei's physical and social crossings in the film.

Peipei's relationship with the smuggling gang, and in particular with one of the dealers, A'Hao, is most heatedly discussed among students.

Students begin by commenting on the fleeting sense of family Peipei finds with these cross-border smugglers. These dealers work, live, cook, and eat together. For someone like Peipei who has been living between two incomplete spaces, this creates a momentary illusion of belonging. Certainly, the dynamic quickly changes when Peipei messes up some deals and refuses to smuggle weapons. Peipei slowly builds an ambiguous but intimate connection with A'Hao, the two both realizing that they are the underdogs who are trying to cross that invisible class line that has bound them in their socioeconomic status. During class discussions, students are not satisfied with simply understanding the smuggling business through Peipei's search for identification and intimacy. Instead, some propose reading Peipei's coming-of-age struggle alongside Hong Kong's struggle in maintaining its role as a global network of transborder exchanges in the 2010s. The illicit, or undesired, crossings of bodies, commercial products, money, and fantasy for social mobility are all concentrated into the everyday passages of thousands of regular people.

My design of this discussion-intensive class on border migration attempts to address the difficulty of creating productive dialogues across seemingly disparate migratory practices and contexts. The structure I outline here initially puts emphasis on collective brainstorming, personal narration, and everyday practices. It gradually comes to involve more conceptual work—defining, differentiating, and adopting new vocabularies—through scaffolded close reading and comparative thinking. In the second half of the class, *The Crossing* offers a shared canvas for students to test out these new analytical languages in understanding border crossing in different sociocultural contexts. Some versions of this class work better than others, in the sense that students are more proactive in making the connections and initiating comparative readings. But ultimately, these pedagogical attempts are meant to encourage both educators and students to journey out of their comfort zones and to engage in a comparative understanding of border migration that might not always translate easily.

Note

1. Parallel traders refer to those who buy popular products in bulk in Hong Kong and resell them in mainland China at a profit. Parallel trading mainly affects the price of daily necessities such as milk powders, diapers, oil, and medicine. This has caused tremendous tension since the 2000s between residents living in Hong Kong's border areas (e.g., New Territories) and mainland travelers.

Works Cited

The Crossing. Directed by Xue Bai, Wanda Media, 2018.

Fojas, Camilla. *Border Optics: Surveillance Cultures on the US-Mexico Frontier.* New York UP, 2021.

Long Arm of the Law. Directed by Johnny Mak, Golden Harvest, 1984.

Mattern, Shannon. "All Eyes on the Border." *Places Journal*, Sept. 2018, https://doi.org/10.22269/180925.

Ten Years. Directed by Jevons Au, Kiwi Chow, Zune Kwok, Ka-leung Ng, and Fei-pang Wong, Ten Years Studio / 109G Studio / Four Parts Production, 2015.

Yau, Esther. "Border Crossing: Mainland China's Presence in Hong Kong Cinema." *New Chinese Cinemas*, edited by Nick Browne et al., Cambridge UP, 1994, pp. 180–201, https://doi.org/10.1017/CBO9781139174121.010.

Zeng, Zilu "Luna." "Film Review: 'The Crossing' A Depoliticized Hong Kong." *China Focus*, 9 July 2019, chinafocus.ucsd.edu/2019/07/09/film-review-the-crossing/.

Darshana Sreedhar Mini

(Un)Reading Jonas Poher Rasmussen's *Flee*

The animated documentary *Flee*, directed by Jonas Poher Rasmussen, focuses on the life of the refugee Amin Nawabi. The staging of the film resembles a psychotherapy session between Nawabi and the filmmaker, with flashbacks taking us down the lanes of Nawabi's childhood memories. Rasmussen encourages Nawabi to take breaks while processing the information and to make himself comfortable with the narration of his life. This helps the viewer understand the emotional toll the revelations can have on Nawabi and prepares us to face the nuances in his truth claims. The sequence then segues to the past, colorful panels intermeshed with archival footage offering us a glimpse of Afghanistan in the 1980s.

Framing the making of the film as a pact of trust between Nawabi and the filmmaker—longtime friends from Nawabi's days as an unaccompanied minor seeking asylum in Denmark—*Flee* captures Nawabi's connection with home as he takes the viewers into his childhood memories of Afghanistan and ends with the home he would eventually set up in Copenhagen with his boyfriend. Interestingly, at some point in that exchange, Nawabi describes home as "somewhere safe, where you know you can stay and . . . don't have to move on. . . . It is not a temporary place" (*Flee* 1:40–2:14). Such questions and assertions about home, place, and the self position the refugee as an unruly subject that troubles the ethicality of sovereignty as a concept that holds up the nation-state.

In her essay "We Refugees," Hannah Arendt responds to the hesitancy among certain Jews who escaped the Nazis to consider themselves refugees. In their willingness to assimilate with the host country, she writes, they tend to forget that their very presence is accommodated within the parameters used by the nation-state to deal with statelessness and displacement (274). In his response to Arendt's essay, Giorgio Agamben considers the refugee as a productive figure that can help us understand the territorial fictions and the identarian performances that scaffold citizenship and the nation-state. The refugee, he says, can initiate "radical crisis to the principles of the nation-state" (115). Sovereign power imagines fixed boundaries and walls that separate true citizens and outsiders. While citizens are imagined as fully human, with the right to partake in civic life and discourse, the refugee, as outsider, is not granted the right to perform such rituals of belonging and identity. Although negatively, the refugee is then conditioned by and defined as the other of the subject formed through the interaction between the nation-state, its sovereign powers, and citizenship. Agamben, however, ends the essay on a hopeful note by suggesting that it is this very denial—and the refugee's constant displacement—that can show us the "reciprocal extraterritorialities" that can reinvent the space of territory (118). In *Flee*, we see one such unraveling of the fixity of birth and belonging, of citizenship and home. The film recuperates the migrant as a figure of relationality that can connect viewers with different kinds of displacement—removal of territorial ownership, or having to remain as an "alien resident," loss of legal status to work, or navigating insecurities that come with getting adjusted to a new place of residence.

In *Unthinking Eurocentrism*, Ella Shohat and Robert Stam argue that "by facilitating an engagement with distant peoples, the media 'deterritorialize' the process of imagining communities" (5). But at the same time, one can also perceive an interplay of power dynamics and media imperialism that reify the normative global world order—the execution of Saddam Hussein is a case in point. The media coverage of the 1990–91 Persian Gulf War showcased how empathy was channeled through a geopolitical grid where the euphoria over victory was premised on a colonial devalorization of non-Western life (24). How are we to make sense of such questions about media and power when it comes to refugee bodies? *Flee*, for example, introduces additional intersectional questions about race, ethnicity, and gender alongside displacement, ensuring that the refugee is not a flat, unmarked body but a body marked by several vertices of identity and power. In *Flee*, a film made by a white, Western filmmaker, a refugee, Nawabi, is able to make a new home through an uncomfortable set of constitutive fictions and frictions. How might we understand a film like this in the context of both contextual and literal deterritorialization?

To understand such questions, I conducted a survey and focus group discussions among college students studying media and communication in the United States. The students' geopolitical location and presence in a major hub of Western power (the United States) and their social presence in the cultural and discursive context of higher education made them an ideal set of subjects to interrogate how geopolitical dynamics influence the way young college adults understand refugee experiences. Conducted in a prominent midwestern university in the United States, the study comprised a survey with 135 survey respondents and focus groups with thirteen participants who were asked to watch *Flee* and respond to a set of questions pertaining to empathy and migrant experiences and to identify the aesthetic techniques used in the film. The aim was to formally understand how the filmmaker uses the form of animated documentary in portraying refugee experiences and how such formal techniques and narrative choices affect the audience's reaction to the film. As a corollary we might also ask, Who is the intended audience of the film? In tracing the range of interpretative possibilities to facilitate conversations around empathy and social justice in classrooms, the study examined how migrant media emerges as an overarching framework in the way students understand the tensions, elisions, and fault lines that construct their perception of the Global South. Considering that the majority of respondents were relatively unfamiliar with the experiences of refugees from the Global South, the study aimed to understand how Afghanistan, as a geopolitical space, is understood in the aftermath of 9/11 and the 2021 Taliban takeover.

The distinction between a "migrant" and "migrant experience" overlaid the survey responses that we received. Some respondents asserted that they had "migrant experiences," although they could not identify as migrants the same way refugees could. Thus, even while the respondents attempted to connect their individual experiences within the broader parameters of migration, they were also trying to ensure that the definition of an asylee figure that the film explores is distinct and cannot be conflated with the experience of displacement. Even so, many international respondents recognized border control as a machine of anxiety that reduces individual identity to a piece of paper (or a set of data points). The experience of border control seemed to provide a baseline from which common understandings of alienation and, hence, empathy toward the refugee other could be forged.

Animation was perceived as a careful and strategic aesthetic choice that lessened the intense feelings associated with the film, which many respondents identified as difficult to watch because of the constant sense of uncertainty that marked the lives of refugees in their efforts to find asylum. Many wondered if the homonormative conclusion of the film, in which Amin and his partner set up a house, thus situating the protagonist as a successful example of asylee integration, would divert the attention from the structural problems undergirding asylum-seeking procedures. In the final sequence, the couple are shown in the yard as their animated versions leave the scene, and the background is replaced by the real location, with the soundtrack capturing the conversation between them (*Flee* 1:22:53–1:24:37). If in the first half of the film animation was used to showcase the emotional distress the characters experienced, with Amin's mother's hair turning grey and the charcoal animation capturing the anxieties around her husband's disappearance, the last sequence is a metatextual move that jolts the audience back to reality. Many respondents mentioned that the film was a provocation to rethink their own structural advantages and privileges, especially in the light of their limited knowledge of Afghanistan as a geographic space, since most knew it only as a site of war and political turmoil. The shift from the geographic terrain of Afghanistan to Denmark via Soviet Russia allowed for a range of emotions that captured varying degrees of precarity that refugees experience in their journeys. Respondents noticed the double edge of visibility, especially the controlled public presence that makes refugees "grow inward" and relearn to occupy public spaces, as one respondent noted. "Like a stone that floats without drawing too much attention, the refugees are forced to learn to pass, so that they don't come across as threatening or dangerous to the natives," wrote one of the respondents. The sequence in the Soviet Union when Amin and his family are holed up in an apartment worrying about the police knocking on the door or hanging out at the opening of a McDonald's in Moscow only to be picked by the police for overstaying showcases the stresses associated with displacement (27:26–33:56, 58:31–1:01:04).

In response to the representation of the vulnerability of a girl who overstayed and was exploited by the police, the survey responses highlighted the ways those who are vulnerable and precariously placed become scapegoats of the system since they are being stripped of their basic rights and are thus subjected to arbitrary regulations. One of the respondents wrote, "A documentary film about a gay Afghan man's escape journey, animated to protect the subject, unexpectedly blurs the line between drama and documentary, and the personalized narration makes the audience unconsciously put themselves in the male protagonist's perspective." Some other responses pointed to the nuances of the asylee determination process, which could make an already stressful refugee experience all the more precarious. As one respondent noted:

> The lack of social capital and money prompts refugees to resort to human traffickers for resettlement in a wealthier, often Western country that has a stable refugee resettlement system. The human trafficking route is dangerous, and refugees face the risk of dying, being spotted by legal institutions, and deportation. They often resort to carefully created stories that would convince officers of refugee registration institutions due to their usually arbitrary standard of refugee admission. Even after a refugee's resettlement, it is unlikely for them to find a high-paying job—Amin's eldest brother only works as a cleaner—despite probably being educated or skilled.

The potential effectiveness of the film as a tool for teaching about intersectional experiences of refugees came through in Amin's identity as an unaccompanied gay minor fleeing war who had to rely on traffickers and the narrative they provided him with. There was an overwhelming agreement that the film's use of empathetic moments connected the viewers with the protagonist and generated empathy for those experiencing displacement (mean 4.52 in response to identifying general feelings to refugee experiences). Despite this, some respondents pointed out the problematics of connecting viewers to the refugee subject through the strategic use of empathy, since there is always the danger that viewers will feel as though they have done their bit by watching the film without feeling a moral responsibility to question the United States' interventions on foreign lands. Interestingly, the sequences that showcased Amin's happy childhood in Afghanistan in which he is shown joyfully running across the street in his sister's dress provided an opportunity for viewers to conceptualize the normalcy of life in Afghanistan before tensions set in (*Flee* 3:50–7:26). Archival footage of televisual images and photographs were seen as adding a new layer to the interpretation, because they were seamlessly interspersed between animated sections to provide historical contextualization.

Because the survey was conducted in 2021, during the Russian occupation of Ukraine, survey participants also commented on the "unequal

rights of the refugees." One of the respondents wondered why the temporary protection directive that the European Union had activated to enable
Ukrainian refugees to remain in Europe for at least a year, with the right
to work and to use social services, would not have been applied for those
fleeing ethnic conflicts in Sub-Saharan Africa or for Rohingya refugees
from Asia. Such responses demonstrated students' perception of the exclu-
sivity of narrative claims that determine who is deemed worthy of entering
Europe. Respondents noted the internal differentiations and gatekeeping
that refute the very purpose of a protective system for refugees. The arbi-
trariness of national borders was also taken up by some respondents. As
one respondent poignantly noted, "A country can be home, and a home
can be erased, and the aching, lovely *Flee* traffics in the space between
belonging and wandering."

In analyzing the sequence in which Amin's father is taken away (*Flee*
13:54–15:13), many respondents identified the use of "faceless" characters to signify how one would recall sad memories. Other respondents
interpreted such "faceless" characters as a statement about the erasure of
refugee experiences in contemporary media, and some argued that the
removal of facial features emboldened the police, seen as faceless pieces of
the governmental machinery that carry out the will of those above them.
Facelessness was also seen as a means of universalizing the issue of the refugee crisis as a problem that transcends Amin and thereby connects him to
a vast number of refugees who had gone through similar experiences. Facelessness was seen as a way of segueing into flashbacks that showcase traumatic memories, thereby giving them an eerie quality. As one respondent
noted, "The technique animates the intangible experience of memory
repression and also illustrates, perhaps, the fact that Amin has had to hide
all these memories for so long that they are becoming blurred."

One of the filmic texts against which *Flee* could be read is *Postcards
from Tora Bora*, directed by Wazhmah Osman and Kelly Dolak, which
offers an Afghan refugee narrative that intricately weaves in the narration
of female migration. While *Flee* is able to poignantly represent a gay refugee figure, Osman and Dolak's film overlays the relevance of more representational examples that can offer a spectrum of vantage points from
which refugees narrate their migration stories. Osman and Dolak complicate the refugee story by dispelling the stereotypes ingrained in the way
Afghanistan was imagined by the Western policymakers. As a personal
documentary, *Postcards from Tora Bora* is narrated by Osman and includes
animated sequences, flashbacks, Super 8 films, and doodles to capture

different facets of Afghan lives and to show how people remember the spaces that were destroyed by the war.

Flee is certainly able to humanize the Afghan refugee subject and make him a likeable character. However, Osman and Karen Redrobe, in a cowritten piece on the storytelling conventions of *Flee*, have pointed out the way that the film plays into a certain tradition of documentary filmmaking that mobilizes star power for marketing and publicity purposes. The use of Nikolaj Coster-Waldau's voice for Rasmussen and Riz Ahmed's for Amin in the English version of the documentary is one case in point. Coster-Waldau and Ahmed were roped in as executive producers of the film shortly after it won the World Cinema Documentary Competition at Sundance (Osman and Redrobe 26). Osman and Redrobe also discuss how the specific storytelling strategies used by the film help foster a certain set of expectations from the audience regarding the film's value and worth (23). They also emphasize how refugee films made by women often struggle to achieve mainstream success or distribution contracts. The Black Latina filmmaker Tamara Shogaolu points out that she was asked whether her film *Half a Life*, an animated documentary about a gay Egyptian activist that was released four years before *Flee*, was inspired by *Flee*. She asks:

> How many awards do Black women directors need to win before we, too, can be considered geniuses? . . . At a time when no single studio feature animated film has been directed by a Black woman, and there is very little representation of Black or Latinx women directors in animation (or women, in general), there are many other stories of erasure out there like mine. Stories of insidious erasure, erasure by exclusion. We are out here directing, but the opportunities are still safeguarded to a few, which does not include many women like me. Women who continue to tell stories, to fight erasure, to be brilliant, to be geniuses and to persevere.

Thus, while the narrative drive to showcase Amin's refugee journey and the use of animated documentary as a form might have added to the success the film has had in the festival circuits, one cannot be totally oblivious to the nuances of the marketing of the refugee narrative as a specific media product that aligns with the expectation of the audience. Osman and Redrobe also discuss how *Flee* excludes female characters from its ambit by not devoting enough space to exploring their interiority, leading to their portrayal as "agency-less immobile objects to be moved by men, almost as failed migrants, lacking mobility" (27). One can read *Flee* as a film-event—one that is celebrated and valorized in very particular ways—

and contrast its reception with that of other filmic texts such as Osman and Dolak's and Shogaolu's to foreground the complex mediations of the figure of the refugee.

In conclusion, then, *Flee* is useful as a narrative text about displacement and asylum and about the interlocked nature of gender identity and citizenship. But we should also be wary of uncritical celebrations of the film that cater to Western liberal notions of citizenship, even the ones that seemingly empathize with those who are left out of its ambit by outsider discourses (Mini). As the critics discussed earlier demonstrate, reading a film such as *Flee* is necessarily a dialectical (and often conflicted) process. The film offers an entry point to discuss structural problems that undergird globalization, migration, and the modern nation-state system, and it is perhaps this that makes *Flee* a teachable text for different constituencies of audiences.

Works Cited

Agamben, Giorgio. "We Refugees." Translated by Michael Rocke. *Symposium*, vol. 49, no. 2, summer 1995, pp. 114–19.

Arendt, Hannah. "We Refugees." *The Jewish Writings*, edited by Jerome Kohn and Ron. H. Feldman, Schocken Books, 2007, pp. 264–74.

Flee. Directed by Jonas Poher Rasmussen, Neon, 2021. *Amazon Prime Video*, www.amazon.com/Flee-Daniel-Karimyar/dp/B09NSFBL2G.

Mini, Darshana Sreedhar. "Narration, Empathy, and the Asylee Body in *Flee*." *Flee*, edited by Jamie Baron and Kristen Fuhs, Routledge, forthcoming. Docalogue.

Osman, Wazhmah, and Karen Redrobe. "The Inclusions and Occlusions of Expanded Refugee Narratives: A Dialogue on *Flee*." *Film Quarterly*, vol. 76, no. 1, 2022, pp. 23–34.

Postcards from Tora Bora. Directed by Wazhmah Osman and Kelly Dolak, DER, 2007. *Amazon Prime Video*, www.amazon.com/Postcards-Tora-Bora-Wazhmah-Osman/dp/B01M6V8TRV.

Shogaolu, Tamara. "Can Black Women Directors Be Geniuses?" *The Medium*, 8 Apr. 2022, medium.com/@tamarashogaolu/can-black-women-directors-be-geniuses-9b07678fa072.

Shohat, Ella, and Robert Stam. *Unthinking Eurocentrism: Multiculturalism and the Media*. Routledge, 2014.

Eva Rueschmann

Traveling Identities:
Migration in Literature and Film
at a Liberal Arts College

In the essay "Reflections on Exile," Edward Said observes, "Exile is strangely compelling to think about but terrible to experience. It is the unhealable rift forced between a human being and a native place" (173). In the last half century, human migrations and refugee flows have accelerated in response to globalization, climate change, and political, ethnic, and religious conflicts. In the early 2000s I developed a college course on migration, exile, and diasporic identities in film and literature for undergraduate students at Hampshire College in Amherst, Massachusetts. The course, titled Traveling Identities, brings together cinematic and literary texts that address the complexities of cultural identity in an age of increasing movement of people across the globe. Taught as a discussion-based seminar, Traveling Identities strongly appeals to a broad range of undergraduates. In a time when the lived experiences of immigrants and refugees are too often stereotyped or politically exploited to arouse fears of (im)migration as social threats, I have found that my students are looking for more complex and authentic narratives of immigration and exile.

In preparing Traveling Identities as an interdisciplinary humanities course, I saw the need to introduce students to novels, memoirs, and films along with selected essays by cultural theorists and literary and film critics that offer diverse perspectives on the multifaceted histories of (im)migration and diaspora. I took as my main inspiration dramatic feature films from around the globe that since the 1980s have told new stories about (im)migration and diaspora communities, many created by filmmakers—or based on the works of authors—who were often (im)migrants or children of (im)migrants themselves. These diverse films altogether broke new ground in world cinema. As the Indian novelist Salman Rushdie observes in *Imaginary Homelands*, contemporary cinema's pluralism and hybridity has offered modern film artists and writers a creative location to explore the loss of "familiar habitats" and the struggles to "make a new imaginative relationship with the world" (125). Rushdie here captures the reason that fictional narratives, especially in cinema, are particularly rich and engaging texts for exploring migration as a topic. Articulating the psychological and cultural consequences of migration and displacement for identity, Rushdie argues that these realities affect aesthetic choices and strategies of representation. This insight is a challenge to static conceptions of national cinemas as insular canons and underlies what Hamid Naficy has called "accented cinema."

The primary learning goals for students in the course are to become familiar with key concepts such as diaspora and (imaginary) homelands, migration, exile, citizenship, hybridity, bicultural identity, double consciousness, transnationalism, trauma, and intercultural and intergenerational differences; to understand specific histories of migration and diaspora communities; and to develop analytical and critical skills through close readings of literary texts and films in their historical and cultural contexts.

The three-part syllabus of Traveling Identities organizes texts topically, thematically, and to some limited extent by genre. An introductory section begins with an exercise designed to encourage dialogue and self-reflection on the part of students about their own assumptions and unconscious biases about migration. Each student is asked to bring to class several images that express for them the meanings of migration. We display the images around the classroom (or, for online courses, in a digital exhibition), and students discuss their responses to the images. As background theory and as a prompt for image selection, I assign Said's "Reflections on Exile," Ketu Katrak's "Colonialism, Imperialism, and Imagined Homes," and Amitava Kumar's introduction to *Passport Photos* (2–15), a multigenre book on the immigration experience. This exercise generates engaged discussion, allowing students to understand one another's positionalities, and it introduces key thematic threads that are developed throughout the course.

The syllabus is structured in three parts: "Historical Journeys of Migration," "Migrant Autobiographies and Memoirs," and "Contemporary Diaspora Communities." The chosen texts and films approach migration as a deeply gendered and racialized experience; explore the effects of colonialism, imperialism, and decolonization; and consider differences between first-generation immigrants and second- or third-generation immigrants who must negotiate their relationship to home and the homeland.[1]

In the first section, we cover three kinds of migrant journeys that highlight the commonalities and differences between men's and women's experiences of migration and displacement. As in the succeeding sections of the course, literary works and films are paired to offer frameworks for comparative analysis. We first look at the Black Atlantic through the French West Indian director Euzhan Palcy's film *Sugar Cane Alley*, based on Joseph Zobel's semi-autobiographical novel about growing up on the sugarcane plantations in 1930s Martinique before leaving for France. We discuss this film as a companion piece to the novel *A State of Independence*, by the Black British author Caryl Phillips, which focuses on a man's return to his native Caribbean home, the island of St. Kitts, after a twenty-year absence on the eve of its transition from colonialism to an uncertain independent future. We also discuss Kayo Hatta's film *Picture Bride* as a fictionalized account of the experiences of Japanese women who came to Hawai'i as arranged brides to husbands they had never met. This section of the seminar ends with Gregory Nava's well-known film *El Norte*, a tale of a brother and sister who undertake the treacherous journey from violence and exploitation in Guatemala for an imagined better life in California only to find their dreams betrayed. The film's epic structure incorporates Mayan myth and effectively employs magic realist scenes to portray the siblings' memories of Guatemala and their cultural disorientation as undocumented workers in the United States.

Sugar Cane Alley, *Picture Bride*, and *El Norte* all treat historical passages and the issue of immigrant labor, lending themselves to a comparison of forced versus voluntary migratory experiences, from the Middle Passage to Asian migration to border crossings from Latin America. In addition to Christine Gaudry-Hudson's essay on Palcy's feminist revision of Zobel's novel, we discuss the cultural theorist Stuart Hall's essay "Cultural Identity and Diaspora." Hall provides two definitions of cultural identity shaped by the Black Atlantic diaspora experience—a sense of exile and displacement and a search for roots. Students compare how these two definitions operate in Caribbean cinema, specifically the film *Sugar Cane*

Alley, and how this filmic representation is similar or different from Phillips's vision of ambivalence and uncertainty in *A State of Independence*. Our analysis of *Picture Bride* is framed by Emma Gee's history of picture brides and Harry Kitano's essay on the Japanese American family structure, which lay the groundwork for discussion questions on gender relationships in *Picture Bride*: How are the relationships between Japanese immigrant men and women on the Hawai'ian sugarcane plantation portrayed? How do traditional Japanese cultural expectations determine the relationship between the central character and her husband, and how do those traditional expectations change? Finally, *El Norte*'s dreamlike images of the trauma of displacement from Guatemala to LA require some background reading in Latinx feature filmmaking and Mayan mythology. Mario Barrera's essay on story structure in Latino feature films, Karl Taube's overview of Mayan myth (*Aztec and Maya Myths* 51–74), and Rosa Linda Fregoso's treatment of female subjectivity as allegory in *El Norte* (106–10) ground our analysis of the film. Five comparative questions weave through this first section's class discussions: In what ways do these films depict migrant journeys as social or psychological rites of passage? Are there common features and patterns in these immigrant journeys? Do specific historical and social factors shape the stories of the protagonists? How do the films portray immigrant labor practices, discrimination, and individual and community resistance to injustice? How do dreams, ghost stories, and magic realist elements function in these films to connect the migrants to their homeland, ancestors, and memories?

The second part of the course examines how memory becomes a recurring trope in migration narratives. Subjectivity, nostalgia, trauma, and loss figure prominently as discussion and writing topics. Julian Schnabel's film adaptation of the Cuban exile writer Reinaldo Arenas's autobiography *Before Night Falls* provides an opportunity to explore a gay writer's sense of exile and imprisonment in his home country, his escape to the United States in the Mariel boatlift of 1980, and his powerful memories of growing up queer in Cuba. Eva Hoffman's memoir *Lost in Translation* recounts her emigration from Poland to Canada and the United States, tracing her memory of constructing a new identity through a different language and culture. The class screens several experimental films—the Armenian Canadian filmmaker Atom Egoyan's *Calendar*, the Hong Kong director Ann Hui's *Song of the Exile*, and the London-based Palestinian artist Mona Hatoum's film *Measures of Distance*—and we read excerpts from Naficy's influential study *An Accented Cinema* (10–39, 118–20,

136–40, 233–34). The following question is central in this section: How do writers and filmmakers probe the tensions of ethnic identity and memory through the richly textured mediums of language and film? Close analyses of passages from the memoirs and film clips address how writers and directors translate through metaphor and imagery both a sense of rupture and loss as well as their reconnection with family and national histories. The films in this section, most made by second-generation directors about their parents or their ethnic history, serve as a transition point to the third section of the course, which considers contemporary diaspora communities in European, Canadian, and US American literature and film.

More specifically, this final part of the course examines intergenerational relationships within diaspora communities. The term *diaspora* is complex; its proliferating meanings in relation to nation, homeland, transnationalism, and cosmopolitanism have been widely debated (Stierstorfer and Wilson; Knott and McLoughlin). However, in the literary fiction and films discussed here, students examine how immigrant families become symbolic microcosms of the tensions between old-world cultural traditions and modernity. Two films set within the British Asian diaspora—Stephen Frears's adaptation of Hanif Kureishi's play *My Beautiful Laundrette* and Gurinder Chadha's *Bhaji on the Beach*—focus on multigenerational Pakistani and Indian families who negotiate their complex ties to their former colonizer, Great Britain. Frears's film works well with Chadha's exploration of three generations of South Asian women on a day trip to the seaside resort of Blackpool, a journey that dramatically captures the collision of tradition and modern cultural life in unexpected ways. The relationship between first-generation migrants and their children and grandchildren is further explored in a pairing of two works devoted to questions of changing values and cultural assimilation in the Chinese diaspora in Canada and the United States: Mina Shum's independent film *Double Happiness*, a semi-autobiographical comedy about asserting one's independence within a conservative Asian immigrant family, and Fae Myenne Ng's novel *Bone*. In the novel, two Chinese American sisters delve into the family secrets of their immigrant parents, the history of San Francisco's Chinatown, and grapple with the aftermath of their third sibling Ona's suicide.

Much has been written on migrant and diaspora film in contemporary Europe. Mathieu Kassovitz's *La haine* (*Hate*) is now a classic example of a French *banlieue* film that depicts the multiethnic, multiracial urban landscape of Paris through the eyes and experiences of three disenfranchised youths from Jewish, Afro-Caribbean, and North African *Beur* immigrant families. *Beur* is a slang term that originated in France to describe the children of North African immigrants, particularly those from the Maghreb region (Algeria, Morocco, Tunisia). *Lone Star*, directed by John Sayles, is an important capstone to the semester because it delves into the history and politics of immigration and interethnic relations along the US-Mexico border. Gloria Anzaldúa's theories of border crossing and mestiza consciousness and Sandra Cisneros's short stories provide a frame for discussion of Anglo-Latinx relations and the connection between storytelling and history in shaping our identities.

The weekly film viewings, readings, and discussions require students to be actively engaged on a regular basis in order to ensure a productive discussion. I provide film notes for all the screenings as well as questions designed to highlight the more complex themes and conflicts addressed in the films and novels, to which students respond in a blog entry in preparation for class discussion. Key theoretical and historical readings by Katrak, Hall, Naficy, Avtar Brah, Said, Iain Chambers, and León Grinberg and Rebeca Grinberg introduce students to different concepts, approaches, and aspects of migration studies, including the history of colonialism and postcolonialism, the social and psychological consequences of displacement, the complexity of cultural identity, and the aesthetic and political choices filmmakers make to capture a sense of living between cultures. I invite students to reflect on these readings in relation to the literary and cinematic texts in their blogs. In addition to these shorter writing assignments, I have students work in pairs on a class presentation about one of the films or literary texts. They frame the issues and provide background materials and prepare a lesson plan with study questions that I review with them ahead of time. For their final project, students choose the topic and format of their research, whether it is an autobiographical narrative, a research paper, an ethnographic project based on interviews with migrants, or a short film or short story about migration.

Teaching migration in literature and film offers valuable lessons and opportunities that extend far beyond the classroom. It allows students to explore complex narratives of identity, belonging, and displacement, fostering empathy and a deeper understanding of the diverse experiences that shape human lives. By engaging with stories that highlight the struggles and resilience of migrants, students can critically examine issues of power, privilege, and social justice. This interdisciplinary approach encourages them to question stereotypes, consider multiple perspectives, and develop global awareness, which is essential in our increasingly interconnected world. Ultimately, the study of migration through literature and film not only enriches students' academic knowledge but also empowers them to become more compassionate and informed citizens.

Note

1. A more recent version of the syllabus features updated texts and films that explore migration from diverse perspectives, providing rich material for discussion. Notable inclusions are Julie Otsuka's *The Buddha in the Attic*, Julia Alvarez's *Afterlife*, and Karla Cornejo Villavicencio's group memoir *The Undocumented Americans* as well as the films *Identifying Features* and *Atlantique* (*Atlantics*).

Works Cited

Alvarez, Julia. *Afterlife*. Algonquin, 2020.

Anzaldúa, Gloria. *Borderlands / La Frontera: The New Mestiza*. 4th ed., Aunt Lute Books, 2012.

Atlantique. Directed by Mati Diop, Ad Vitam Distribution / mk2 Films, 2019.

Barrera, Mario. "Story Structure in Latino Feature Films." *Chicanos and Film: Representation and Resistance*, edited by Chon Noriega, U of Minnesota P, 1992, pp. 218–40.

Before Night Falls. Directed by Julian Schnabel, Fine Line Features, 2000.

Bhaji on the Beach. Directed by Gurinder Chadha, First Independent Films, 1993.

Brah, Avtar. *Cartographies of Diaspora: Contesting Identities*. Routledge, 1996.

Calendar. Directed by Atom Egoyan, Zeitgeist Films, 1993.

Chambers, Iain. *Migrancy, Culture, Identity*. Routledge, 1994.

Cisneros, Sandra. *The House on Mango Street*. Vintage Books, 1991.

Double Happiness. Directed by Mina Shum, Fine Line Features, 1994.

Fregoso, Rosa Linda. *The Bronze Screen: Chicana and Chicano Film Culture*. U of Minnesota P, 1993.

Gaudry-Hudson, Christine. "'Raising Cane': A Feminist Rewriting of Joseph Zobel's Novel *Sugar Cane Alley* by Film Director Euzhan Palcy." *CLA Journal*, vol. 46, no. 4, 2003, pp. 478–93.

Gee, Emma. "Issei Women: 'Picture Brides' in America." *Immigrant Women*, edited by Maxine Schwartz Seller, State U of New York P, 1994, pp. 53–59.

Grinberg, León, and Rebeca Grinberg. *Psychoanalytic Perspectives on Migration and Exile*. Yale UP, 2009.

La haine. Directed by Mathieu Kassovitz, Janus Films, 1995.

Hall, Stuart. "Cultural Identity and Diaspora." *Transatlantic Literary Studies: A Reader*, edited by Susan Manning and Andrew Taylor, Johns Hopkins UP, 2007, pp. 131–38.

Hoffman, Eva. *Lost in Translation: A Life in a New Language*. Penguin, 1990.

Identifying Features. Directed by Fernanda Valadez, Alpha Violet / Kino Lorber, 2020.

Katrak, Ketu. "Colonialism, Imperialism, and Imagined Homes." *The Columbia History of the American Novel: New Views*, edited by Emory Elliott, Columbia UP, 1991, pp. 649–78.

Kitano, Harry. "The Japanese American Family." *Ethnic Families in America: Patterns and Variations*, edited by Charles Mindel et al., Elsevier, 1988, pp. 258–75.

Knott, Kim, and Sean McLoughlin, editors. *Diasporas: Concepts, Intersections, Identities.* Zed Books, 2010.

Kumar, Amitava. *Passport Photos.* U of California P, 2000.

Lone Star. Directed by John Sayles, Sony Pictures Classics, 1996.

Measures of Distance. Directed by Mona Hatoum, Women Make Movies, 1988.

My Beautiful Laundrette. Directed by Stephen Frears, Mainline Pictures, 1985.

Naficy, Hamid. *An Accented Cinema: Exilic and Diasporic Filmmaking.* Princeton UP, 2001.

Ng, Fae Myenne. *Bone.* Hyperion, 2008.

El Norte. Directed by Gregory Nava, Artisan Entertainment, 1984.

Otsuka, Julie. *The Buddha in the Attic.* Vintage Books, 2012.

Phillips, Caryl. *A State of Independence.* Vintage Books, 1986.

Picture Bride. Directed by Kayo Hatta, Miramax, 1994.

Rushdie, Salman. *Imaginary Homelands: Essays and Criticism, 1981–1991.* Granta / Penguin Books, 1992.

Said, Edward W. "Reflections on Exile." *"Reflections on Exile" and Other Essays*, by Said, Harvard UP, 2000, pp. 173–86.

Song of the Exile. Directed by Ann Hui, Golden Harvest, 1990.

Stierstorfer, Klaus, and Janet Wilson, editors. *The Routledge Diaspora Studies Reader.* Routledge, 2018.

Sugar Cane Alley. Directed by Euzhan Palcy, Carlotta Films / JMJ Productions, 1983.

Taube, Karl. *Aztec and Maya Myths.* U of Texas P, 1993.

Villavicencio, Karla Cornejo. *The Undocumented Americans.* One World, 2020.

Marilén Loyola

Migrating Scenes: Teaching an Undergraduate Seminar on Migration and Movement in the Hispanic World

While designed primarily with upper-level Spanish and Latin American studies majors in mind, my special topics course, Migrating Scenes: Migration and Movement in the Hispanic World, has an interdisciplinary appeal that draws Spanish-speaking students from other humanities disciplines and the social sciences. Migrating Scenes, taught in Spanish, is framed by theories of migration and culture and organized around a series of modules dedicated, respectively, to the following migration trajectories: Africa to Spain (module 1), Latin America to Spain (module 2), Europe to Latin America (module 3), and Latin America to the United States (module 4).[1] Course materials include theoretical readings, news articles on current events, and a variety of cultural productions including theater, film, novels, and short stories, all of which address the rupture and losses inherent in migration while emphasizing the roles of resilience and creativity.

The semester opens with a course introduction that exposes students to key terminology and concepts related to migration, such as cultural hybridity, transculturation, and *la otredad* ("otherness"). Among the articles students read in the first class sessions are Néstor García Canclini's "No sabemos cómo llamar a los otros" ("We Do Not Know What to Call Others") and María Fabiola Pardo's "La inmigración y el devenir de las

236

sociedades multiculturales: Perspectivas políticas y teóricas" ("Immigration and the Future of Multicultural Societies: Political and Theoretical Perspectives").[2] The first assignments of the semester ask students to identify and explain the significance of at least three key terms (in Spanish) per article that have to do with migration. From García Canclini's essay, for example, students might identify terms such as "imaginarios" ("imaginaries"; 35), "hegemónica" ("hegemonic"; 35), "etnocentrismo" ("ethnocentrism"; 35), "bárbaros" ("barbarian"; 36), "integración nacional" ("national integration"; 36), "interculturalidad globalizada" ("globalized interculturality"; 37), and "multiculturalismo conservador/liberal" ("conservative/liberal multiculturalism"; 38). Students also choose a sentence or fragment from each essay and write a brief analysis explaining how the concepts presented in the selection, and the essay in general, might help shape their approach to the study of migration. Students then share and discuss their findings and, based on this in-class exchange, work together to develop a collective working list of key concepts they deem relevant to a critical understanding of migration. Including shorter assignments such as these during the first two or three weeks of the course helps build students' conceptual arsenal, increasing their familiarity with specialized terminology in Spanish while encouraging their engagement and serving to frame the regional migration modules that follow.

As a part of this introductory module, students also do a dramatic reading in class of the short play *El buen vecino* (*The Good Neighbor*), by the Spanish playwright Juan Mayorga. The play addresses the insecurity, anxiety, and potential for manipulation that can corrupt the relationship between those who are undocumented and those who are citizens.[3] This type of embodied reading recasts students' awareness of the human experience of migration, compelling a more empathetic approach to the stark power differentials and potential suffering and discrimination that can emerge through migration. *El buen vecino* in particular also tends to awaken students' curiosity about individual and real-life stories of migration, inviting them to think critically about the unspoken conflicts that can frame considerations of legality and legitimacy in the migratory context. During this introductory unit, the course also identifies key framing questions. For instance, how does the experience of migration challenge the tension between center and periphery and expand notions of belonging, alterity, and reciprocity? To what extent can we speak of an ethics of migration? Finally, how might resilience and resistance function as creative means of survival?

Considering these questions, students embark on the first of four content modules, Africa to Spain,[4] which is anchored by the Basque writer and artist Javier de Isusi's graphic novel *Asȳlum*. *Asȳlum* is framed as a series of five visually interwoven vignettes featuring migration stories and the search for asylum because of persecution and violence. One is a story of exile from Spain to Venezuela via France set during the Spanish Civil War, while the other four take place in the twenty-first century—three from Africa and one from Mexico—all converging in a warm gathering around a table in an apartment in the Basque region of Spain. Students also watch *Las cartas de Alou* (*Letters from Alou*), the first feature-length film to depict African migration to Spain, about a young Senegalese man who migrates to Spain and faces a series of obstacles while attempting to integrate into Spanish culture. Rounding out this module is the Claymation short film *El viaje de Saïd* (*Saïd's Voyage*), which features the dreamscape of a young Moroccan boy who imagines crossing the Mediterranean and arriving on Spain's shores. As with each of the modules that follow, at the end of module 1, students write a two- to three-page essay in which they analyze critically the module's works of fiction, in this case the graphic novel and two films, and nonfiction (documentaries, current events research, etc.). By reflecting on selected works in their historical and cultural context, students begin to approach migration as a multifaceted experience, the nuanced understanding of which is enriched by a variety of perspectives and genres.

In module 1, students consider the factors that can motivate migration—on the one hand, violence, corruption, persecution, and poverty, and on the other, a longing for new opportunity and even a dreamlike idealism regarding the future. At the same time, the combination of de Isusi's graphic novel, *Las cartas de Alou*, and the short Claymation film ground students in the realities, often nightmarish, of attempting to belong in a foreign land. *Asȳlum* is especially effective in this regard since, alongside its fictionalized migrants, it refers to real-life victims of violence and persecution in Africa, Spain, and Mexico. There is a powerful theme that emerges in this first module that also becomes critical in subsequent modules and contexts and can be articulated as another layer of questions: How do friendship and interpersonal ties heal and potentially save the migrant? How can these relationships nurture new forms of identification and expression in an unfamiliar place characterized by strangeness and strangers?

Module 2, Latin America to Spain, features discussions of how generational differences and gender roles affect the migration experience. Students begin by reading the coming-of-age novel *Una tarde con campanas*

(*An Afternoon with Bells*), by the Venezuelan writer Juan Carlos Méndez Guédez. Written as a sort of diary, the novel features the voice of a young Latin American boy who, together with his family, has fled a repressive regime in an unnamed country in Latin America and now lives in Madrid, Spain. After reading this novel, students watch the feature-length film *Flores de otro mundo* (*Flowers from Another World*), in which women from the Spanish-speaking Caribbean and other parts of Spain arrive in a rural Spanish town with the goal of being romantically paired with the town's men. A useful sociological study that addresses the context in *Flores* is "El rapto de las Latinas: Migración latinoamericana y mercado matrimonial en España" ("The Sequestering of Latinas: Latin American Migration and the Matrimonial Market in Spain"), by Andreu Domingo and colleagues. Another insightful scholarly resource for the study of migration to Spain in modules 1 and 2 is Raquel Vega-Durán's *Emigrant Dreams, Immigrant Borders: Migrants, Transnational Encounters, and Identity in Spain,* particularly the introduction.

Module 3, Europe to Latin America, focuses on the novel *Los informantes* (*The Informants*), by the Colombian writer Juan Gabriel Vásquez, about Nazi and Jewish post–Second World War migration to Colombia.[5] Complementing this novel is the feature documentary produced by Univision titled "Desafiar el olvido" ("Defying Forgetting"), part of Univision's *Aquí y ahora* (*Here and Now*) series, which traces the history of post-Holocaust European migration to Latin America.[6] Students also read Diego Acosta's "Free Movement in South America: The Emergence of an Alternative Model," an article that encourages readers to question how immigration policies in Latin America compare to those that govern relations between the United States and other countries. The comparative approach in Acosta's article serves to frame module 4, in which migration to the United States from places like Mexico and different countries in Central America can be read in contrast to migration between Caribbean islands and to the United States from places like Cuba, the Dominican Republic, and Puerto Rico.

Key texts for the last and longest module, Latin America to the United States, include novels such as *How the García Girls Lost Their Accents*, by the Dominican American writer Julia Álvarez; *De donde venimos* (*Where We Come From*), by the Brownsville native Oscar Cásares; *The House on Mango Street*, by the Mexican American writer Sandra Cisneros; and *Of Women and Salt*, the debut novel of Gabriela García, the daughter of Cuban and Mexican immigrants.[7] All four novels focus on the lives of children and teenagers who are part of immigrant families in the United States struggling to hold on to their respective cultures. Two movies that capture elements of contemporary Cuban migration to the United States and take place almost entirely in Havana are Alejandro Brugués's *Personal Belongings* and Lucy Mulloy's *Una noche* (*One Night*). These films pair well because of their shared focus on Cubans in their teens and twenties in Havana and their desire to leave the island. Students also read the self-published novel *Sueños ilegales* (*Illegal Dreams*), by Constantino Urzaiz, the painful story of a Yucatec man who crosses illegally into the United States and faces devastating trials. Module 4 can also include the recent film *Sueños ilegales: Las estrellas no conocen fronteras* (*Illegal Dreams: The Stars Know No Borders*), unrelated to the aforementioned novel but similarly based on true events, featuring the stories of two brothers from El Salvador who cross into the United States and experience drastically different fates. Complementing these films are the short stories from Eduardo Cabrera's *9 cuentos de inmigrantes en los Estados Unidos* (*9 Stories about Immigrants in the United States*) and authentic accounts of migration recounted by undocumented immigrants in the United States, such as those found in Val Rosenfeld and Flor Fortunati's edited volume *Voices of the Undocumented*.[8]

Each module described above includes an analytical essay, a combination of oral presentations and student-led discussions, and frequent assignments in which students do research and exchange ideas on the course's online discussion board. For example, to ground our class discussions throughout the semester, I integrate current events research by having students search for online news articles, videos, or images referencing migration that pertain to a specific module's particular national or cultural context. I then ask students to use an online class discussion board to post the results of their research, which should include a link to the online source, a brief critical summary and reflection written by the student, and a response to the posts of at least two other students. This type of low-stakes interactive work develops students' research and writing skills in Spanish, further contextualizes each module's assigned readings and viewings, and works to sharpen students' intercultural competence and global awareness of experiences of migration in today's world.

For the course's final project, students write a critical analysis of migration in relation to a topic of their choice. Examples have included how migration relates to memory and the imagination; gender and sexual identities; language and bilingualism; generational differences and coming of age;

concepts of home, family, and refuge; resilience and creativity; and the impulse to reconnect with the country of origin. All are topics that the course touches on throughout the semester and all deepen students' understandings of the complexity, rupture, and resilience that inhere in experiences of migration.

Notes

1. Module 4 can be subdivided into distinct migration contexts, including Caribbean migration to the United States, Central and South American migration to the United States, and Latinx immigrant communities in the United States.

2. There are many ways of establishing the theoretical framework for this course. The two articles I mention have worked well in the past to shape students' learning and target discussion toward understanding key terms and concepts. Another reading I will add in the future is an excerpt from Patrick Chamoiseau's *Migrant Brothers: A Poet's Declaration of Human Dignity*, which has been translated into Spanish as *Hermanos migrantes*.

3. Mayorga later developed *El buen vecino* into a full-length play titled *Animales nocturnos* (*Nocturnal Animals*), first published in 2003.

4. As with the other modules, the first module can be expanded into a semester-long course. Possible additional resources here are the films *Bwana* and *Adú*; the first season of the television series *Mar de plástico* (*Plastic Sea*), which features North and sub-Saharan African immigrants as secondary characters; and the documentaries *Les sauteurs* (*Those Who Jump*) and *Hijos de las nubes, la última colonia* (*Sons of the Clouds: The Last Colony*), about the postcolonial challenges faced by Saharawi refugees in Western Sahara. Another possibility is adding a more robust theater component. An excellent resource on race, theater, and immigration from a variety of regions to Spain is Jeffrey K. Coleman's *Necropolitical Theater: Race and Immigration on the Contemporary Spanish Stage*.

5. For historical context, see Friedman.

6. Module 3 could be expanded to include, for example, Japanese immigration to Brazil and could feature Bernardo Carvalho's *O sol se põe em São Paulo* (*The Sun Sets in São Paulo*), provided that students can read Portuguese. Time permitting, the course could also include the novel *El libro de los recuerdos* (*The Book of Memories*), by Ana María Shúa, which focuses on European immigration to Argentina through the lens of family.

7. All four novels were originally written in English. Only Álvarez's, Cásares's, and Cisneros's novels are currently available in Spanish translation.

8. If expanded into a semester-long course, module 4 could also include a selection of films such as *Sin nombre* (*Nameless*), *Paraíso Travel*, *A Better Life*, and *Ya no estoy aquí* (*I Am No Longer Here*), among many others. Another volume that could be of interest in module 4 is the self-published *Náufragos en una Yola: Cruzando de Santo Domingo a la Isla hermana Puerto Rico* (*Shipwreck Survivors*

on a Dinghy: Crossing from Santo Domingo to the Sister Island of Puerto Rico), a novel by Orliz Espiritusanto, a writer of Puerto Rican and Dominican descent.

Works Cited

Acosta, Diego. "Free Movement in South America: The Emergence of an Alternative Model." *Migration Policy Institute*, 23 Aug. 2016, www.migrationpolicy.org/article/free-movement-south-america-emergence-alternative-model.

Adú. Directed by Salvador Calvo, Ikiru Films, 2020.

Álvarez, Julia. *How the García Girls Lost Their Accents*. Algonquin Books, 2007.

A Better Life. Directed by Chris Weitz, Lime Orchard Productions, 2011.

Bwana. Directed by Imanol Uribe, Aurum Producciones, 1996.

Cabrera, Eduardo. *9 cuentos de inmigrantes en los Estados Unidos*. 2017.

Las cartas de Alou. Directed by Montxo Armendáriz, Elías Querejeta, 1990.

Carvalho, Bernardo. *O sol se põe em São Paulo*. Companhia das Letras, 2007.

Cásares, Oscar. *De donde venimos*. Penguin Random House, 2019.

Chamoiseau, Patrick. *Hermanos migrantes*. Translated by Adalber Salas Hernández, Editorial Pre-Textos, 2020.

———. *Migrant Brothers: A Poet's Declaration of Human Dignity*. Translated by Matthew Amos and Fredrik Rönnbäck, Yale UP, 2018.

Cisneros, Sandra. *The House on Mango Street*. Vintage Books, 1984.

Coleman, Jeffrey K. *Necropolitical Theater: Race and Immigration on the Contemporary Spanish Stage*. Northwestern UP, 2020.

de Isusi, Javier. *Asÿlum*. Comisión de Ayuda al Refugiado en Euskadi / Fundación Gernika Gogoratuz, 2015.

"Desafiar el olvido." *Aquí y ahora*, Univision, 27 Oct. 2019.

Domingo, Andreu, et al. "El rapto de las Latinas: Migración latinoamericana y mercado matrimonial en España." *El género en movimiento: Familias y migraciones*, edited by María Eugenia Zavala de Cosío and Virginie Rozée Gomez, Colegio de México, 2014, pp. 41–66.

Espiritusanto, Orliz. *Náufragos en una Yola: Cruzando de Santo Domingo a la Isla hermana Puerto Rico*. 2019.

Flores de otro mundo. Directed by Icíar Bollaín, Alta Films, 1999.

Friedman, Max Paul. "There Goes the Neighborhood: Blacklisting Germans in Latin America and the Evanescence of the Good Neighbor Policy." *Diplomatic History*, vol. 27, no. 4, Sept. 2003, pp. 569–97.

García, Gabriela. *Of Women and Salt*. Flatiron Books, 2021.

García Canclini, Néstor. "No sabemos cómo llamar a los otros." *Global/Local: Democracia, memoria, identidades*, edited by Hugo Achugar and Sonia D'Alessandro, Ediciones Trilce, 2002, pp. 35–56.

Hijos de las nubes, la última colonia. Directed by Álvaro Longoria, Candescent Films, 2012.

Mayorga, Juan. *El buen vecino. Teatro para minutos*, by Mayorga, Ediciones La Uña Rota, 2020, pp. 145–52.

Méndez Guédez, Juan Carlos. *Una tarde con campanas*. Alianza Editorial, 2004.

Una noche. Directed by Lucy Mulloy, Una Noche Films, 2012.

Paraiso Travel. Directed by Simón Brand, Paraíso Producciones, 2008.

Pardo, María Fabiola. "La inmigración y el devenir de las sociedades multiculturales: Perspectivas políticas y teóricas." *Las migraciones en América Latina: Políticas, culturas y estrategias,* edited by Susana Novick, Catálogos, 2008, pp. 153–71.

Personal Belongings. Directed by Alejandro Brugués, Producciones de la 5ta Avenida, 2006.

Rosenfeld, Val, and Flor Fortunati, editors. *Voices of the Undocumented.* First Edition Design Publishing, 2015.

Les sauteurs. Directed by Moritz Siebert and Estephan Wagner, Final Cut for Real, 2016.

Shúa, Ana María. *El libro de los recuerdos.* Editorial Sudamericana, 1994.

Sin nombre. Directed by Cary Joji Fukunaga, Canana Films, 2009.

Sueños ilegales: Las estrellas no conocen fronteras. Directed by Fernando Lemus and Ángel Camilo, Latino Media / Ícono Producciones, 2022.

Urzaiz, Constantino. *Sueños ilegales: Imigracion ilegal.* 2013.

Vásquez, Juan Gabriel. *Los informantes.* Alfaguara, 2004.

Vega-Durán, Raquel. *Emigrant Dreams, Immigrant Borders: Migrants, Transnational Encounters, and Identity in Spain.* Bucknell UP, 2016.

El viaje de Saïd. Directed by Coke Riobóo, Jazzy Producciones, 2007.

Ya no estoy aquí. Directed by Fernando Frías de la Parra, Panorama Global / PPW Films, 2019.

Megan Thornton Velázquez

Learning through Service: Migration in the Spanish-Language Classroom

An understanding of migration is crucial for learners of Spanish because of an ever-growing and diverse Latinx (im)migrant community in the United States as well as a divisive political climate that negatively portrays this community. Representations of (im)migrant stories in literature and film offer a unique opportunity to analyze personal experiences, physical borders, and identity politics. Furthermore, combining the classroom experience with a required service learning activity that engages the Latinx (im)migrant community allows students to connect on a more personal level with the subject matter. This essay, therefore, discusses my pedagogical approach to teaching a course titled Migrant Voices at John Carroll University that requires students to engage with authentic cultural materials in Spanish, primarily short stories, movies, and documentaries, while teaching ESL to Latinx (im)migrants in the Cleveland area through a non-profit organization called Esperanza. I offer suggestions for relevant texts in Spanish and also review student reflections and assessment results to highlight the value of experiential learning.

Service learning, a form of experiential learning, has sparked much scholarly interest in higher education. Robert Bringle and Julie Hatcher provide a detailed definition of this type of learning as "a credit-bearing educational experience in which students participate in an organized service activity that meets identified community needs and reflect on the service activity in such a way as to gain further understanding of the course content, a broader appreciation of the discipline, and an enhanced sense of civic responsibility" (222). With specific respect to the study of non-English languages, community-based service learning projects address the goals established by ACTFL in the *World-Readiness Standards for Learning Languages* by moving the educational experience beyond the classroom and by creating globally competent citizens (National Standards Collaborative Board). Furthermore, a service learning pedagogy answers the call to reimagine the humanities and to bridge the so-called town-and-gown divide, providing students with real-world experiences and instilling in them a sense of social responsibility (Carney; Barreneche; Larson).

Providing a connection between the classroom and the community with a focus on cultural competence and civic engagement, particularly as it pertains to social justice, are essential components of my service learning course Migrant Voices. This is an advanced course taught in Spanish designed for students at an intermediate-high or advanced-low proficiency level who are majoring or minoring in Spanish. Part of the university's core curriculum, Migrant Voices is also designated as a course that explores issues related to social justice. As a Jesuit institution, advocating for social justice through service is one of John Carroll's overarching learning goals, and the Center for Service and Social Action provides instructors with a framework for incorporating service learning into the classroom experience. I am indebted to the center for establishing a connection with our community partner Esperanza and for handling the logistics of the service experience. With the support of the center, my course thus integrates students' experiential learning with improving their Spanish skills and raising their awareness about (im)migration.

According to the Pew Research Center, the origins of the US immigrant population have shifted dramatically since the passage of the 1965 Immigration and Nationality Act, which ended a quota system based on national origins in exchange for privileging certain occupational skills, those with relatives in the United States, and political refugees (Kohut). It essentially opened the door for immigrants from Latin America and Asia. In 1960, for example, the majority of immigrants (84%) were from Europe, Canada, or other North American countries, while only 6% were from Mexico, 4% from Asia, 3% from the rest of Latin America, and 3% from other areas ("Facts"). In 2018, however, Asians (28%), Mexicans (25%), and other Latin American nationalities (25%) accounted for more than three-fourths of the nation's immigrant population ("Facts"). This dramatic shift has contributed to the growing Latinx community in the United States, whose population totaled approximately 62.5 million (foreign- and US-born) in 2021, up from nearly 15 million in 1980 (Moslimani and Noe-Bustamante). Furthermore, this growth can be seen in all parts of the United States, and the Cleveland metropolitan area is no different. Our community partner Esperanza is a nonprofit organization that has served this growing population in northeastern Ohio since the early 1980s, with the primary goal of promoting educational achievement. The center's ESL classes depend entirely on volunteers, thereby providing my students with the perfect service learning opportunity.

During the fall 2019 semester, nine students enrolled in my Migrant Voices class logged a combined total of 218 hours of service at Esperanza.[1] They taught beginning ESL to a mix of students, both young and old as well as new arrivals and longtime residents of the United States. The ESL students were from a variety of places: Mexico, Puerto Rico, Ecuador, the Dominican Republic, Honduras, Peru, Cuba, Guatemala, and El Salvador. This rich diversity provided my students with the opportunity to negotiate the cultural and linguistic differences between Latin American countries and among members of the US Latinx community. To reflect this diversity, the course materials also represented a variety of (im)migrant experiences. Topics included the experiences of documented and undocumented (im)migrants, border crossings, family fragmentations, linguistic and cultural assimilations, identity politics, and the illusive American dream. Texts were presented contextually within their historical and cultural milieus and provided an overview of US immigration policy and important vocabulary in Spanish (for a list of texts, see Thornton Velázquez). Classroom conversations were also guided by discussion questions that students prepared before coming to class. Students took a midterm and a final exam to assess their overall comprehension of the course material and also wrote two papers in which they analyzed the text of their choice. The papers were graded with a rubric that considered the quality of the analysis as well as the use of grammar and vocabulary in Spanish. The final assignment was a reflection piece, with both an oral and a written component, that allowed students to integrate the classroom experience with their service learning experience.

A variety of themes emerged from the reflections, such as thoughts about (im)migration, social justice, personal growth, and future plans.

Several students emphasized how the weekly service activities helped bring the classroom discussions to life because the stories and statistics were personalized by people at Esperanza. Discussing and trying different foods was one cultural exchange that students cherished, and it reminded them of the cultural representations of food, family, and cooking in texts like Francisco Jiménez's *Cajas de cartón* (*The Circuit*) and Esmeralda Santiago's *Cuando era puertorriqueña* (*When I Was Puerto Rican*). In addition, students reflected on their personal growth, often noting that they were pushed beyond their comfort zones. Both my students and the ESL students could share in the frustrations and joys of learning a second language, which provided a unique opportunity to bridge cultural gaps, overcome language barriers, and build community. Furthermore, the overall positive experience of teaching ESL at Esperanza motivated students to learn more about (im)migration issues and Latin America in general. Two students, for example, decided to participate in immersion trips organized by the university, one to El Salvador and the other to the US-Mexico border, and several students continued to volunteer at Esperanza after the class had ended.

The course evaluations completed by students at the end of the semester offer an indirect assessment of the benefits of including a service learning component in the course. Written comments were positive, with one student writing that Migrant Voices was one of her favorite classes at John Carroll. Nine out of eleven students completed the evaluation, and of those students who completed the evaluation, all reported either meeting or exceeding the course goals. The results were as follows:

"I can read and analyze cultural texts in Spanish": 78% exceeded; 22% met.

"I can write essays in Spanish using connected sentences and appropriate vocabulary pertaining to (im)migration": 78% exceeded; 22% met.

"I can demonstrate knowledge of the historical, political, and socioeconomic conditions related to Latin American (im)migrations that have given rise to injustices and discrimination": 67% exceeded; 33% met.

"I can understand cultural differences between and among Latinx (im)migrant communities": 67% exceeded; 33% met.

"The course stimulated my interest in learning more about the subject": 89% strongly agreed; 11% somewhat agreed.

By helping students meet the course goals, service learning aligns with ACTFL's proficiency guidelines and *World-Readiness Standards for Learning Languages*. For my students, working with ESL students at Esperanza translated into a deeper understanding of Latin America and the US Latinx (im)migrant community while also helping improve their Spanish skills. It allowed them to make connections with people who had lived the very experiences they were reading about in texts and watching on screens, and I would argue, it is the personal connections that will continue to inform their lives and shape their civic engagement.

I would encourage those considering a service learning component as part of a Spanish-language course on migration to engage in the process of identifying a community partner that would enrich the course material. Instructor flexibility and student adaptability are key, and building time into the course for reflection and preparation are essential. Reflection allows students to process their experiences, and preparation gives them the tools to meet the challenges of service learning. The main request I had from my students was more time to do lesson planning because they felt unprepared to teach ESL, so the next time I offer the course I plan to invite a guest lecturer from the Department of Education to give my students more teaching tools. Overall, service learning requires an extra time commitment from instructors and students, but promoting the experiential benefits and resume-building opportunities encourages students facing a tough job market to enroll in the course. Furthermore, community partnership and student engagement are important steps toward bridging cultural gaps in today's polarized society.

Note

1. There were eleven students enrolled in the course. Two students were unable to commit to the Esperanza schedule because of work and conflicts with other classes. Consequently, they translated sponsorship letters from Spanish to English for COAR Peace Mission, a Cleveland nonprofit organization that has supported a children's village—a school and orphanage—in Zaragoza, El Salvador, since 1980. Because the time commitment was considerably less and the work was completed virtually, their experiences are not analyzed here.

Works Cited

Barreneche, Gabriel Ignacio. "Language Learners as Teachers: Integrating Service-Learning and the Advanced Language Course." *Hispania*, vol. 94, no. 1, 2011, pp. 103–20.

Bringle, Robert G., and Julie A. Hatcher. "Implementing Service Learning in Higher Education." *Journal of Higher Education*, vol. 67, no. 2, 1996, pp. 221–39.

Carney, Terri M. "How Service-Learning in Spanish Speaks to the Crisis in the Humanities." *Hispania*, vol. 96, no. 2, 2013, pp. 229–37.

"Facts on U.S. Immigrants, 2018." *Pew Research Center*, 20 Aug. 2020, www .pewresearch.org/race-and-ethnicity/2020/08/20/facts-on-u-s-immigrants.

Jiménez, Francisco. *Cajas de cartón: Relatos de la vida peregrina de un niño campesino.* Houghton Mifflin, 2000.

Kohut, Andrew. "From the Archives: In '60s, Americans Gave Thumbs-Up to Immigration Law That Changed the Nation." *Pew Research Center*, 20 Sept. 2019, www.pewresearch.org/short-reads/2019/09/20/in-1965-majority-of -americans-favored-immigration-and-nationality-act-2/.

Larson, Kajsa C. "Uniting Hispanic Film Studies with Civic Engagement: A Chance for Personal Transformation." *Hispania*, vol. 98, no. 3, 2015, pp. 533–48.

Moslimani, Mohamad, and Luis Noe-Bustamante. "Facts on Latinos in the U.S." *Pew Research Center*, 16 Aug. 2023, www.pewresearch.org/race-and -ethnicity/fact-sheet/latinos-in-the-us-fact-sheet.

The National Standards Collaborative Board. *World-Readiness Standards for Learning Languages.* 4th ed., ACTFL, 2015.

Santiago, Esmeralda. *Cuando era puertorriqueña.* Reprint ed., Vintage Español, 1994.

Thornton Velázquez, Megan. Syllabus for Migrant Voices. *Teaching Migration in Literature, Film, and Media*, 17 July 2024, https://doi.org/10.17613/ 5vne-w961.

Emily S. Davis and Délice I. Williams

We Need More Stories:
Disrupting Dominant Narratives of
Migration through Digital Collaboration

The advent of humanitarian crises in Syria, North Africa, and Central America in recent years has brought new moral and political urgency to the many questions that accompany the figure of the migrant: Who is the migrant? What claims do they have on a receiving country? To what extent do they require policing and surveillance? What, if anything, do we owe them? Responses to these questions are not only matters of law, ethics, or policy but also matters of story. Put another way, our answers to these questions are closely tied to the stories we hear and tell about who migrants are and why they seek to move within and between countries.

Such stories circulate (and dominate) through headlines, sound bites, images, and official government statements. Importantly, many of these stories converge into disturbing narratives about migrants as potential threats: Syrian refugees are invading hordes seeking to replace native-born Europeans in a "Muslim invasion" comparable to that of the eighth century. Sub-Saharan Africans crossing the Strait of Gibraltar are carriers of infectious disease. Mexicans crossing the southern US border are rapists, gang members, and drug traffickers. Large "caravans" of Guatemalans, Salvadorans, and Hondurans are making their way up to the Rio Grande, using children as covers to allow them a free pass into the United

States. Those purporting to be refugees are in fact "economic migrants" who threaten labor markets or plan to exploit the generous social welfare systems of European democracies.

Even when these narratives do not depict migrants as threats and invaders, they often portray them as unwitting victims of coyotes, human traffickers, and shady lawyers who teach them the key words to request asylum. In these kinds of narratives, none of these people are who they say they are. They are bad people. They should be denied legal entry and met with armed sea patrols, visa denials, barbed wire fences, and walls.

These dangerous and increasingly prevalent narratives continue to inform ethical, legal, and economic responses to migrants in various categories. Agreements such as the Dublin Regulation mean that there are fewer legal routes to asylum or refugee status. According to the American Immigration Council, spending on border security and immigration enforcement in the United States alone increased by eight billion dollars between 2015 and 2021 ("Cost"). And recent reports have shown that "[i]n the same period as it spent €2bn euros on border security, the EU spent only an estimated €700m on reception conditions for refugees" (Trilling). As Claudia Tazreiter explains, in "the contemporary manifestations of new bordering regimes . . . value is attached to persons in ways that manifest in state practices of exclusion and social distancing, as well as in the technologies of the border" (193).

While decisions about law and resource allocation clearly involve a number of complex considerations, we maintain that narratives about migrants form a crucial part of the matrix from which these decisions emerge. Thus, we contend that it is more urgent than ever that we work to circulate narratives about who the migrant is and why they are in one place and not in another, narratives that work against the racialized process of devaluing that Tazreiter describes. We believe imaginative literature and literary nonfiction have an important role to play in that circulation.

Historically, and especially in the United States, narratives of migration have trafficked in relatively benign clichés about plucky dreamers moving northward or westward in search of opportunity that is scarce or unavailable in their home countries. As noted, however, that romantic image of the migrant has lost much of its appeal in countries in the Global North. Today the migrant is more threat than dreamer. Indeed, in the US context, the Dreamer is often labeled as a threat to law and order.

The web project we describe here, *Moving Fictions: Exploring Migration in Modern Literature* (sites.udel.edu/movingfictions), aims to provide a resource for students and scholars to discover and engage with other narratives of migration. We offer it as an example of a multimodal intervention into public storytelling about this topic. The site was developed by a world literature course in fall 2018 with the goal of providing a public humanities resource for schools and other groups reading fiction about migration. For the last several semesters, different undergraduate English classes have helped select texts and develop content about literature depicting the experiences of migrants. The site includes a variety of subpages for each text, including "Reception," "Discussion Questions," "Historical Relevance," "Teaching Materials," and "Scholarly Research," though students have at times developed additional pages to contextualize unique features of a particular book. For example, the subpage detailing the historical relevance of Julissa Arce's memoir *Someone Like Me* offers information about the Texas Dream Act, and clicking on the link for research leads to an annotated bibliographic entry for Marta Caminero-Santangelo's review of the edited collection *Documenting the Undocumented: Life Narratives of Unauthorized Immigrants*.

Rather than attempt to provide a single story of migration, the site presents an assortment of different literary modes, reasons for migration, and personal experiences through a wide array of texts. Collectively, the works featured here defy both the romanticized vision and the more destructive conceptions of the migrant as cultural, economic, and physical threat. As Chinua Achebe once argued, and as Chimamanda Adichie famously echoed, the best way to address the limitations of a single story is a proliferation of stories. For Achebe, such proliferation constitutes part of the unfinished and ongoing work of the twenty-first century (79). We believe that opening up pathways for new migration stories can invite inquiry, catalyze curiosity, and lay the groundwork for more complex discussions, not only about those who inhabit the position of the migrant but also about the dynamic and increasingly powerful forces, such as US imperialism, economic globalization, and climate crisis, that drive migration in the twenty-first century. We also believe that providing more opportunities to know and imagine migrant experiences is a crucial part of creating conditions for more ethical responses to those who have chosen or been forced to become migrants themselves.

Part of what we model here is also the potential of this kind of project for public engagement, which we describe in more detail below. As the project continues, we aim to play a meaningful role in discussions of migration in the local community as well as in the wider digital networks a website allows. At all levels, this project invites collaborations that involve larger migrant communities in the production of knowledge about migration rather than define them simply as objects of discussion in and outside the classroom. Ultimately, we hope that our account of this project and its evolution will inspire other forms of digital scholarship and community collaboration to allow more migrant stories to emerge, circulate, and challenge dominant narratives.

Course Structure and Scaffolding

To date, five different undergraduate English classes have played a role in developing the structure and content of *Moving Fictions*. Our website is a *WordPress* site hosted by our institution, which means that we do not have to pay for the site and that we have access to some in-house tech support. Since the technical elements might vary widely depending on the platform or scale of faculty projects, we focus on larger questions of structure and ethos here.

For upper-level English classes we have found that it is most effective to have all students participate in reading and discussing each of the texts but to then designate smaller working groups to develop the web content for a text at the end of the semester. For example, one group (often the English education majors in the class, who are most familiar with the format and standards of lesson planning) will develop the "Teaching Materials" page, another will dive into the secondary research and pick three or four appropriate sources for the "Scholarly Research" page, and so on. All the content for each book is written by undergraduates, who also then work with supervision to get that material uploaded onto the *WordPress* site.

We have experimented with organizing the workload in different ways. One approach is to designate working groups to develop content for a book immediately after each book and before moving on to the next. This approach has the benefit of getting students started developing content and gaining familiarity with *WordPress* early in the semester. However, we have ultimately found that it benefited all the groups to participate in larger discussions about a text and to write about it individually before breaking into working groups for each course text as a final project.

There are a few important reasons we have settled on this approach. For one thing, there is an ethical dimension to using student labor for a public humanities project. Students understandably respond badly to the idea that they are simply drones producing content for something that is not theirs, even if they are enthusiastic about the website itself. Students feel more empowered with the material if they have been allowed to write about it individually first and their grade is not completely determined by their work on the website. When it comes time for students to contribute to the site, we refer to "A Student Collaborators' Bill of Rights," developed by the University of California, Los Angeles, as a touchstone (Di Pressi et al.), aiming to provide students with as much editorial control as possible over their content while minimizing the amount of technical knowledge required for them to do their work. Student collaborators are named on every page they develop, and those who have completed more advanced editorial or design work on the site are credited on the "About Us" page. Group work is also difficult to structure and assess effectively, and we have learned through trial and (significant) error to provide two forms of evaluation at the end of the process: an individual self-assessment and an assessment of other group members. On different occasions, we have used a hard-copy document and a Qualtrics survey for this purpose, and both work well.

In many ways the ideal course for this is a senior capstone, which Emily has taught twice on the topic of migration literature. Since our capstone is designed for students to produce significant research projects, we structure this course so that students work in groups on two books earlier in the semester to get used to the site and the types of content included on it. They then select their own book for their final project and produce all the content for that book individually. This gives students a real investment in their content, and they are able to share their work with the university community at the public symposium that concludes every capstone in English. The seniors in these capstone courses have been overwhelmingly enthusiastic about how developing an assortment of web-based resources on the same text makes them better writers by requiring them to translate their ideas about migration and literature for a general audience. While the senior capstone students develop the most advanced *WordPress* skills, students in all versions of this class leave knowing that both the content they produce and their web development skills can go on their résumés and are immediately applicable to jobs in nonprofits and community advocacy.

Scale, Growth, and Sustainability

As we describe above, different versions of the *Moving Fictions* courses have operated at different scales. In upper-division courses, we typically develop material for five new books during a semester, while in a capstone of eighteen students we add material for approximately twenty texts. As an instructor it becomes overwhelming to teach entirely new books every semester, so we have experimented with having groups return to a text already on the site in order to revise and expand existing material. As the project continues, we expect to scale back the amount of work devoted to new texts and focus instead on other elements we would like to develop for the site. In this section we briefly describe some of those plans.

The original intent of the website was not to keep adding more and more texts, of course, but to provide a dynamic, public-facing resource to facilitate conversations about migration and literature. Now that there is a substantial body of work on the site, we have begun to shift our focus to laying the groundwork for such conversations at the local, national, and international levels. For our particular project, the most logical immediate avenue for public engagement is to collaborate with our local public school system. Thus far that has entailed leading a seminar for teachers through our state-based affiliate of the Yale Teacher's Institute and beginning the process of establishing partnerships with high school teachers that might allow high school and college students to work together to develop content for the site. This move is important to us because it would help strengthen pipelines between local high schools and the flagship state university where we teach. At the same time, Ainehi Edoro's site *Brittle Paper* (brittlepaper.com) has inspired us to think about the potential for showcasing writers by having students conduct interviews with writers about how and why they write about migration. We have worked directly with one author so far, the Ivorian short story writer and activist Edwige-Renée Dro. Students read two of her short stories and developed interview questions, which they then posed to her during a virtual class visit. That interview will be housed on the site and will eventually be joined by others. In addition, we have begun to develop a social media plan to inform the public of resources already on the site and to connect with (and amplify) similar projects.

We would also like the website to include a resources page that directs readers to other relevant projects, such as the *Undocumented Migration Project* (undocumentedmigrationproject.org), *Words without Borders* (words withoutborders.org), and *Re-imagining Migration* (reimaginingmigration .org). As we continue to apply for funding, we also hope to bring speakers to campus for events that will be captured on the website for the general public. This vision may be specific to our particular project, but the general idea of involving students in public-facing digital work on migration could take a variety of forms, from individual assignments within particular classes to storytelling advocacy projects with local immigrant communities to research-based writing about detention and asylum practices in a specific area local to a particular institution. Our goal in this essay is to offer an example of a methodology and ethical framework rather than a prescriptive sense of what other instructors should do in their own classes.

In designing our own project, our goal was for the website to function as a virtual gathering space that would inspire a range of conversations and events that could then be digitally preserved. The site might be a potential repository for local community storytelling projects about migration that emerge from workshops involving both students and community members. As our state's writer's project, which has been dormant for several years, gets back off the ground, we aim to collaborate on writing initiatives specifically about migration storytelling. There are already existing initiatives around human rights storytelling and migration at our institution with which we can imagine productive collaborations. The environmental humanities research cluster at our university is rapidly expanding, and we have begun to build a cluster of texts that consider climate migration as a specific focus for interdisciplinary research and teaching. Moreover, our site at present does not consider visual storytelling such as feature and documentary film, murals, and photography. We have considered how developing a new section of the site (perhaps titled "Moving Pictures") might open up a different set of conversations that engages with fields such as media studies, art history, and art conservation. While the scale of such a project can become overwhelming without an engaged editorial team and long-term planning, it also provides a much-needed flexible space to teach, research, discuss, and, most importantly, imagine the value of storytelling about migration beyond the narrow confines of academic disciplines. Our ultimate hope is that these collaborations could lead to the establishment of a center at our institution that could bring together students, faculty members, and community members around this shared set of interests and commitments.

Works Cited

Achebe, Chinua. "Today, the Balance of Stories." *Home and Exile*, by Achebe, Oxford UP, 2000, pp. 69–100.
Adichie, Chimamanda Ngozi. "The Danger of a Single Story." *TED*, July 2009, www.ted.com/talks/chimamanda_ngozi_adichie_the_danger_of_a_single_story.

"The Cost of Immigration Enforcement and Border Security." *American Immigration Council*, 14 Aug. 2024, www.americanimmigrationcouncil.org/research/the-cost-of-immigration-enforcement-and-border-security.

Di Pressi, Haley, et al. "A Student Collaborators' Bill of Rights." *UCLA Humanities Technology*, 8 June 2015, humtech.ucla.edu/news/a-student-collaborators-bill-of-rights.

Tazreiter, Claudia. "The Emotional Confluence of Borders, Refugees and Visual Culture: The Case of Behrouz Boochani, Held in Australia's Offshore Detention Regime." *Critical Criminology*, vol. 28, 2020, pp. 193–207.

Trilling, Daniel. "Five Myths about the Refugee Crisis." *The Guardian*, 5 July 2018, www.theguardian.com/news/2018/jun/05/five-myths-about-the-refugee-crisis.

Juan Llamas-Rodriguez

The Migrant Reality Treatment

The Migrant Reality Treatment, the in-class assignment described in this essay, asks students to role-play as producers pitching a new media production centered on migrants. Through an applied real-world scenario, students have to contend with the aspects that I argue are indispensable to understanding media about migration: the formal conventions, sociohistorical contexts, genre and format conventions, and institutional politics that establish what counts as realistic representations of migrants.

The in-class assignment is the culminating activity for Encounters, a section of my undergraduate global media seminar. This section concerns the uses of media around the world to stage encounters between people from different backgrounds, across different settings, or with contrasting points of view. I taught some version of this assignment in various iterations of the course between 2019 and 2022. Throughout these iterations, I have refined the assignment prompt and scaffolding so that the assignment led to more interesting proposals. Some of the specific readings may change from year to year, but consistently this section of the course has the following structure:

Week 1

DAY 1: Leshu Torchin, "iWitnesses and CitizenTube: Focus on Darfur" (*Creating the Witness: Documenting Genocide on Film, Video, and the Internet*, U of Minnesota P, 2012, pp. 172–215); Angharad Valdivia, "Othering" (*Keywords for Media Studies*, edited by Laurie Ouellette and Jonathan Gray, New York UP, 2017, pp. 133–34)

DAY 2: Jeff Himpele, "Reality Affects: Cultural Strategies and the Televisual Public Sphere" (*Circuits of Culture: Media, Politics, and Indigenous Identity in the Andes*, U of Minnesota P, 2008, pp. 137–63); *Radio Ambulante*, "La Concursante," 16 May 2017 (podcast)

Week 2

DAY 1: Kaarina Nikunen, "Media, Passion, and Humanitarian Reality Television" (*European Journal of Cultural Studies*, vol. 19, no. 3, June 2016, pp. 489–504); *On the Media*, "Breaking News Consumer's Handbook: Migration Edition," parts 1 and 2, 29 July 2016 (podcasts)

DAY 2: Eszter Zimanyi and Emma Ben Ayoun, "On Bodily Absence in Humanitarian Multisensory VR" (*Intermediality: History and Theory of the Arts, Literature and Technologies*, no. 34, fall 2019, pp. 1–16)

Week 3

DAY 1: Matthew Kelly, "The Game of Politics: Examining the Role of Work, Play, and Subjectivity Formation in *Papers, Please*" (*Games and Culture*, vol. 13, no. 5, July 2018, pp. 459–78); *Papers, Please* (Lucas Pope, 2013)

DAY 2: The Migrant Reality Treatment in-class activity

The Migrant Reality Treatment borrows the structure of a traditional TV show treatment. In television production, a treatment presents the main ideas about a show before a script is written. Treatments must highlight the most important information about the series, including the title, episode format, story summary, and descriptions of its various narrative and production elements. As a writing format, treatments allow creatives to flesh out an idea in a systematic way, approaching the media production from a macro perspective before developing individual episodes or stories. The process also enables writers to summarize their creative goals in a pithy, compelling way to pitch to studio executives who might want to produce the series.

The format for the in-class assignment is a pared-down version of a more traditional treatment format. The prompt asks only for the title of the media production, examples of existing media that could serve as inspiration or reference points, a description of the target audience, an outline of the narrative or episode format, and a storyboard. The storyboard includes six frames where students can draw or describe sample scenes, the setting, or their intended production design (e.g., costumes, props, sets). Because we have read Torchin's work on "witnessing publics," I encourage students to address the description of their target audience in terms of publics instead of demographics, as would be common in a traditional industry pitch. That is, rather than describe a group of people based on identity (e.g., "women eighteen to thirty-four years old," "Latinos"), they must describe the intended audience as a public: for instance, "people who believe X," "people who care (or do not care about) about X issue," "people who want X to happen." Throughout the global media course, we critically analyze and break down essentialist representations of people based on national and other forms of identity. Although the assignment borrows the structure from a common industry practice, formulating an intended audience as a public is one way to push back on industry dynamics that see audiences as homogeneous, identity-based groups.

I set up the activity by assigning groups of four or five students. Each group receives a type of media genre (reality TV show, *YouTube* series, or a narrative-focused virtual reality experience) and a framework for how migrants should be depicted in their media production (as victims, villains, or ordinary people). These frames are borrowed from the helpful breakdown of media frames for migrants presented in the *On the Media* podcasts covered in previous weeks. Groups assigned the villain framework often tend to balk at the prompt, either noting their discontent while writing up the treatment or stating during their presentations that they do not personally agree with the ideas they propose. I have found that this reaction leads to productive insights when redirected toward a reflection on the politics of the media production process. For instance, students quickly realize that it is fairly easy to find examples of existing media that portray migrants as villains. Likewise, students who find examples of current media that purportedly portray migrants as ordinary people quickly recognize the villain-and-victim frame seeping into these representations. In the activity debriefing, we build on the ideas from the *On the Media* podcasts to explore how realistic narrative media often include multiple, contradictory ideologies.

For a class of twenty-five to thirty students, this activity takes up an entire class session (seventy-five minutes in my case). For six groups of four to five students each, groups have twenty-five to thirty minutes to work on the treatment and five minutes each to present a two-minute pitch and answer questions or receive feedback. Finally, fifteen minutes are devoted to general class discussion.

The Encounters section of the course features a number of examples that could be considered humanitarian-themed media. In its original version, the prompt for the assignment also asked students to describe the intended social effects of their media production, as humanitarian media tends to do. It is implied in the assignment prompt that the media production they come up with should be entertaining in some capacity since students are pitching to producers in order to get a green light on the project. The question about the production's humanitarian dimension was originally intended to ask students to make explicit the politics in any representation of migrants. However, I soon found that this question ended up reproducing one aspect that continues to plague students' interrogations of mediated depictions of migrants: the recourse to empathy as a solution to social problems. Students would often default to attempting to elicit empathy for the migrants depicted in their media production, regardless of whether their assigned frame was migrants as victims or migrants as ordinary people. For instance, one proposal was a virtual reality game that would take players through a regular day in the life of an immigrant; another was a human-interest documentary series that interviewed migrants with the stated goal of showing that they are just like everyone else. In these first iterations of the assignment, the ideology of empathy loomed large in students' proposals, often overshadowing more critical engagement with the other ideas raised in the course.

My initial attempt to address this was to add course materials that specifically broke down the ideology of empathy. In the past, I tried using excerpts from Paul Bloom's *Against Empathy* (19–60) and Olivia Banner's chapter "Against the Empathy Hypothesis" (*Communicative Biocapitalism* 125–50), but a more recent publication could be Lisa Nakamura's "Feeling Good about Feeling Bad: Virtuous Virtual Reality and the Automation of Racial Empathy," which specifically targets the promise of empathy in virtual reality. Whether through psychological studies or textual analysis, these authors all demonstrate how empathy hinders critical reflection on structural inequalities by centering the individual user's experience in the here and now. To evoke empathy in a reader or viewer, creators adapt stories to the emotional expectations of their audience, twisting or altogether erasing the messy nuances of their subject. In migration media, appeals to empathy almost always end up framing migrants as victims in order to make us feel good about ourselves for momentarily feeling bad about the plight of those less privileged. Empathy projects, especially those marketed with new media technologies, implicitly concede that our caring about a social issue depends on whether we appreciate the immersive, interactive experience teaching us about such an issue. In short, aiming for empathy is a problem because empathy will always privilege the empathizer's feelings at the expense of the real lives of those empathized with.

There was some improvement in students' critical reflection on the limits of empathy after tackling the issue head-on. A notable student submission was titled *The Empathy Meter*, a virtual reality reskinning[1] of the video game *Papers, Please* where players would take on the role of port-of-entry agents and would be evaluated based on their ability to keep their "empathy meter" down when interacting with migrants. Although students at first did not pitch it as such, through the general class discussion we were able to think about how this reskinned game could offer a structural critique not only of the empathy ideology but also of the institutions that regulate migration. By making explicit the regulatory function of bureaucratic management with a literal empathy meter, this example commented on the ways that state institutions themselves shape how subjects interact despite individual intentions.

In subsequent iterations of the assignment, I concluded that asking students to speculate on the social impact of their media production and develop the treatment in such a short period of time limited both their creative thinking and the subsequent critical conversation. As a result, I refocused the activity on the production aspects, limiting the audience component to identifying interested publics. Again, despite borrowing an industry framework, this new focus allowed us to push back on the idea that producers are the ultimate arbiters of the intentions and meanings of a media text. The examples of proposals that came out of later iterations evidenced much more nuance in the stated goals of the media productions. At the same time, the ensuing class discussion allowed us to explore myriad ways in which each of the productions, despite their intended frame for representing migrants, could function as critiques of mainstream portrayals of migration.

One of the most successful examples from these later iterations was *American Foods*, a *YouTube* series in the style of food-testing videos where the host tries new, often unusual, dishes every episode and records their reaction to eating them. In the students' version, the hosts would be a group of migrants who had recently arrived to the United States from different parts of the world. Each episode would feature these migrants trying a dish purportedly typical of the United States (e.g., apple pie, biscuits and gravy, turkey stuffing). The rather simple format of the series and its episodic nature made it a successful pitch that many could see being produced. In terms of the goals of the activity within the Encounters section of the course, this series achieved two main goals. First, it successfully made use of the format requirements of the *YouTube* series to introduce migrants as ordinary people. By making the migrants the hosts, the series would allow them to interact with one another and introduce aspects of their experiences as well as their commonalities and differences while keeping every episode's focus squarely on the dish being sampled. Second, by presenting "US-style" dishes in a format known for exoticizing local cuisines, the series would defamiliarize foods well-known to US audiences and expose the Orientalist underpinnings of this type of programming. In some ways, the series gestures toward the idea that immigrants are just like everyone else, but it did not have to articulate that idea explicitly. By not being forced to acknowledge this gesture, the series could lead to more interesting depictions and critique: defamiliarizing the implied US experience while also allowing for the participants' lives to come through.

The Migrant Reality Treatment illustrates three aspects that are central to the teaching of migration media. The first aspect is understanding realism as dependent on a set of formal conventions and on sociohistorical contexts. At the beginning of the Encounters section, I do a brief lecture on realism in cinema and ask students to identify the formal elements that they associate with realistic representations (e.g., shaky camera, invisible editing) across the media they regularly watch. Establishing the constructedness of realism at the outset is important because all the examples in the section are of the reality variety: reality television, realistic virtual reality, and *YouTube* documentary videos. Focusing on this commonality provides a through line even as we move across media formats throughout the weeks. The second aspect is thus learning to parse out the expectations set up by medium, genre, and format. Students are usually familiar with reality television, virtual reality experiences, and *YouTube* series, so as we work through the examples in weeks 1 and 2, I make sure to ask them to list out the genre expectations in each of the case studies. The third aspect central to teaching migrant media is dissecting the dominant representational frames of migrants and considering how these serve specific political projects. While the *On the Media* podcasts tackle the biases of news reports and official government statements, the narrative media examples addressed in our scholarly readings—*CitizenTube* (*YouTube* series), *Go Back to Where You Came From* (reality television), *Carne y arena* (*Flesh and Sand*; virtual reality)—all make their political intentions explicit. As we discuss these examples in class, we tie their formal decisions to specific ideological frameworks.

The more successful student pitches reflect a careful understanding of these three aspects and their practical applications. For example, groups can often ably dissect the key narrative and formal elements in existing shows like *Live PD* and *Border Wars* that naturalize their depictions of migrants, or people of color generally, as villains. The assignment thus reveals the value of media studies approaches to teaching migration. The insights of media studies into the genre-specific nature of realism offer a critical reappraisal of the construction of popular images about migrants. Students are able to break down and explain the specific formal and narrative elements that lead to what is often reductively described as "accurate" or "inaccurate," "positive" or "negative" representations of migrants. The narrative need for dramatic tension, the differing time constraints inherent in television or web video programming, the limited scenarios imposed by an adherence to realism—understanding how these aspects interact better equips us to evaluate how mainstream discussions about migrants emerge from traditional expectations. In the best-case scenario, students may even come up with creative alternatives to these mainstream forms of representation.

Note

1. Here I refer to what Mary Flanagan calls "reskinning," the practice of taking the same mechanics of a game but changing its "skin" (i.e., the aesthetics and symbols) to convey a critical message (60).

Works Cited

Banner, Olivia. *Communicative Biocapitalism: The Voice of the Patient in Digital Health and the Health Humanities.* U of Michigan P, 2017.

Bloom, Paul. *Against Empathy: The Case for Rational Compassion.* HarperCollins Publishers, 2016.

Flanagan, Mary. *Critical Play: Radical Game Design.* MIT Press, 2009.

Nakamura, Lisa. "Feeling Good about Feeling Bad: Virtuous Virtual Reality and the Automation of Racial Empathy." *Journal of Visual Culture*, vol. 19, no. 1, Apr. 2020, pp. 47–64.

Torchin, Leshu. *Creating the Witness: Documenting Genocide on Film, Video, and the Internet.* U of Minnesota P, 2012.

Karen Little

A Macro-Micro Approach to Migration through Digital Exploration

A framework that I emphasize with undergraduates when teaching texts representing mass cultural movements—migrations, artistic movements, schools of thought—is what I refer to as the macro-micro approach, a means of shifting focus from generalizations and broad trends of cultural experience in a particular context (i.e., the macro) to the particular (i.e., micro) experience of individuals who cannot in their singularity exhibit all the features or the gestalt of the macro. One classic example is the retrospective nomenclature and literary periodization of the "Harlem Renaissance," which sounds much more cohesive and formal, more intentionally collective and grandiose, than would have been accurate to any single Black American author's experience of producing literature. While terminology like the "Harlem Renaissance" or the "Great Migration" makes swaths of history digestible, it obscures the fact that people do not think of themselves as single data points in a mighty stream with a teleology and an expiration date when movement ceases. This is an argument for the value of literature (fiction, biography, autobiography, poetry, drama) as the representation of what loses focus when we talk generally about a phenomenon like migration, even a specific snapshot of migration at one moment in time and in one location or node.

266

Theories rooted in the macro representation of migration—say, Thomas Nail's classifications of movement in *The Figure of the Migrant* or Jason De León's geographic analysis of necropolitics in US border policy in *The Land of Open Graves*—depend on the micro to humanize what appear theoretically in their work as flows of circulating bodies or unidentifiable corpses in the desert.[1] Dominika Baran and colleagues refer to this macro-micro relationship as "the grammars linking the one and the many . . . the dynamic between the statistics of mass migration and the individual story that might compel identification." These grammars undergird the ethical appeal of representing migration in literature and of teaching those representations in the humanities classroom to undergraduates who may primarily encounter migrants as statistics or patterns in less humanistic disciplines as well as in mass media. At the same time, data points—even in the form of homogenizing statistics—can be used intentionally to guide the humanistic reflection of zeroing in on the micro.

A migration studies research collective I joined at Duke University offers a case study in how a methodology that pairs digital humanities tools with archival material (and other primary texts) in an environment of open-ended exploration can illuminate for students the macro-micro grammar of migration, the interplay between data and individual narratives.[2] The research style undertaken by the collective, what is trendily referred to as a sandbox-style project, centered experimentation and inquiry rather than products or publications.[3] One research subgroup, Black Mobilities and the Archive, explored the Blunt Family Papers.[4] This small archive, housed in the David M. Rubenstein Rare Book and Manuscript Library at Duke University, consists of personal correspondence, photographs, and mementos belonging to members of a Black American family and primarily spans the 1940s through the 1960s, overlapping with the period of US history known as the Second Great Migration. We avoided, however, trying to extract proof that the Blunt family in some way exemplified this broad trend of movement northward and into urban areas, from the agricultural landscape to the industrial; this agenda would have made it difficult to uncover the micro level of the family's experience. Instead, we began by sifting through letters and learning the writers' personalities and their accounts of movement. While many members of the Blunt family moved from rural Virginia to Norfolk and then to Philadelphia, consistent with the trend of the Great Migration periods, one woman moved on from Philadelphia to Indianapolis and back, and a segment of the family moved permanently to Florida.

In reaction to the complexity of the narrative emerging from the archival letters, the many different trajectories of migration within the Blunt family, we developed a spreadsheet documenting as thoroughly as possible the dates, addresses, and names recorded on the family's correspondence. Putting the letters in order chronologically with geographic details was necessary for reading their content effectively, to begin seeing migrations and motivations unfold. We used *Palladio* software developed at Stanford University to map communication networks within the family across space and time, which gave us a snapshot of the whole family's whereabouts at the time of any dated letter.[5] Having a data-based visualization allowed us to generate more humanistic questions. Zooming in on Philadelphia in *Palladio* showed a burst of movement within the city over time, a series of intracity relocations, which seemed to complicate the Great Migration narrative. I returned to our data to produce a smaller, less sophisticated project using *Google My Maps* to locate the Philadelphia addresses and label them with known dates of residence for core family members. This exercise suggested narratives I had not previously considered. The family moved several times within a small neighborhood; one move was as short as a ten-minute walk. Visualizing the Blunt family's movement this way and being able to manipulate the maps fleshed out my speculative resources by providing context for certain archival items. For example, the archive included a furniture down-payment coupon at one of these addresses, which together with the insignificant change in location suggested a financial strain and a need, perhaps, to shop around for the best rental deal. When I used Street View to examine the locations as they are today, I found luxury condos and construction projects in lieu of modest apartment buildings, which speaks to gentrification and places the Blunt family in a longer narrative of housing development and migration in US cities. A simple mapping project contained rich possibilities for further research. Engagement at the granular level of one family's migration encourages students to consider, for example, what would persuade a family to relocate so often in such a small neighborhood, why a young woman would move cross-country despite her preference for the city she knew as home, or how the dearth of employment opportunities for young Black men determined where Black families took root, sometimes against the grain of the northward tide.

I describe this project in detail because it speaks to the generative possibilities for students that emerge from pairing data visualization with close reading techniques and from toggling between the individual narrative and the general context. Not only can this type of digital spatial analysis be used to model or launch a classroom research project, it can also model how career academics conceptualize and produce research. Paul Jaskot, an architectural historian, has done painstaking archival research with the Holocaust Geographies Collaborative, collecting data on the construction time line of buildings in the Auschwitz-Birkenau concentration camp. The data is extensive, covering roughly fourteen hundred buildings, and yet also granular within the geographic, temporal, and human scope of the Holocaust. One of Jaskot's collaborators, Chester Harvey, used Jaskot's data to produce an animated visualization, and Jaskot described how he was "shocked" to see "chaos" even though he had compiled the data himself, because the scale of the data made it impossible to digest. The animation generated a new research question for him, "Why is the built environment so chaotic?," which further led him to questions about "labor, about people in that space." The architecture in motion communicated a singular texture of life in the death camps and showed how inmates were "constructing this space and experiencing this process" (Jaskot). Viewing its "chaos" complicates the broader narrative of Auschwitz as an orderly cog in the Nazi machine of genocide. The digital model, instead of being the main product or capstone of the collaborative research, becomes an analytical tool for humanistic questions about the interplay between architecture and the Third Reich's genocidal project as it evolved.

Britt Rusert's "New World: The Impact of Digitization on the Study of Slavery" is an especially useful essay for introducing undergraduate students to the process of using digital tools to explore the relationship of the particular to the general. Rusert provides a concise, accessible history of archival research techniques and makes a provocative argument about the widely circulated data visualization "The Atlantic Slave Trade in Two Minutes" (Kahn and Bouie), which speedily represents the forced migration of African captives over centuries using dots to signify slave trade voyages. Rusert claims that "digital projects create particular imaginaries of slavery itself" and that "the representation of slave ships—as black dots—moving across the map without the colonial actors, sailors, buyers, traders, and other agents that made the trade happen on a day-to-day basis, presents an image of Africa that gives itself and its people freely to the world" (274, 276). She also describes how this visualization resonates with the imagery of the slave ship operating by invisible "magic" in Olaudah Equiano's autobiography (275). Presenting her work here as an "experiment in reading," Rusert models for students the questions that emerge from carefully and critically reading data (in this case processed by other researchers) and by asking what perspectives and particularities are lost when people and their life-shattering narratives are distilled into tiny parts of tiny dots (274). Framing her interpretation as an exercise invites potentially hesitant undergraduate readers to challenge her conclusions, to perform their own exercises, and to see the possibility of play in critical analysis. Rusert finds flaws in the data visualization, but she clearly communicates the value of its provocation for humanistic migration studies.

Having been introduced to the methodology of engaging in critical play with digital tools, of putting macro trends in conversation with the micro of individual experience, students can imagine their own analytical experiments with data visualizations or take part in class-wide exploratory projects. I especially like digital mapping projects for teaching migration topics in the undergraduate classroom because they are deceptively simple to produce and endlessly customizable. One example of a mapping project that I developed as part of the migration-focused research collective emerged from my engagement with the Robert A. Hill Collection, also part of the Rubenstein Rare Book and Manuscript Library, an archive of papers related to Hill's career-long study of the Jamaican-born political activist Marcus Garvey. Migration narratives loom large in this archive given Garvey's movements to and from the Caribbean as he immigrated to the United States and traveled to recruit members for his United Negro Improvement Association (UNIA); his members' own immigration stories; the concept of the Back-to-Africa movement; and the Black Star Line, Garvey's unsuccessful steamship corporation meant to enrich Black Americans. The archive includes a list that Hill generated of key public locations, Black businesses, and important UNIA members' homes in New York. Like the Blunt Family Papers spreadsheet, this list is opaque to anyone unacquainted with the geography of Harlem until plotted on a map. Once plotted, the proximity of many UNIA leaders' homes becomes clear. This activity locates the sprawling Garveyite movement while also hinting at how the UNIA members circulated within the city. Lists of Black-owned businesses provide a wealth of points to map and give a snapshot of Black commerce during the First Great Migration. Basic mapping exercises with these lists of data beget questions about the landscape of the migrant community in New York: Why did Black people live and open businesses where they did? Why were some types of businesses more likely to be Black-owned than others? These questions would then return students to archival sources like digitized Black newspapers, perhaps to advertisements of businesses they mapped to see how Black entrepreneurs represented their services and products as well as how they appealed to their diverse Black patrons— some migrants within the United States, some Caribbean migrants, some longtime residents. What begins as a very specific set of points on a map expands to a broader investigation of Black life in Harlem that far exceeds the topic of Garvey.

Although this sort of exercise would be worthwhile as a stand-alone project in a history course, activities like this add richness to literary courses by immersing students in the worlds of texts that are in unfamiliar terrain (often the case in migration narratives). The activity of mapping Garvey's New York described above would, for example, contextualize texts such as Chester Himes's 1965 detective novel *Cotton Comes to Harlem*, which begins with a parodic representation of a Back-to-Africa rally and portrays the Garveyite movement as an elaborate swindle. The significance of the detectives' movements through Harlem would come to life, and the centrality of Garveyism in Harlem's geography would be clearer. Digital mapping, too, gives students a record, even an archive, of their own movement through texts and accretion of spatial knowledge. Multiple texts that share a setting could even be layered into one map to generate questions about how different authors make use of the same spatial framework. The process of manipulating space on a digital map puts students in literal touch with the processes and effects of migrations that may seem abstract, general rather than particular, on the page.

If migration is an experience of orientation and disorientation, of encountering novel spaces in succession, of discovery, an experience of being one among many, a part of a pattern, and yet wholly individual, then mapping as a process can impart to students a taste of this indeterminate mood, a shift from bounded and finite literary texts to uncharted paths of inquiry.

Notes

1. See Little for more on the use of Nail's migration theory in the undergraduate classroom.

2. Duke University's English Department housed a three-year (2017–20) collective research program entitled Representing Migration Humanities Lab. More information about the lab's activities and participants can be found on its website (sites.duke.edu/representingmigration).

3. As Baran and colleagues attest, "[I]deas seeded in the [Representing Migration] lab are taking root and flourishing in each of our scholarly and pedagogical

practices. This intellectual growth was made possible, we think, because of the way the [research collective] allowed us the space to sit with different experiences of migration without the need for outcomes."

4. John Gartrell, director of the John Hope Franklin Research Center for African and African American History and Culture at Duke University, recommended the Blunt Family Papers for work on the Second Great Migration.

5. Brian Norberg, a digital humanities technology analyst at Trinity Technology Services, Duke University, was invaluable to this project; he taught the research team how to use *Palladio* and produced the location coordinates that *Palladio* required to map the letters.

Works Cited

Baran, Dominika, et al. "Keywords for Humanities Labs." 30 Sept. 2019. Unpublished article manuscript.

De León, Jason. *The Land of Open Graves: Living and Dying on the Migrant Trail.* U of California P, 2017.

Himes, Chester. *Cotton Comes to Harlem.* Vintage Books, 1988.

Jaskot, Paul B. "Forced Movement and Migration of Jews in/from Nazi Occupied Europe: Digital Approaches to the Holocaust." Digital Humanities Series: Digital Research in Progress. Representing Migration Humanities Lab, 19 Oct. 2018, Duke University, sites.duke.edu/representingmigration/pedagogy. Lecture.

Kahn, Andrew, and Jamelle Bouie. "The Atlantic Slave Trade in Two Minutes." *Slate*, 16 Sept. 2021, slate.com/news-and-politics/2021/09/atlantic-slave-trade-history-animated-interactive.html.

Little, Karen. "Mobilizing Home: Thomas Nail and the Literature Classroom." *Cultural Dynamics*, vol. 30, no. 3, 2018, pp. 219–24.

Nail, Thomas. *The Figure of the Migrant.* Stanford UP, 2015.

Rusert, Britt. "New World: The Impact of Digitization on the Study of Slavery." *American Literary History*, vol. 29, no. 2, summer 2017, pp. 267–86.

Notes on Contributors

Paige Andersson is senior assistant vice provost of experiential learning and outreach at Indiana University, Bloomington. Previously, she served as executive director for student success and as assistant director of the Global Gateway for Teachers program in Indiana University's School of Education. From 2019 to 2022, she was part of the faculty of Hispanic studies at DePauw University. Her research focuses on the colonial legacies of modern-day Mexico, Central American and Mexican migration, and the environmental humanities.

William Arighi was associate professor of world literature at Springfield College. He has published in *Comparative Literature Studies*, *Hispanic Review*, *MELUS*, and other venues. He was previously a fellow at the Walter Chapin Simpson Center for the Humanities at the University of Washington and a Fulbright-Hayes Group Project scholar in the Philippines.

Bruce Bennett is professor of film studies at Lancaster University. His research focuses on national and transnational cinemas, film history, pedagogy, and media technology. His publications include *Cycling and Cinema* (2019) and *The Cinema of Michael Winterbottom: Borders, Intimacy, Terror* (2014). He coedited a special dossier on the films of Michael Bay in the journal *Senses of Cinema* (2015) and, with Katarzyna Marciniak, a special issue of *Transnational Cinemas*, *Aporias of Foreignness: Transnational Encounters in Cinema* (2018). Also with Marciniak, he is currently writing *Refugee Cinema* (forthcoming from Oxford University Press).

Manuel Chinchilla teaches Spanish language and culture at University School in Hunting Valley, Ohio. Previously, he was associate professor of Spanish and Italian at Sewanee: The University of the South, where he taught Latin American literature and culture, Italian language, and collaborative seminars in the humanities program. He has published on contemporary literature and culture from Mexico, Central America, and Italy. His current research focuses on translation studies. He has finished a draft of an English translation of the Honduran author Jorge Medina García's *Cenizas en la memoria* (*Ashen Memories*) and is currently translating a selection of works by the poet Juana Pavón.

Emily S. Davis is associate professor of English and women and gender studies and director of the graduate program in English at the University of Delaware.

Alexander Dawson is assistant professor of world literature at Bard High School Early College in Washington, DC. His research, which examines the intersections of migration and disability in postcolonial African literature, has been published in *Disability Studies Quarterly*. His writing has also appeared in *Twentieth-Century Literature* and *African Studies Review*.

Lisa Dolasinski is senior lecturer of Italian and an affiliate faculty member in the Institute for Women's Studies at the University of Georgia. She works on contemporary Italian cinema and culture and is particularly interested in the topics of migration, aging, and masculinity. She has designed courses on Italian immigration and second-generation Italians at Bucknell University, Dickinson College, and the University of Pittsburgh. Her publications interrogate the fluid sexual and racial identities of migrant protagonists on-screen. She has presented in the Humanities Forum at the University of Scranton and at the NEMLA and MLA annual conventions. In addition to preparing her first monograph for publication, she is currently working on a project that investigates representations of aging in Italian films.

Kester Dyer is a settler scholar and assistant professor in film studies in the School for Studies in Art and Culture at Carleton University. His teaching and research focus on Québec and Indigenous film and media. His current book project, "Otherworldly Incursions: The Supernatural in Québec Cinema," is funded by a Social Sciences and Humanities Research Council Insight Development grant and offers a broad exploration of the Québec film corpus since the 1990s, analyzing how supernatural tropes reveal key information about the struggle of the Québec social imaginary to delineate relationships between historically dominant and marginalized groups. With Liz Miller, Dyer is cofounder of Circle Visions, a community-building project that features media-making workshops aimed at emerging Indigenous filmmakers.

Jocelyn Frelier is associate director of Brown University's Brown in Washington program, a program that supports university students in experiential learning opportunities. She is also the author of *Transforming Family: Queer Kinship and Migration in Contemporary Francophone Literature* (2022). Previously, she was a program manager at Vital Voices Global Partnership, a nonprofit organization in Washington, DC, that advocates for women leaders in international development. Jocelyn held two faculty positions, including an Accountability, Climate, Equity and Sustainability Fellowship at Texas A&M University. Her research interests include literature, migration, family, and gender theory.

Jutta Gsoels-Lorensen is associate professor of German, English, and comparative literature at Penn State University, Altoona College. Her current research focuses on forced migration in literature and film. Her scholarship has appeared in publications including *Comparative Literature Studies*, *New German Critique*, *Arethusa*, *Mosaic*, *African American Review*, *Germanic Review*, *Critique*, and *German Quarterly*. She is also interested in undergraduate teaching innovation, including the creation of open access materials and interinstitutional public humanities initiatives.

Malini Guha is associate professor of film studies at Carleton University. She is the author of *From Empire to the World: Migrant London and Paris in Cinema* (2015) and coeditor of *London as Screen Gateway* (2023). Her research interests include film and the city, diasporic and postcolonial cinemas, and world cinema and other moving image practices, such as public projection. Guha's essays have been published in *Feminist Media Histories*, the *Canadian Journal of Film Studies*, *NECSUS*, *Screening the Past*, and the *Journal of British Cinema and Television*. As a contributing editor for the online journal *Mediapolis*, she writes a regular column, "Screening Canada," which explores Canada's mediated place-making, global role, and domestic negotiation of racial and ethnic difference. She recently joined the editorial board of the journal *Screen*.

Spencer R. Herrera is professor of Spanish and Chicana/o/x studies in the Department of Languages and Linguistics at New Mexico State University. His most recent coedited book is *Querencia: Reflections on the New Mexico Homeland* (2020). He is also coauthor of *Sagrado: A Photopoetics across the Chicano Homeland* (2013). He has published in and guest-edited and curated issues of leading journals such as *Aztlán* and *Casa de las Américas*. He was born and raised in Houston, Texas, but has lived in New Mexico for over twenty years.

Rebecca H. Hogue is assistant professor of English at the University of Toronto, where she writes and teaches on empire, militarization, and the environment. Her work has been published in *Critical Ethnic Studies*, *Amerasia*, and *International Affairs*, among other venues. She is currently working on her own manuscript on the arts and literatures of the nuclear free movement in Oceania.

Hsuan L. Hsu is professor of English at the University of California, Davis, where he writes and teaches about environmental humanities, American literature, cultural geography, critical ethnic studies, and sensory studies. His recent books include *The Smell of Risk: Environmental Disparities and Olfactory Aesthetics* (2020) and *Air Conditioning* (2024).

Karen Little works in administration at Wild Labs, a start-up formed to provide COVID-19 testing and immunization services through government contracts with the Commonwealth of Kentucky. Prior to summer 2021, she was a PhD candidate in English at Duke University, where she worked for the Representing Migration Humanities Lab and held a fellowship at the Kenan Institute for Ethics.

Juan Llamas-Rodriguez is assistant professor in the Annenberg School for Communication and affiliate faculty member with the Center for Latinx and Latin American Studies at the University of Pennsylvania. He is also associate director of the Center for Advanced Research in Global Communication, where he leads the research theme "Mobile Borders: Media, Migration, Diasporas." His work has appeared in the journals *Social Text, Feminist Media Histories, Television and New Media, Communication, Culture, and Critique, Journal of Cinema and Media Studies, Lateral,* and *Catalyst: Feminism, Theory, Technoscience* as well as in several edited collections. His first book, *Border Tunnels: A Media Theory of the US-Mexico Underground*, was published in 2023.

Marilén Loyola is assistant professor of Spanish at Lake Forest College, where she teaches courses in language, literature, and culture. She specializes in contemporary Spanish theater, with a focus on memory, migration, and transatlantic studies. Her most recent publication, "Memory and the Ethical Imagination: The Holocaust and Deportation to Mauthausen in Twenty-First Century Spanish Theater," appeared in the edited collection *Spain, the Second World War, and the Holocaust: History and Representation* (2020). Two forthcoming articles analyze the representation of migration in Spain in the graphic novel *Asýlum* and the television series *Mar de plástico*, respectively. Her current project examines cultural representations of the Almerían region in the Spanish imaginary.

Katarzyna Marciniak is professor of transnational and global media in the Media Arts and Culture Department at Occidental College. She researches the aesthetics and politics of transnational visual cultures, particularly representations of foreignness, immigration, national belonging and unbelonging, and the construction of border zones as sites of contention. She is the author of *Alienhood: Citizenship, Exile, and the Logic of Difference* (2006) and *Streets of Crocodiles: Photography, Media, and Postsocialist Landscapes in Poland* (2010) and coeditor of *Transnational Feminism in Film and Media* (2007), *Protesting Citizenship: Migrant Activisms* (2014), *Immigrant Protest: Politics, Aesthetics, and Everyday Dissent* (2014), *Teaching Transnational Cinema: Politics and Pedagogy* (2016), and *The Oxford Handbook of Com-*

munist Visual Cultures (2020). She is also editor of the Palgrave series Global Cinema. With Bruce Bennett, she is currently writing *Refugee Cinema* (forthcoming from Oxford University Press).

B. Judith Martínez-García, originally from Monterrey, Mexico, is assistant professor in the Department of English and World Cultures in the Judith Enyeart Reynolds College of Arts and Humanities at Missouri State University. She is also a certified diversity professional and recently earned a certificate in public leadership and service from Harvard University. She has been recognized with the Board of Governors Award, the Excellence in Teaching Lawrence Award, and the Missouri State University Research Award. Her research focuses on representations of violence in contemporary Latin American literature and culture as well as poverty, narco-narratives, patriarchy, and forced migration.

Darshana Sreedhar Mini is assistant professor of film at the University of Wisconsin, Madison. She is the author of *Rated A: Soft-Porn Cinema and Mediations of Desire in India* (2024) and coeditor of *South Asian Pornographies: Vernacular Formations of the Permissible and the Obscene* (2024).

Weixian Pan is assistant professor in the Department of Film and Media at Queen's University in Canada. Her research interests include politics of visuality, critical media infrastructure, and environmental media. She examines media's textual, material, and sociopolitical dynamics mainly through the situated experience of China but is gradually expanding this scope to trace transregional linkages across Asia.

Elizabeth Rich is professor of English at Saginaw Valley State University and specializes in contemporary literature. Her book *Authority and the Historical Document in Late Twentieth-Century Literature* (2021) examines six late-twentieth-century pieces of historiographic metafiction that critically employ archival documents. She has published articles and presented papers on such writers as Elizabeth Bishop, Mohsin Hamid, Naveed Noori, Penelope Lively, and Louise Erdrich.

Eva Rueschmann is professor of cultural studies at Hampshire College. She is the author of *Sisters on Screen: Siblings in Contemporary Cinema* (2000) and the editor of *Moving Pictures, Migrating Identities* (2003). She has also published articles in journals such as *Post Script* (on Jane Campion) and the *Journal of New Zealand and Pacific Studies* (on Taika Waititi) and in several essay collections. She is currently working on a book on the screen adaptations of the British writer Daphne du Maurier's gothic fiction.

Claudia Sadowski-Smith is professor of English and American studies at Arizona State University. She is the author of *The New Immigrant Whiteness: Neoliberalism, Race, and Post-Soviet Migration to the United States*

(2018) and *Border Fictions: Globalization, Empire, and Writing at the Boundaries of the United States* (2008). She is the editor of *Globalization on the Line: Culture, Capital, and Citizenship at U.S. Borders* (2002) and of special journal issues on the cultures of global post/socialism, comparative border studies, and postsocialist literatures in the United States. Sadowski-Smith has also published on climate migration, comparative US migration, transnational adoption, and transnational reality television.

Masha Salazkina is professor of film studies at Concordia University, Montreal. She is the author of *In Excess: Sergei Eisenstein's Mexico* (2009), *World Socialist Cinema: Alliances, Affinities and Solidarities in the Global Cold War* (2023), and *Romancing Yesenia: How a Mexican Melodrama Shaped Global Culture* (2024). She is coeditor of *Sound, Speech, Music in Soviet and Post-Soviet Cinema* (2015) and *Global Perspectives on Amateur Film Histories and Cultures* (2022).

Yumna Siddiqi is professor of English at Middlebury College, where she specializes in postcolonial literature and theory, diaspora and migration studies, and literary theory. Her book *Anxieties of Empire and the Fiction of Intrigue* (2008) explores the contradictions of postcolonial modernity in turn-of-the-nineteenth- and turn-of-the-twentieth-century detective and spy fiction. She has published articles on postcolonial literature and culture in *Cultural Critique, Victorian Literature and Culture, Renaissance Drama, Alif, South Asia Research, Textual Practice,* and *The Minnesota Review.* Her current research is on postcolonial literature, migrants, and the city.

Kristen Stern is assistant professor in francophone studies at the University of Massachusetts, Lowell. Stern regularly presents and publishes on contemporary francophone African literature, performance studies, and the sociology of the author. She teaches all levels of language and literature in French and has published work in *Research in African Literatures, Journal of the African Literature Association,* and *Postcolonial Text.* Her first book, *Performative Authorship: Francophone African Novelists in French Spaces,* is forthcoming with Liverpool University Press. Her writing can be found on the blog *Africa in Words,* where she is also an editor.

Megan Thornton Velázquez is associate professor of Spanish at John Carroll University. She specializes in twentieth- and twenty-first-century Latin American literature and culture, with a particular interest in Mexico and Central America. Her work has focused on representations of migration and mobility in literature, music, and film. She is also interested in border studies, women writers, and testimonial narratives. She has published scholarly articles in *Hispania, Letras Femeninas, Hispanic Journal,* and *Studies in Latin American Popular Culture.*

Délice I. Williams is associate professor and director of the undergraduate program in English at the University of Delaware.

Gaoheng Zhang is associate professor of Italian studies at the University of British Columbia. His first book, *Migration and the Media: Debating Chinese Migration to Italy, 1992–2012*, is the first detailed media and cultural study of the Chinese migration from both Italian and Chinese migrant perspectives. His next two books examine cultural representations and dynamics pertaining to food and fashion mobilities between China and Italy that migration and tourism help deepen. From 2022 to 2023, he was a Jean Monnet Fellow at the European University Institute in Florence, where he studied media debates between Western Europe and China regarding the latter's Belt and Road Initiative in certain East African countries.

Eszter Zimanyi is senior research manager at the University of Pennsylvania's Center for Advanced Research in Global Communication. She specializes in documentary studies, migration and refugee studies, and global media cultures. Her work on topics such as refugee selfies, humanitarian immersive media, and migrant documentaries has been published in *Journal of Cinema and Media Studies*, *Feminist Media Studies*, and *Transnational Screens*, among other venues. She is also a film programmer and curator and most recently curated *Discarded Visions*, a virtual exhibit exploring the political, cultural, and mediating qualities of waste.